Live a Conscious Life

Reconnect mind, body, heart and soul for personal and spiritual growth

Carolyn Moody

Clink Street

London | New York

Published by Clink Street Publishing 2017

Copyright © 2017

First edition.

ISBN: 978-1-911525-07-3 paperback
978-1-911525-08-0 ebook

Dedications

I would like to thank my husband, family, friends, clients and students for their encouragement and support over the many years it took me to complete this project.

I particularly want to thank the two Daves, Dave Skinner and David Monkcom, both of whom kindly agreed to do a copy-edit/proofread on an earlier version of the book. Guys, your suggestions, comments, questions and grammatical corrections were brilliant! I changed and explained a lot based on your feedback. Though it pained me to do so, I even reinstated many hyphens after Dave S. pointed out, *"You really don't like hyphens much, do you?!"*

I offer my thanks and gratitude to all at Authoright, to Gareth and Hayley, without whom this book would never have made it out there in published form. I have a tendency to procrastinate (but only big time) and they gave me professional and human care to help nudge me along. Their expertise in all aspects of publishing impressed me and went beyond my expectations. Thank you all.

About the author

Carolyn trained at the Institute for Optimum Nutrition (ION) in London, qualifying as a Nutrition Consultant in 1990. Since then she has helped thousands of people, both in Belgium and internationally, recover their health by making more balanced nutritional and lifestyle choices.

A writer since childhood, Carolyn has written many articles for a variety of publications. She has also written all her own course material, nutrition programmes and articles for her website.

In 2003, she wrote and self-published her first book, *Nurturing Superwoman*, about women's health and natural healing, which sold well among her clients and students.

Fascinated by the link between mind, emotion and our habits, Carolyn decided to learn more about the psychology of eating. In 2004, she created and launched *Body Balance*, a weight management group programme that tackled WHY people ate, as well as WHAT they ate. The programme was based on the principle of integrated mind, body and emotional health, and helped participants break the dispiriting cycle of dieting and weight gain.

Over the next few years, Carolyn heard time and again how spiritually lost and disconnected her clients and students felt. They had achieved so much but, at a heart and soul level, they felt empty. She created the *Live a Conscious Life* coaching programme, an approach that helps people reconnect their mind, body, heart (emotions) and soul self. The coaching manual formed the basis for this book. *Live a Conscious Life* is about self-empowerment, self-trust and self-worth. Carolyn guides her students and readers to listen to their intuition and divine guidance, and to discover their purpose(s) in life.

Contents

The journey begins

Introduction   1
   To live a conscious life   2
   A cry from the soul   3
   A personal journey   3
   Mind, emotions, body and soul   4
   Spiritual growth gently   5

1: Seeking my own truth   7
   Being a highly sensitive person   8
   Transcending rationalism   9
   Reincarnation and past lives   9
   Natural health and healing   10
   Our journey through life   11
   Wait and the teacher will appear   12
   The psychology of eating   13
   The birth of Body Balance   14
   Reading my soul   15
   Raising women's consciousness   16

2: Know yourself   18
   The dis-integration of self   20
   Suppressing anger   22
   Self-enquiry and our lost self   23
   The mind, body and spirit connection   25
   Reclaiming our integral self   27
   Learning through joy   29

Spirit in human form

3: A foot in both worlds   31
   Soul or spirit – defining the indefinable   32
   Spirituality and religion   34
   Spiritual beings   36
   Doing and being   38
   Reconnecting with our divine self   39
   Stillness   40
   Daydreaming   41
   Contemplation   42
   Meditation   42
   Mindfulness   43
   Intuition   45
   Guided visualisations   46
   Leap of faith   49
   Finding the balance   50
   Acceptance   51

4: Fear and love   54
   Tribal influence   56
   Sterile science   58
   Fear disconnects   60
   Understanding fear   61
   The different levels of fear   62
   Guilt   62
   Disapproval and rejection   63
   Abandonment and death   64
   Love   65
   Love is unconditional   66
   Nobody's doormat   67
   Love drives out fear   68
   The language of fear and love   70
   Self-love   72

Mind and emotions

5: Unravelling the mind   74
    Attachment to thoughts   75
    The mind and personality   76
    The brain   77
    Ego as a concept   78
    Exploring the diagrams   80
    Moving from diagram 1 to 2   82
    Making friends with the ego   83
    Stuck in our stories   85
    Track to nowhere   87
    Drama addiction   88
    Drama monster   90
    Why we suffer   91
    Revising the internal map   92

6: Emotional guidance   96
    Feelings and emotions   97
    Stoicism   98
    Human design   99
    The Observer   100
    Loving detachment   101
    The range of emotions   102
    Numbed down   106
    Anger   108
    Releasing emotion   111

7: Buttons and beliefs   112
    Beliefs   112
    Mind filter   113
    Self-sabotage   113
    Always right   114
    Excavation   115
    Hot buttons   116
    List of hot buttons   117
    Emotional charge   118

Pulling the threads   119
I think or I feel   121
How old am I?   121
Reacting or responding   122
Emotional need, expectation and self-esteem   122
The blame game   124
Projection and blame   125
Reflection   127
Changing habitual patterns   129
Releasing our deepest fears   130

Exploring power

8: Dare to be authentic!   132
    Self-image   132
    Creating personas and roles   133
    Persona or authentic self?   135
    Letting others define us   137
    Shining our light   139
    The theatre of life   141
    Patience and self-acceptance   141
    Stillness and solitude   143

9: Self-empowerment   144
    Exploring external power   144
    You are already wise   146
    Giving away our power   148
    Victim consciousness   150
    Pseudo-power   151
    Selfless, selfish and self-hood   151
    Selfish   152
    Self-hood   152
    You have a choice   153
    Circle of influence and the illusion of control 155
    The desire for love, approval and appreciation 156
    Organisation and too much busyness   158

Self-discipline, commitment and willpower   160
Success and failure   162
An opportunity to learn   164

10: Confident communication   166
Emotional oxygen   168
Mis-communication   168
Great communicators   169
Fudging communication   170
Passive behaviour: suppressing   171
Passive-aggressive behaviour: sniping   171
Aggressive behaviour: exploding   172
Fuzzy boundaries   174
Assertiveness   176
In the face of hostility   178
The sound of silence   179
Compassionate communication   180
Active listening   180
Confrontational situations   182

Divine purpose

11: The need to fall apart   184
The nature of depression and burnout   185
Spiritual breakdown   187
Letting go   188
The need to retreat   189
Forgiveness   190
Self-forgiveness   191
Surrender to higher guidance   192
Dream Team   193
Trust   193
The middle way   194
Timelessness   196
Falling apart again and again   197

12: A time for every purpose   199
   What is my life purpose?   199
   Being a lightworker   201
   Divine Timing   203
   Different phases of life   203
   Absolute clarity   205

Introduction

"And the day came when the risk to remain tight in a bud was more painful than the risk it took to blossom." Anaïs Nin

The time has come. We are going for personal and spiritual growth at a roller coaster rate. The trend towards enlightenment picked up pace in the 1960s and '70s with the hippy movement, flower power and Woodstock. Pop and rock bands led the way in having their own personal gurus, and we started exploring Eastern philosophy and spirituality with great enthusiasm. There was an explosion of interest and research into the paranormal. Suddenly people were learning yoga, Reiki, crystal healing, aromatherapy, reflexology, shiatsu, kiniesiology and meditation. When we got a backache we went to an osteopath or chiropractor. Organic gardening and healthy eating were being adopted by a growing minority of the population. Health food shops sprung up in every town. In 1973 I discovered brown rice and herbs.

It was the birth of consciousness. In the twenty-first century it is hard to imagine that once upon a time these things were very new and very much on the edge of 'normal'. Talking about a visit to an acupuncturist got you labelled as a 'crank'. Today, while many areas of mainstream thinking are still trying to push back this tide of rising consciousness, even the UK NHS (National Health Service) is offering patients acupuncture for pain relief. In Belgium many doctors will happily talk about herbs, homeopathy and diet, long before they get out the prescription pad. Telling someone that you are learning to channel your guides has become less shocking than even twenty years ago. While there still remains a large army of doubting Thomases who want to put us back into the mainstream box, the 'New Age' has arrived and with it a sense of urgency as we rush to raise our own self-awareness.

To live a conscious life

To live a conscious life is to wake up as if from a deep sleep. Everything that seemed normal now seems crazy. We realise that we were adding to the craziness by being attached to our thinking and reactions to the same provocations in the same old way, and all the while nothing changes. We are no longer mindless, but are becoming mindful of who we really are and our purpose(s) for being here. We are learning to live in the present moment, aware that everything else is all in the mind.

When we live consciously, we can choose whether or not to live according to generations of programmed conditioning, the need to conform to the norms and standards set by others. We stop blaming others and take full responsibility for how we think, feel and react to any given situation. We gain clarity about what we really want and we are willing to follow our own unique path through life, no matter what the opinion of others may be. We become authentic.

As we begin to live consciously, we are able to connect with our wise or soul self so that we may trust our instincts and believe in ourselves. We become conscious of our interaction with others and with our environment, and how we are all interconnected – for good or harm.

Living a conscious life isn't an easy road to follow, at times it can feel incredibly lonely. On the way it is just too easy to doubt ourselves, and fall back into old habits of thinking and behaviour. This is especially so when we encounter the disbelievers who challenge our new way of thinking and being, the *"Oh, you're not still following that spiritual stuff are you?!"* types. There are times when we painfully fall apart, cast adrift from everything we thought was real. We no longer know who we are or our place in the world. It takes a great deal of courage and conviction to allow ourselves to go through the metamorphosis from living unconsciously to stepping into the light of consciousness.

If you are already in the process of choosing to live a conscious life, you may be assured that you are not alone. We are living in a time of great awakening as human beings reach a new level of consciousness. This is a vital time in humanity's history: a crossroads where, if we choose to keep doing what we have always done, the outcome will probably be disastrous. Each and every one of us can grasp this opportunity to change our individual and collective future.

A cry from the soul

At the time of writing I am based in Belgium, near Brussels, a crossroads in Europe where many nationalities come together to work and live. My coaching clients and students come from all over the world. They are well educated, high-achieving individuals, yet irrespective of nationality, language or culture, they tell me that they feel stuck, don't fit in, have lost their sense of joy and purpose, and they want to know why they are here.

This loss of a sense of meaning or purpose to life is a cry from the soul. People are searching for clarity about who they are and what they really want out of life. They want to feel confident about trusting their own instincts, and to stop trying to please or measure up to the demands of other people. They want to be able to deal with conflict situations, and to stop giving in to other people's manipulation. They feel the loss of connection to nature, and are all too aware of the effects of man's destruction of Mother Earth. They want to be part of the solution, not part of the cause.

More than anything, they want to be at peace with who they are. Many feel the lack of a deeply meaningful connection both with themselves and with 'something more', whatever they perceive that to be: a Super-Consciousness, Spirit, God, a Divine Power, their own soul. Many of us feel alone, suffering from a lack of spiritual nourishment, and have no idea how to go about finding it.

A personal journey

In 2003 I self-published my first book, *Nurturing Superwoman*, about nutrition and health for women. While *Nurturing Superwoman* dealt with the physical aspects of women's health, in *Live a Conscious Life* I wanted a book that reflected my own journey and those of the many people it has been my privilege to help.

This is not a textbook, referenced with countless scientific studies designed to prove what I am saying. There are many books out there that already do this, and I have very much enjoyed reading them. Instead I have used anecdotes throughout the book based on amalgamations of many people's experiences (including my own). I have protected individuals' identities by changing names and many details, while keeping the essence of their story. Even when they have asked specifically to be quoted, I have kept their contribution anonymous.

I have also liberally quoted authors and philosophers who have inspired me to continue my quest towards seeking my own truth.

My coaching and teaching style seems to appeal more to women, especially those who are already waking up to a conscious life. The small percentage of men that make up my client base tend to be those who are not constrained by an orthodox view of science. They are very much aware of the mystical and metaphysical, and want that aspect back in their lives. They also tend to be discontented with the conventional male roles assigned to them by society and want to explore their own unique way of being masculine.

Mind, emotions, body and soul

In *Live a Conscious Life* I hope to pass on wisdom, inspiration and philosophies that have helped me and my clients. My approach is down-to-earth, while encouraging people to reconnect with their soul self. I have met many lovely people who are on their spiritual path but find life in the practical world rather challenging. They can meditate to an altered state of consciousness or communicate with their angels, but can't balance their bank accounts, or they have one disastrous relationship after another.

My aim is to help each person realign their mind, body, emotions and their soul self to create a more peaceful and harmonious life. In the process, I am of course helping myself as I too tread this path towards the light, and freedom from the constraints of the mind and emotions.

The mind and emotions are everything. They can work for us, leading us quietly on our paths to a fulfilling life, or they can control us and lead us astray. When the mind takes over we forget who we really are: spirits in human form.

During our coaching sessions, I find that many people at some point in the process take a colossal leap in their understanding and awareness. It is as if they have stepped through a portal, from the darkness of fear and insecurity, into a bright and sparkling place full of light, hope and love. Having taken that giant step, they find there is no going back. It isn't always a comfortable place to be, at least until they get used to the peace and quiet inside their mind. It changes their perception of themselves and their world.

Spiritual growth gently

I believe that spirituality is a very personal thing and that we are all capable of connecting to our own soul self, and the Source or Spirit from whence we came. There are many methods that human beings use to make this connection. I explore these later in the book.

I am convinced that we do not have to suffer to reconnect with our innate spirituality. The quest to find Spirit is often made into a journey of discomfort and deprivation. While that may suit some people, I can feel spiritual when I am teaching, coaching, writing, walking in nature, spending time with my family, dancing, singing, tending my garden or standing on the seashore watching the sunset.

Spirit is in everything. It is love. Our spiritual self is the part of us that is love. All we need is an open heart and to feel love or gratitude in everything we do: to feel our connection to Spirit. Even when we are unable to feel love or gratitude, we can still accept ourselves with loving kindness for all our human frailties. I don't think the spiritual quest has to be more complicated than that, but already this is a tall order for most of us.

I hope in these pages you will find insights, information and inspiration. The message is not new, but perhaps like me, when you hear the same message expressed in a different way, eventually something clicks, and you really understand at both a head and heart level.

Chapter 1

Seeking my own truth

"I seek the truth ... it is only persistence in self-delusion and ignorance that does harm." Marcus Aurelius

The wisdom of ages has been passed down to us over millennia to inspire our evolution towards personal and spiritual growth. I have been inspired and helped by the wisdom, compassion and enlightened thinking of many authors, as well as by those with whom I have connected on this path. They have all in their way held a beacon of light for me on my journey towards seeking my own truth.

As a young woman, I felt like a displaced spirit, disenchanted with all the imperfection I saw around me: wars, conflict, brutality, violence, greed, exploitation, self-interest and general mean-mindedness. I was living in the wrong world and the wrong time. I didn't belong here. I felt like a bystander watching an X-rated horror movie where everyone had logical and rational reasons for the insanity of human atrocities, against each other and against their home, planet Earth. As Eckhart Tolle says in *A New Earth*:

> *"If the history of humanity were the clinical case history of a single human being, the diagnosis would have to be: chronic paranoid delusions, a pathological propensity to commit murder, and acts of extreme violence and cruelty against his perceived 'enemies' – his own consciousness projected outward. Criminally insane with a few brief lucid intervals."*

I realised that I saw life differently to the way others did. As a teenager I wasn't interested in going out and getting drunk, taking drugs, being rebellious or promiscuous. In those days my apparent conformity was regarded as being 'goody two shoes', but I just didn't see the point of potentially self-harming behaviour. From a young age I was asking questions that didn't seem to concern 'normal' people. I wanted *"The Answer to Life, the Universe and Everything"*, to quote Douglas Adams in his *The Hitchhiker's Guide to the Galaxy*.

I wanted to know who I was and why I was here. I wanted answers to all sorts of questions about health and healing, because health and healing meant so much more than getting rid of an infection or surviving cancer. For me, healing encompassed body, mind, emotions and spirit, not just for each individual, but for the whole planet.

Being a highly sensitive person
My parents and teachers referred to me as *'an old head on young shoulders'*. I know now that I am what Dr Elaine Aaron calls an HSP, a highly sensitive person. Also known as emotional empaths, or, in Carl Jung's personality types, introverts, HSPs make up an estimated 15% to 20% of the world's population. We are therefore in the minority and always feel different. HSPs feel everything more intensely than non-HSPs. Our brains and nervous systems are wired slightly differently and can become overstimulated very quickly. Being in overcrowded places can be an overwhelming experience for an HSP. We need a lot of quiet time to recover our equilibrium after too much stimulation from noise, people and bright lights. We may love rock music, but a stadium-filled rock concert can be overpowering.

HSPs tend to be very sensitive to other people's moods and energies. We feel other people's suffering as our own, so that watching the news or violent movies can be a painful experience.

HSPs are usually compassionate, hard-working, creative, imaginative, and empathic listeners. From the age of thirteen, people seemed to gravitate towards me to tell me their problems or their innermost secrets. I think the Dalai Lama XIV was addressing HSPs directly when he said:

"The planet does not need more successful people. The planet desperately needs more peacemakers, healers, restorers, storytellers and lovers of all kinds."

I started on my truth-seeking journey when I was twenty. I wanted explanations that transcended mainstream, orthodox thinking about life, health and spirituality. I found conventional thinking very limiting: it left too many unanswered questions. There was so much knowledge and wisdom lost or suppressed through the ages. The truth was out there and I wanted to find it.

This was the early 1970s and I was inspired by three books of the time: *The Occult* by Colin Wilson, *The Bloxham Tapes* by Arnall Bloxham and *Let's Eat Right to Get Fit* by Adele Davis.

Transcending rationalism

The Occult explored alchemy, mysticism and the supernatural as though they were a normal part of life. In his introduction, Colin Wilson sums up how the human race has gone down an evolutionary blind alley as it allowed rationalism and realism to suppress the spiritual side of being human:

> *"[with the Age of Reason] ... man became a thinking pygmy and the world of the rationalists was a daylight place in which boredom, triviality and 'ordinariness' were ultimate truths ... human beings have a tendency to become trapped in the 'triviality of everydayness' ... man needs a sense of meaning to release his hidden energies."*

I wanted more than the rationalist's world of trivia and everydayness. Most of us spend our lives concerned with just a tiny corner of the image, believing that this is all there is to life: the external everydayness. We fail to see the bigger picture, the 'something more' of purpose, meaning and a Divine connection. Human beings need a sense of purpose and meaning to realise their spiritual potential. This was my quest, to find my path and follow it, wherever it might lead.

Reincarnation and past lives

Arnall Bloxham, author of *The Bloxham Tapes,* was a Welsh hypnotherapist who regressed his subjects to past lives under hypnosis. The rationalists at the time dismissed his findings. They said that his subjects had been exposed, even subconsciously, to the historical information that came through in their hypnotic regressions, therefore their accounts of past lives were not reliable. That is except for one of his subjects, Jane Evans, who agreed to be hypnotised on BBC television in 1976. Under hypnosis she gave a detailed description of her life as a Jew in York, England, in 1190. She said that during the time of the massacre of the Jewish people by the local townsfolk, she and several of her kind had been forced to hide in a crypt in a church outside the castle in York. They were found by the mob and that is where she died in that lifetime. From Jane's description of the church where she hid, it sounded as though it was most probably St Mary's, Castlegate. The snag was that this church did not have a crypt. Then a few months after the television programme was aired, workmen, who had been working at St Mary's on a renovation project, uncovered a crypt below the floor.

Neither Judaism nor Christianity believes in reincarnation, yet interest in past lives has gained in popularity among Western truth-seekers since the 1960s. Much of the influence has come from Eastern traditions with reincarnation being a central tenet of the majority of Indian religions, such as Hinduism, Jainism, and Sikhism.

I didn't come from a particularly religious background, although, like many children of that era, I attended Sunday School and Christmas church services. Religious instruction was also part of the school curriculum and I learned a lot about Christianity and its beliefs. While being interested in the subject, by the time I had reached my teens I was already sceptical about many aspects of organised religion, which seemed to be more focused on dogma and blind faith than in encouraging an individual's spiritual growth.

Colin Wilson and Arnall Bloxham inspired me to continue my search for the link between our physical existence here on Earth, and where we go between our incarnations. Mainstream science did not appear to be interested in discovering explanations for the unexplainable. Things that didn't fit with current scientific logic were treated as an anomaly and unimportant. Worse, unexplained phenomena like ghosts, telepathy, energy or faith healing were ridiculed and denied existence.

Despite mainstream scientific thinking, I remained convinced that the supernatural and reincarnation were important dimensions of life on Earth.

Natural health and healing
I wanted to know more but it seems my 'higher self' (the soul or wise part of ourselves that already knows our purpose and potential) had other plans and my first priority seemed to be a concern with the physical body. I became interested in natural health and healing.

Adele Davis was the American pioneer in nutrition and health in the 1970s. I picked up a copy of her book, *Let's Eat Right to Get Fit,* in a hospital waiting room of all places. I thought this rather ironic as mainstream medicine gave no credibility to healthy nutrition in those days. As I read her book I felt excited. Having been prescribed antibiotics for everything from a sore throat to intestinal bloating, I knew there had to be another route to good health. Doctors seemed to have no idea how we create health or disease in ourselves. Adele Davis explained the importance of nutrition on the workings of the body. Eating is absolutely fundamental to life. I just had no idea that this approach could be so powerful. Nor, it seems, did the many doctors I consulted about my ailments. Adele Davis was my inspiration to learn more.

I became fascinated with 'alternative' health, and in particular with nutrition. I had no idea then that I would do anything with this interest, other than change my own eating habits and learn to get rid of my niggling health problems. Very soon my interest for healthy eating and lifestyle turned into a passion. I still had no sense of this being part of my destiny, but all of that was about to change.

Our journey through life
The ancient wisdom of life as a journey has been around since pre-biblical times but, as most of us have no conscious idea how our lives are going to pan out, life can seem more like a magical mystery tour with plenty of challenges en route. How we rise to those challenges is all part of the journey of life and the creation of wisdom.

This is our path, it takes courage and a strong sense of purpose and trust that everything is happening exactly as it should, even if we don't understand the reasons why. It is so easy to be deflected by the 'rationalists', the 'there is nothing else except your five senses' brigade.

Where the journey starts depends on your own beliefs. If you believe that life starts at conception or birth, then your journey will be the time between then and physical death. If you believe in reincarnation, then your journey may have been ongoing over many lifetimes. This is a concept that can be both liberating and daunting.

I see the journey of life as made up of zillions of baby steps with the occasional giant leap – those 'ah' moments of understanding as another piece of the jigsaw falls into place. Sometimes these moments hit us out of the blue, while at other times they happen as part of the process of conscious self-enquiry.

Wait and the teacher will appear
A quote attributed to both the Buddha and the Tao says: *"When the student is ready, the teacher will appear."* Looking back, it is clear to me that when I was on my right path the teachers would appear to help me on the next step of my journey. I am sure the rational explanation is simply that, as soon as we have decided we want something, we notice when opportunities arise. I think this is also true. Whatever the explanation, I eventually found the right teacher in Patrick Holford and changed the course of my life.

I first met Patrick in the early 1980s when I lived in Buckinghamshire, UK. His then wife, Liz, ran the local health food shop and had a passion for healthy eating. She and I got talking and went through our first pregnancies together, comparing notes on diet, supplements and the local antenatal facilities. She introduced me to Patrick, who at that time was holding nutrition consultations in a room at the back of her shop. I immediately signed up for a nutrition consultation, a novel experience for me. I honestly can't remember what advice he gave me, and I do remember thinking that his manner was a bit rushed and impersonal. However, I was impressed and inspired by his in-depth knowledge of nutrition and its impact on mental and physical health. Patrick had a vision of a different kind of medicine, science-based, but independent from the control of pharmaceutical companies and drug-based (allopathic) medicine. Patrick saw nutrition as a vital component of healing because of the powerful biochemical effect it has on cellular function. Nutrition as medicine also means that the practitioner treats the individual as a whole person, rather than just focusing on their symptoms or disease. I knew then that I would sign up for his Nutrition Consultants training programme at his recently formed Institute for Optimum Nutrition (ION) in London.

In 1987 I moved to Belgium as a trailing spouse with two young children aged two and five. A year later I applied to ION to start their training course. They seemed to be perplexed that someone could do the course from outside the UK, despite the fact that they had a satellite programme already in place for people travelling from other parts of the country. I had to assure them that with the advent of Virgin Express I would have no problems getting over for all the tutorial weekends (these were the days long before the Channel tunnel). For what it's worth, I can lay claim to being the first ever student from outside the UK to follow the ION Nutrition Consultant programme. I qualified in 1990 and that was the next stage of my journey.

For the next thirteen years I worked as a Nutritionist in the Brussels international expatriate community. Most of my clients came from referrals and I even had doctors sending their patients to me. Unfortunately, financially it wasn't enough. I was now divorced with two young children, and money was tight. To pay the bills I combined a full-time job in the daytime with nutrition consultancy work, and running courses during evenings and weekends. The full-time job was for a Belgian business aviation magazine as their English-speaking proofreader and editorial assistant. They soon asked me to write regular articles about health matters within the business aviation community, which was fun and good experience.

The psychology of eating
For some time I had wanted to add another skill to my health practitioner tool kit. Working with my clients provided the signpost.

My nutrition clients achieved some good, sometimes even amazing, results with the advice I gave them. They would lose weight, get better, feel great, and in many cases be able to reduce or stop prescribed medication. Then I would hear from them a year or two later that they had gone back to their old habits, put the weight back on or started feeling unwell again. I asked them why they went back to their previous, harmful eating and lifestyle habits. The answers were always the same: it was just too hard to stick to their new habits due to partners, family, social obligations, eating out, eating away from home, feelings of deprivation, or they couldn't cope with being different.

As I always worked with my clients' own food preferences and lifestyle constraints, clearly something else was going on here to do with mind and emotions. Many people's eating habits are driven by emotion and programmed conditioning from childhood. Here was the new skill I wanted to acquire: the psychology of eating to help people understand WHY they ate, as well as WHAT they ate. At this point I had no idea where I would go for this kind of training so I waited for the answer to come to me.

I was teaching my ten-week nutrition evening class in Brussels to a group of about twelve women. We were talking about weight when one of my students showed us a manual produced by a weight loss programme that was big in Australia and the USA but unheard of in the UK or Europe at that time. This programme included plenty of advice about health and nutrition, and tips on emotionally driven overeating. I found the manual confusing. I also saw that I could provide better, more up-to-date nutrition advice. I wanted to address food obsession and emotional eating at a more profound level than this system was able to cover.

The weight loss business is worth billions of dollars. In 2014 Weight Watchers alone had a net income of US$204.72 million (although by 2015 that was down to US$32.94 million). New diet books are snapped up, especially if they are celebrity-endorsed. Some methods do attempt to deal with the underlying eating habits and emotional drivers that lead to weight gain. Many do not. The statistics for the success of most dietary advice shows that 65% to 80% of people who lose weight on a weight loss programme put it all back on within two to five years. The statistics vary according to which study you read. Some studies say the regain rate is as much as 95%. Those who follow meal replacement diets, where they replace a meal with a formulated drink, do even worse. Not only do they regain lost weight, but they gain a whole lot more than when they first started the diet.

The birth of Body Balance
I thought then that I would like to create a new approach to weight management that delved deeply into the psychology of eating. There were no training courses that fitted my requirements. I needed people with very specific skills to help me develop a psychological coaching programme that would help people understand why they sabotaged themselves with food and drink. I also needed someone with similar nutritional knowledge and experience to help me develop the nutritional side of the programme.

I met Eva when I attended her public speaking workshop. Eva was a psychotherapist who specialised in weight management. She is also a German with a sense of humour (her joke), and a yoga and Pilates teacher who eats meat, manicures her nails, wears make up and always dresses immaculately. She told me that she attracted plenty of criticism from her more traditional fellow yoga teachers who believed that the spiritual path

requires a scrubbed-down approach to beauty and an adherence to a vegetarian way of life. Eva had tried being a vegetarian but went back to eating
meat because she had much more energy on a Stone Age diet (these days
called a Paleo diet) which is high in animal protein and low in grains. I
am also healthier on a Stone Age diet and knew that this was exactly my
kind of woman, one who was not afraid to be different. Eva provided the
material for the first coaching modules of the Body Balance programme
and she taught me what I needed to know to help people understand their
emotionally-driven eating habits.

I got chatting to Helen, a newly trained ION nutritionist living in
Brussels, who said she would like to join us. Helen had experience of
nutrition geared towards weight loss. Both she and Eva had personal experience of eating habits driven by emotion and early conditioning. They
were ideal women to help me create and run the first Body Balance group
programme, which we launched in 2004 with great success.

As I put together the four-hundred-page manual for the initial Body
Balance programme, Jo, someone I had known since our sons went to
school together, used her inestimable skills to help me layout the material
into a beautiful student manual.

After running several programmes with me, Eva and Helen left Body
Balance to continue their own careers. Margaret, a brilliant self-mastery
coach, joined me to help develop the programme further. Later, Margaret
returned to the UK where she grew her successful international career as
a corporate trainer and coach.

I am very grateful to these four amazing women from whom I learned
so much.

Reading my soul

A year into running the first Body Balance groups, I heard about a 'soul
reader', Julie, who visited Brussels from time to time. My curiosity was
piqued and I made an appointment with her. Julie is a very warm, down-
to-earth person. There were no special effects or props and she didn't go
into a spooky trance state like you see in the movies. She welcomed me
with a hug. We sat down face to face in comfortable chairs and then
she held my hands briefly with her eyes closed. After about a minute she
opened her eyes, looked at me and said: *"What they are telling me is this
…"* and then proceeded to tell me all about myself. The 'they' were my

spirit guides and angels, of whom she told me I have plenty. They told her that I (my soul) *"came from the angelic realms and that I found this world so imperfect that it is hard for me to be here. A part of me would like to just go home now (home being not of this Earth)."* At this I promptly burst into tears. Nobody, but absolutely nobody, knew how I felt about being here, or got that close to knowing me this intimately in over fifty years. I really felt as if she had looked into my heart and soul.

She also told me that my guides remarked that I never asked them for help although they were here whenever I needed them. At that time, these were very new concepts for me: my own personal spirit guides and angels who wanted to help me?! That my soul had been somewhere else called an 'angelic realm', whatever that meant?! And that she could hear my guides talking to her and telling her such intimate information that nobody else on earth knew about me … Blimey!

Julie told me that the reason I am here is to *"help raise women's consciousness: this is your purpose"*. I really had no idea what she was talking about and protested that I had just launched a weight management pro-gramme that I intended to franchise. In any case, I wouldn't have the first clue how to raise women's consciousness. What did it mean? I didn't understand the words she was using. Julie just smiled her all-knowing and loving smile and said, *"That's just what they are telling me"*.

I came away with my cassette recording of that first session feeling emotional, perplexed, daunted and yet somehow relieved. More than any-thing, I felt completely seen and heard for the first time in my life. This was an amazing experience for me. But as for my purpose in life, hmm, I still had no idea what that meant or how it might happen.

Raising women's consciousness

For the next two to three years I pushed ahead with developing my Body Balance programme into a franchise. Just when I thought I was on the path of becoming a 'business woman', I had problems with the nerves in my teeth. I had been suffering from insomnia for a couple of years and now my teeth were aching, even though there was nothing medically wrong with them. I didn't hear the message from my body that I was on the wrong path and doing too much, and that I needed to take better care of my physical and emotional self. I was on a roll and couldn't bear the thought of stopping. I ended up having extensive dental work and my amalgam fillings removed. This was such a mistake. Three weeks after the treatment, I went from being energetic and full of enthusiasm (despite insomnia) to hardly being able to get out of bed. I crashed. I had no energy, my brain was fuzzy and I couldn't think straight. It was as if someone had plugged into my energy source and drained it away. I was burnt out.

I wondered if I was suffering from mercury toxicity from having my amalgam fillings incorrectly removed, and if this had triggered adrenal exhaustion. I went from doctor to doctor asking them to check for mercury toxicity but couldn't get anyone to take me seriously. They did however confirm that I was suffering from a complete endocrine (hormone system) collapse, translated as adrenal fatigue. I spent the next four years pushing myself to keep working while trying to get my health back.

The Body Balance business slowed down: I just didn't have the energy to run a franchise business or big group programmes on my own any more. I worked more with individuals and gradually I realised that, even though people were coming to me with weight issues, in the end I was helping them to go within and discover who they really were. My role seemed to be evolving from nutritionist, to emotional eating specialist, and now to a coach who helped people become aware of the way their mind and emotions worked to either keep them stuck, or push them forward. I was providing a safe place where they could reconnect to their authentic or soul self, when they felt ready to do so. It dawned on me that, slowly but surely, I was raising my own consciousness while helping others on their path towards personal and spiritual growth. Soon I was coaching women, and some men, of all ages who wanted to know who they were, why they felt different or why they felt a longing for 'something more'. Many had the gift of sixth sense, were psychic, telepathic and natural healers, but were afraid of their abilities. Mostly I found that I was helping people to accept themselves and be happy with who they were.

I suddenly got it. Here I was on my true path helping people to live a conscious life. Whoever would have thought it?!

Chapter 2

Know yourself

"Be yourself. Everyone else is already taken." Oscar Wilde

"Know yourself" is the first tenet of most philosophical thinking and spirituality. It has apparently been uttered by Greek philosophers, the Oracle at Delphi and the Buddha. Yet how many of us really know ourselves? We think we do, but we tend to be very selective in what we will acknowledge about who we are. Many are hypercritical of some aspects of themselves, while being afraid to admit to other parts they don't like.

When I first started working with women in the Body Balance group programmes, I was surprised and saddened at the amount of self-criticism and even self-loathing among the participants. They were all bright, intelligent women, holding down high-powered and responsible jobs, and some were also bringing up families. They ranged in age from early twenties to well into their sixties. I thought they were all wonderful and inspiring, and I felt privileged that they wanted to work with me on their emotional eating problems. I found them fascinating, but they didn't see themselves that way. They came to the group programmes because they were tired of constantly worrying about their weight. Many had been on diets for most of their lives. Their self-doubt led to low self-esteem, despite all their successes. They ate and drank to suppress their feelings, and they gained weight. Their weight gain caused them to hate themselves, so they ate more because they were miserable. They were caught in a vicious cycle and felt helpless to stop.

During the Live a Conscious Life group coaching programmes, I found the same issues of self-doubt and lack of self-trust among the participants. I started each new programme by asking participants to look into a mirror and talk about what they saw. I asked how many of them had a full-length mirror in their home. I also asked them how much they loved or valued themselves on a scale of one to ten, with ten being the highest.

Each of these gorgeous women stood in front of the mirror criticising the bits she didn't like about herself. Not one of them commented on anything they liked, although, when pushed, they might say their hair or nails were alright. Some couldn't bear to look at themselves at all, despising what they saw. Usually their self-love or self-value registered between zero and five. Most of them didn't have a full-length mirror in their home. Those that did said it was hidden away in a spare room and never used.

This is such a waste of human potential. Here we are in the twenty-first century with women holding their own in a male-dominated world, and inside they are pulling themselves apart with self-doubt. The group participants were highly successful women, and yet they were unable to accept their true worth because they believed that there was something inherently wrong with them. This is energy draining and disempowering.

Why do we doubt ourselves so much? So many of us go through life feeling as though we are not quite good enough and must continually prove ourselves. No matter what our achievements may be, we always think we should do and be better. How do we go from bonny, bouncy baby to a self-doubting or self-loathing adult?

A study carried out by a toiletry manufacturer showed that only 4% of women globally consider themselves beautiful. The study also found that anxiety about looks begins at an early age. Generations of women have grown up with a distorted self-image and low self-esteem. Even the most confident of women suffer from varying degrees of self-doubt. We all grow up with a certain amount of conditioning about who we are and our intrinsic value or self-worth, some of it encouraging and some of it discouraging. The erosion of identity and self-image often starts at a very young age. It can stem from the messages we receive at home, from parents and siblings, but also in school, the playground, or from the culture at large. We have had thousands of years of male dominance, with men telling us who and what we can be, and it has become part of the female psyche to limit our expectations. Thanks to many courageous, campaigning women, many of us now have much more freedom and respect than even a hundred years ago, yet the messages are still there. Girls are still being brought up to please others, to do what is expected, and to conform to other people's ideas of who and how they should be. Women are bombarded with media images telling them that to be beautiful and desirable they must look, behave and dress in a certain way.

Men don't have it that much easier as they may be brought up in the macho image of what it is to be a man. This causes them to become unbalanced as they learn to focus on being tough, while suppressing their softer, more female energy.

The dis-integration of self

Most of us, male or female, grew up learning to deny our 'authentic' or 'integral' self. This is the wholeness or true essence at the heart of being human, the 'real me' hiding behind the different masks, roles and personas that we call 'me'. It is often hard to remember who we really are under all those layers of negative programming, even for those who had a relatively loving upbringing. We can end up feeling empty, alone and anxious. To suppress these uncomfortable feelings, we distract ourselves with constant busyness, excessive food and alcohol, too much television, the latest gadgets, playing and working too hard, unsatisfying relationships, the pursuit of wealth, disregarding our health and wellbeing, holding ourselves back, smoking, recreational drugs: all manner of activities and behaviours that can never nurture our heart and soul.

We are pretty good at making sure we don't have to spend too much time alone with ourselves just feeling whatever we feel. I discovered through the group programmes just how much people use food and drink to run away from uncomfortable feelings. I saw how our Western obsession with busyness meant that the word 'boredom' provoked real anxiety, as though life would come to an end if we had nothing to do and felt bored. We even say *"I could have died of boredom"*. Yet boredom can so easily be turned into a real opportunity to reflect, contemplate and be still without the need for external distraction.

After we are born, we rapidly learn to adapt to our caregivers and society in order to survive. In the process our authentic self becomes fragmented as we attempt to fit in with the society in which we were raised. Our integral self dis-integrates. In his book, *Getting the Love You Want*, Harville Hendrix PhD, psychologist and co-creator of 'Imago Relationship Therapy', says:

> *"Each society has a unique collection of practices, laws, beliefs and values that children need to absorb. Our parents and teachers are the main conduits through which they are transmitted. This indoctrination*

> *process goes on in every family or institution in every society. There seems to be a universal agreement that unless limits are placed on the individual, the individual becomes a danger to the tribe."*

As children we are socialised in order to fit in, with the result that many of us reach adulthood believing that we are not quite lovable or good enough as we are. We then spend our lives trying to prove our worthiness.

Growing up, we are told who we are, how to behave, what we should think, and even what we should feel. Perhaps you recognise some of these: *You are so lazy! You are the intelligent one, your sister is the pretty one. You are such a bad boy/girl! Big boys don't cry. Be quiet! Sit still! Stop running around! Do as you are told! Don't speak like that! You don't really mean that. You mustn't think that about your sister. We don't discuss those sort of things in this family. You aren't really angry. It was just a little bump – not enough to upset you. Of course you are well enough to go to school! You aren't frightened of that dog, he's much smaller than you.*

I believe that all children need firm boundaries to feel safe and to learn healthy self-discipline. They also need to know how to function within their society so they can grow up to be self-supporting, confident adults with a good sense of who they are. When children learn values like honour and respect for self and others through loving kindness, it creates a core strength of self-trust, honesty and integrity. The danger comes when socialising our children means indoctrinating them against their innate intelligence and nature. Too many of us learned to suppress and deny natural behaviours, talents and abilities if they did not fit with the tribal beliefs of our family and culture. For example, the little boy who wants to learn to dance but whose father thinks dancing is sissy, or the little girl who wants to help fix the family car, but whose mother thinks this is unladylike.

We soon picked up the taboo subjects or emotions in our family or culture: what is polite or not polite; how, what and when to eat; to eat even if we are not hungry; how to lie or tell half-truths to please others; what we can say or not say; what beliefs about ourselves we should have; and how to compare ourselves with others and find ourselves wanting. We suppress aspects of our innate nature, whether quiet and thoughtful, or outgoing and enthusiastic, to fit in with those who can't handle the way we are.

Parents might have used clear-cut 'do', 'don't' and 'be' directives, or they may have used more subtle invalidation by ignoring or rewarding certain behaviours, depending on the value they placed on those behaviours. So, if a parent doesn't value intellectual development, the child might have toys but no books. Conversely, parents who value intellectual development over manual work will provide books but no construction toys. Or they may only reward their child for gender-appropriate behaviour: *You look so pretty in that dress. You play so nicely with your dolls. What a strong boy you are carrying that big, heavy box. I bet you can kick this football really hard.* Harville Hendrix again:

> "*Children instinctively observe the choices their parents make, the freedoms and pleasures they allow themselves, the talents they develop, the abilities they ignore, and the rules they follow. All of this has a profound effect on children: 'This is how to live'. 'This is how we get through life'.*"

As our growing sense of self became distorted, we became anxious. Over time the anxiety seeps into the subconscious and becomes our automatic way of reacting to certain trigger events in life, such as dealing with authority figures or conflict situations, or taking care of our finances.

Suppressing anger
Even with the most sensitive of parenting, the need to survive is such a primal drive that we learned to lose a part of ourselves. We couldn't risk alienating the grownups because our survival depended on their approval. How many of us have held back from telling parents our truth about our experiences of childhood for fear of hurting them? Children protect their parents. As adults, we continue the same behaviour, carrying the burden of anxiety and unresolved stress.

During childhood there would have been many times when we felt anger or even rage towards our caregivers, but most of us weren't allowed to express these emotions safely. Even the most conscientious of parents often have no idea how to handle their child's anger, having never been taught to handle their own anger. A child's rage triggers anxiety, guilt, feelings of inadequacy and anger in the parents, who then fall back on old patterns learned during their own childhood:

punishing, shouting, criticising, putting down, giving in, distracting, ignoring and bribing – anything but helping the child to manage its anger in a positive way.

Many of us learned that anger is unacceptable and we quickly suppressed our angry thoughts and feelings as unladylike, unmanly, unacceptable, impolite or downright dangerous. Feeling hurt is just another shade of anger. We pushed our anger and our hurt deep down inside where they festered, only to re-emerge in our teens and adult life as self-doubt, a sense of loss, people pleasing, aggression, arrogance, rebellion and self-sabotaging behaviours.

None of us received perfect parenting. It is impossible because each child comes with its own set of needs and no adult can possibly fulfil every need in their child. It may not even be healthy to do so because a child who is supported in solving their own problems grows up with a strong sense of self-esteem and good life skills.

Many of us were socialised from the perspective of the needs and anxieties of our parents and society, rather than our own emotional needs. At best we would have received sensitive, intelligent, child-centred parenting and schooling. At worst we may have experienced the opposite: insensitive, selfish, neglectful, critical, bullying, overbearing or abusive parenting or schooling.

Self-enquiry and our lost self
To some extent we all carry around some hurt from our childhood. All traumas, both the big and the apparently insignificant (at least to the adult mind), leave wounds in our psyche. We learned to adopt personas or masks to cover up our wounded sense of self. If we were not lovable or acceptable just as we were, then we needed to behave in a way that brought us approval, grudging acceptance, or at the very least we were noticed. We compromised a part of who we were and complied to survive. The more high-spirited decided that compliance was not an option. They became the rebels, constantly kicking against the traces, being angry, but never showing the hurt and pain of rejection simmering beneath the surface. The result is that we all have parts of ourselves that we have hidden from consciousness. This is our lost self. Our challenge is to wake up, become conscious and regain our integral self.

On the road to seeking our own truth it is important to recognise the influences of our formative years: the positive and negative messages about who we are, our lovability and our value. Identifying the ways that we adapted to survive and thrive gives us insights into how our thinking, emotions and beliefs influence us now.

Self-enquiry – going into our childhood experiences – is a conscious process using the power of the mind to question all our assumptions about how we view ourselves and our interaction with the world. It involves delving around in the murky depths of our subconscious, wherein lie all the beliefs we laid down when we were too young to discriminate between suppressive or supportive beliefs. Self-enquiry can be our first step on the journey to finding our lost self. We use self-enquiry with the intention of getting ourselves unstuck from our current position, and moving ourselves forward towards personal and spiritual growth.

There is a danger that we might use the traumas and pain of the past as an excuse for our behaviour now. For example: *Well it's no wonder I can't succeed at my job when my father told me I would never amount to anything. I can't possibly leave my husband because my mother told me I would never find anyone else to love me.* Having discovered how childhood bullying or abuse has contributed to our lack of self-esteem, we can become attached to our wounds. In her book, *Anatomy of the Spirit*, Caroline Myss uses the term 'woundology' to describe how some people define themselves by their emotional and physical wounds. She explains that the language of woundology creates a connection of shared pain and suffering among people, which can provide friendship, companionship and ongoing compassionate support: something that the most wounded would have never received while growing up. No wonder it is easy to unconsciously fall into the comfortable niche of wounded victim.

When I sat and cried for the umpteenth time with Marcie, my straight-talking psychotherapist, about the man in my life and his apparently uncaring behaviour towards me, she went quiet for a moment and then asked me one question: *"Why do you collude with him in his behaviour?"* After a thirty second stunned silence I suddenly got it. *"Oh no, I'm being a victim aren't I?"* Marcie nodded very slightly. *"But I have never seen myself as a victim. This is horrible!"* I exclaimed. This was a pivotal moment for me as I genuinely had not seen or understood that I had any power to change my situation. I was playing the part of wounded victim to perfection. This was my first step on my own journey towards self-empowerment and personal healing. I could have continued wallowing around in the wounds of my younger years, looking for validation from therapy. Instead I began the process of reintegrating my lost self at a time when I had absolutely no concept of an integral or dis-integrated self.

The mind, body and spirit connection
We are all made up of a physical, mental, emotional and spiritual body. Ancient healing systems from the East, such as Chinese Traditional Medicine and Ayurvedic medicine (the Hindu system of healing), also include the existence of an etheric body. This is an energy body, often referred to as our aura, that surrounds and is connected to our physical body by meridians and chakras (energy channels and centres). Unless we have tried energy healing like Reiki or acupuncture, most of us are unaware of an energy body. Currently it does not appear in conventional medical training.

The body, mind and emotions are intrinsically linked: each influences the other. For the most part, conventional medicine compartmentalises the human body, treating it as though it were separate from the mind and emotions. When we live consciously, we begin to understand that our self-perception has a profound effect on our physical health. The stress created by our negative, repetitive thoughts, subconscious beliefs and emotions carries an energetic charge which influences our energy body, either draining energy or increasing its flow. This in turn affects our physical and biochemical health, and can eventually lead to health problems.

As human beings living in an industrialised world, we have lost connection with all the different aspects of ourselves as human, energy and spiritual beings. The huge rise in heart disease, cancer and strokes are no doubt due to the dis-integration of the whole being. We have lost the connection with our innate wisdom and power to heal, dis-integrating not only from our soul self, but also from our physical body and emotions. As a result, we poison our soil, food, water and air with all manner of legal pollutants; we inject and consume toxic chemicals (many of them prescribed); and we create massive stress in our lifestyles. We are not taught how our bodies work, not even the fundamentals of nutrition, stress management or healthy living. Being knowledgeable about our physical body is not deemed important. We are passive recipients of treatment and advice from current mainstream medical beliefs, often to be told decades later that the advice and treatment has changed due to the dangers they pose to health.

I am just hopping on my nutritionist soapbox here to give an example of a huge about-turn in medical advice on saturated fats and cholesterol. Published in the BMJ (British Medical Journal) in 2013 was an article entitled '*Saturated fat is not the major issue. Let's bust the myth of its role in heart disease*'. The article then went on to say that while trans fats increase the risk of cardiovascular disease through inflammatory process, the mantra that we should remove saturated fat from our diets has "*paradoxically increased our cardiovascular risks*". They also tell us that "*the government's obsession with levels of total cholesterol has led to the over-medication with statins of millions of people*".

Nutritionists have been saying for the last forty years that we need saturated fat (it is the heart's preferred form of fuel), but the medical profession's obsession with cholesterol (let's face it, the government just follows medical advice), fuelled by the pharmaceutical industry's greed for profit at any cost to our health, has affected many people's cardiovascular health.

Conventional medical training is geared towards teaching doctors how to recognise disease states and suppress symptoms. They are not taught to create health through an understanding of the interconnectedness of all the aspects of being human.

Mentally, we are stuck in minds that were not designed to deal with all the complexities of a fast-changing world. Our mind is only a part of who we are. We are meant to live and act as a whole person, mind, body, emotions and spirit all connected and working as one. No wonder we are suffering from stress-related health problems and burnout.

But the tide is changing. There is a groundswell of energy coming from people who want something different. At a grassroots level people are tired of feeling less than whole. Others perceive that there is a part of them that is suppressed and must be released before they can truly be themselves, whatever that might mean. They all want good physical, mental and emotional health. Integrating mind, body, emotions and spirit leads us back to wholeness and peace.

This holistic element of addressing the physical and biochemical imbalances is missing from most coaching and psychotherapy. Working at all these different levels can bring about transformation in individuals who think there is something inherently wrong with their mind or emotions. They may be dealing with childhood baggage, but they may also be relieved to find other factors contributing to their depression, such as, for example, food intolerance, a lack of B vitamins and zinc, candidiasis (systemic fungal infection) which can cause huge hormonal fluctuations, or they have subclinical low thyroid function. Knowing there is something positive they can do about their health is already very empowering for people, and is a good start to healing.

Reclaiming our integral self
The path to really knowing ourselves and reclaiming our integral self meanders through understanding how the mind and emotions work together to drive behaviours; going beyond the mind and emotions to get in touch with who we really are; reaching a place of fearlessness and love to create serenity; and being true to ourselves, which means feeling comfortable with every part of who we are, even the bits we think we don't like.

To our minds, trained in instant gratification, this can seem like an awful lot of hard work, especially when we have no idea if we will achieve any results. It takes time, courage and a committed conscious effort to understand and change a lifetime of thinking and emotional habits. I have met plenty of people who go straight for spiritual development, believing that this is the higher path to follow. Years later they still feel stuck men-tally and emotionally, and are often still physically unwell.

For twenty years, Angie had studied tai chi, shiatsu and meditation, lived in an ashram and worked with a number of spiritual masters. Now in her fifties, she still felt totally stuck. Despite all the different things she had done for her spiritual development, she kept arriving at the same self-destructive patterns that she could not shift, particularly around emotional overeating. Her path through life was very unclear. She felt resentful that she had sacrificed herself to her family. Her physical health was suffering: she was depressed, tired, lacked energy, had digestive problems, and felt angry all the time but didn't seem to understand the cause of her anger. She had lost all sense of purpose, was fearful of change and felt rebellious against anyone who tried to help her.

We talked about her willingness to uncover the unconscious beliefs that were driving her behaviours and health problems now, but Angie decided that she wasn't yet ready to tackle her mind and emotions. She felt scared even thinking about delving into her programmed conditioning and was not prepared to explore her mind, even with plenty of guidance, coaching and support. She decided to keep up her spiritual practices and live with her discontent.

I think each of us has to be ready to start the journey of self-discovery. The time is right when we are so sick of being out of balance that we can't stand another day feeling this way. It is exhausting hanging on to old self-sabotaging behaviours. Often there is a trigger that drives people to find the courage to examine what is going on: it can be depression, a burnout, a serious illness or a life crisis. It sometimes comes with age. The menopause can be a time for taking stock, galvanising women to make life-changing decisions.

Living a conscious life means being willing to face our shadow side wherein lie our personal demons. To become a truth-seeker we must be prepared to delve into all the dark crevices of our mind and emotions. It can feel perilous. Many of us are brought up hearing the expression: *"Better the devil you know"*. It is easy to feel desperate to change on the one hand, but on the other hand scared stiff to risk moving out of our dis-comfort zone into areas where we have no experience. As Pema Chödrön, Buddhist teacher and author of *When Things Fall Apart*, tells us:

> *"No one ever tells us to stop running away from fear – the advice we usually get is to sweeten it up, smooth it over, take a pill or distract ourselves, but by all means make it go away."*

No wonder we don't know how to deal with our fears. Most of us grew up with no real training in fear: what it is and how to deal with it. Fear is a primal emotion designed to keep us safe from harm. Pema Chödrön adds:

> *"Fear is a natural reaction to moving closer to the truth."*

Each of us has to reach a point where we are ready to move closer to the truth if we are to reintegrate with every part of ourselves.

Linda came to see me initially to lose weight. In her mid-fifties, she wanted to be slim, healthy and to feel in control of her eating habits. Since she was forty, she had been exploring her spirituality through yoga, mindfulness and meditation. That was going well, but she was still distracting herself through food in an attempt to run away from her fears about who she really was. Her other wants were to heal the relationship with her brother and integrate the two parts of herself that she called 'good and bad Linda'.

Over the course of the next fifteen months, she started to take back control of her mind. She learned to recognise the games it was playing by making a conscious effort to monitor her mind's thought and behaviour patterns. She was committed to not fall back into familiar thinking. She realised that her belief *"I am not worthy or lovable"* was totally untrue. She finally understood how her father had encouraged a split between her and her brother, and decided that, even though her father was dead, she understood and forgave him. She also forgave herself and her brother, which led to their becoming very close again, just as they had been when they were younger. In the process of putting down her burden of self-doubt and resentment, Linda was able to completely reintegrate all the different parts of herself. She knew she was free when she was finally able to say with absolute conviction, *"There is only ONE Linda, neither good nor bad!"*

Linda lost the eight kilos she wanted to lose, looked radiant and continued with her healthy eating habits. She had faced many of her fears, and came to know and value herself in a way that she hadn't thought possible. After retirement from her office job, she decided to retrain as a kinesiologist and energy healer so she could help others.

Learning through joy
There is no compulsion to do anything. Each person takes their own time to follow their spiritual path wherever it leads. It can be a joyful experience, taken slowly and peacefully, although as human beings we do have a tendency to want to suffer before we make the desired changes. The idea of forcing, nagging, shouting or beating oneself up to become a spiritual person is totally cockeyed, yet it is deeply embedded in our collective psyche. I am thinking here of the old religious practices of wearing hair shirts and self-flagellation. Out of curiosity, I once attended a workshop run by a group of people who specialised in personal growth programmes. I knew their material to be very good but at this workshop their approach was to bully the participants into feeling their emotions. The weekend started on a Friday evening with everyone feeling very apprehensive, which already rang an alarm bell in my head: for me personal growth and discovery is an exciting proposition, full of love and compassion. We were kept up late, and suffered from exhaustion over the long weekend in order to 'break us down' and make us feel our 'blocked feelings', the idea being

that we would then step into our power. I came away from the experience feeling very angry (no trouble getting in touch with that emotion). It enabled me to clarify my own beliefs that the road to personal and spiritual growth does not have to be aggressive or bullying. It can be soft and gentle, like a spring breeze or the touch of a feather on skin.

Chapter 3

A foot in both worlds

"The Earth is our playground.
We have chosen to be here." Gill Edwards

I first came across the phrase, *"Walking with a foot in both worlds"* in Gill Edward's book, *Stepping into the Magic*. A gifted spiritual teacher, Gill Edwards believed that we are all beings of light and love. As spiritual beings we are here to learn to walk with a foot in both worlds, the outer world of everyday reality, and our inner world of the soul and divine connection.

According to ancient astrological and New Age wisdom, we are in a period of human history when we are waking from a deep sleep. Bob Frissell, in his book: *Nothing in This Book is True, But it's Exactly How Things Are,* tells us that this is due to the precession of the equinoxes. He explains that the precession of the equinoxes is caused by the Earth's axis which is on a rotational wobble with the North Pole, tracing an ellipse over a period of nearly twenty-six thousand years through the constellations of the zodiac. It passes through each constellation approximately every two thousand one hundred and fifty years. The further we move away from the centre of the galaxy, we fall asleep: we forget who we are and from whence we came. As we move past the halfway mark, we begin to wake up.

Some believe that we are waking up because we are entering the Age of Aquarius, a more harmonious time of rising consciousness, although I could find no consistency in thinking about which age we are in right now.

I am neither an astronomer nor an astrologer, but I do observe that many of us seem to be moving from a time when we were content to be told what to think and believe, to a period of realisation that there is 'something more'. We are becoming aware that there is more to life than material success and approval. It's as if the blinkers are being removed from our eyes and, instead of seeing the narrow view of life through our cultural and family indoctrination, something in us wants to open up to 360° vision. We want to see and feel everything.

Soul or spirit – defining the indefinable

Pierre Teilhard de Chardin was a French philosopher, Jesuit priest and mystic who died in 1955. He is often quoted as saying:

> *"We are not human beings having a spiritual experience. We are spiritual beings having a human experience."*

I understand that he meant that we are much more than our physical body. We are spiritual beings that have come here to experience human emotion and three-dimensional living in a dense human body.

For a long time, I was confused by the words, 'soul' and 'spirit'. Some religions try to make a distinction between the two concepts, but when I searched for a definition of the two words, there seemed to be conflicting ideas and no real agreement.

Dr Michael Newton, author of *Destiny of Souls*, tells us that, through his experience of regressive hypnotherapy with hundreds of patients, he discovered that we have the ability to remember our soul's life between lives. After death we return 'home' to a place that could be called 'soul world' (my words not Dr Newton's) or the heavenly place described by many religions. He consistently uses the word 'soul' to describe that part of us that is immortal.

In *The Magus of Strovolos*, Kyriacos C. Markides documents the life and work of Stylianos Atteshlis, a twentieth-century Cypriot mystic, healer and spiritual teacher. Daskalos (the Greek word for teacher), as he preferred to be called, also uses the word 'soul', telling us that:

> *"The soul is that part of ourselves which is pure and uncoloured by earthly experience. The soul is our divine essence, unchangeable and eternal. We have a permanent personality, a part of ourselves upon which the incarnational experiences are recorded and transferred from one incarnation to the next."*

The Oxford English Dictionary defines spirit as: *"The soul: the non-physical part of a person regarded as their true self and as capable of surviving physical death or separation."*

Because there is no clear consensus, I have used the words interchangeably throughout this book.

We bring a part of ourselves, our 'permanent personality', or perhaps our soul personality, into each incarnation. It fuses with the inherited traits of our new human persona. According to Dr Newton's regressed patients, our soul chooses our next incarnation and knows our purpose for coming here. When we are born, the veil drops and most of us become immersed in this physical reality of the five senses, forgetting who we really are and why we are here. Our current human persona takes over and we lose the connection with our soul and the Source from whence we came. Shakti Gawain, in her book, *Living in the Light*, observes:

> *"The physical world still exists at a relatively primitive level of creation compared to the consciousness of our spirits."*

Our human mind and body are concerned with primitive survival issues: food, shelter, territory (the right to live in a place), harm to health and life, reproduction, and emotional nurturing. Once we are here and we forget our soul's existence, we take on the survival consciousness of the physical world: we lose touch with our true power as spiritual beings. Our focus is on the external world of doing, achieving, and belonging to a tribe or cultural group.

Many of us feel lost and alone, living a life that seems mundane and devoid of meaning or satisfaction. Daskalos says:

> *"We are gods but we are not aware of it. We suffer from self-inflicted amnesia. The aim is to reawaken that which we have always been and we shall always be."*

Apart from a few already enlightened individuals, for most of us waking up and becoming conscious is a process of spiritual and personal growth that can last a lifetime. The more consciously evolved among us are multi-sensory and able to reach altered states of consciousness where they become aware of other energies beyond the three-dimensional. These people are the healers, psychics, mediums and true spiritual teachers of the world. The rest of us, caught up in survival consciousness but aware of something more, could be termed 'spiritual intellectuals' (Daskalos uses the term *"intellectual mystics"*). We may feel the pull of Spirit quite strongly at times, but mostly we begin the process of walking with a foot in both worlds at an intellectual level.

Spirituality and religion

When I first started bringing spirituality into my teaching, I found that people were confused because of religious doctrine which says that only organised religion and its priests can be the source of spirituality. I came up against this attitude when I was renting a consulting room in Brussels from an American Christian group who were doing valuable work in the community. They had no church building and no preachers. I admired their approach to helping those less fortunate, and I liked their apparent openness to my work in natural health and raising people's consciousness. However, after a while things became uncomfortable and it transpired that one of their younger members was very unhappy with me talking about spirituality in my group programmes. He proclaimed that only Christians can talk about spirituality and what I was doing was equivalent to the work of the devil. I was stunned, and left to find new premises with the British Quakers who welcomed me and my holistic approach to life, health and spiritual growth.

Similarly, I was listening one day to the God spot on BBC radio and heard someone high in the ranks of the Church of England being very derogatory about *"so called New Age spirituality"*. He said that it was nonsense to think that we can *"cherry-pick what we believe in"*, stating that *"there is only one set of beliefs as defined by the Anglican Church"*. I started grumpily telling this guy that spirituality is so much more exciting, mystical and amazing than the 'truths' cherry-picked for his religion by the Romans in the fourth century AD (or CE common era which some use instead of the old AD). Unfortunately, he couldn't hear me. As truth-seekers we must listen to our inner guidance. As Elizabeth Gilbert says in *Eat, Pray, Love*:

> *"You have the right to cherry-pick when it comes to moving your spirit and finding peace in God. You take whatever works from wherever you can find it, and you keep moving toward the light."*

Here are some thoughts on the subject of spirituality and religion. Feel free to agree or disagree. Go with what resonates with you as your own truth.

While historically we associate spirituality with organised religion, the two are not necessarily the same. Religion can be a route to spiritual learning and comfort, but it can also put an obstacle in the way of people finding their own soul connection and truth.

Traditionally, religion provided rules for living and a moral code that gave structure to communities. In societies all over the world, organised religion still represents a focal point for people to come together, to connect with each other, and to share comfort and caring. For many, religion can be the vehicle through which they discover their spiritual self. Without a doubt there are many gifted healers and spiritual teachers in all organised religions.

Our beliefs about ourselves and our own spirituality have been shaped by centuries of religious interpretation of what is right and wrong, and what constitutes 'spiritual'. Someone who is 'good' measured against religiously defined norms could be regarded as spiritual or even saintly. Conversely, someone who does not live up to those norms would never be 'good enough' to be seen as spiritual. As what is deemed acceptable or spiritual behaviour changes with the times, and from culture to culture, how we see ourselves through the eyes of our chosen religious order is a constantly changing dynamic.

Throughout history until more recent times, we have been controlled by religion, which has traditionally been run by powerful men who wanted us to believe that we could never be good enough to join their God in his kingdom. The Catholic Church's concept of 'original sin' was designed to keep us in a place of self-doubt and low self-esteem, and therefore more easily manipulated to the thinking of religious leaders.

At the centre of all religions that developed from the teachings of wise men and women (although women have historically been either written out of religion, or their role has been diminished) is the message of love, compassion, tolerance and connection to a powerful Source or God. Far too often the message has been misinterpreted, or conveniently forgotten, as the ego took over, operating from its most primitive setting of survival fear and a need for power over others. Seeing others as different or wrong has led to centuries of atrocities carried out by organised religions that claim exclusivity to the truth, the justification being that if their beliefs are the one and only, then everyone else's must be wrong.

Discussing spirituality and Christianity at length with a lively Anglican vicar, I soon realised that organised religion is like a club. To be a member you must accept their rule book, traditions and teachings. Most religions dictate what we should believe. They demand faith in those beliefs and expect complete loyalty to the club. In times gone by, being excommunicated if you didn't adhere to the rules was a big deal as you were shunted to the wilderness on the edge of society, lonely and unprotected.

Nowadays, in many countries, religion and politics have been separated sufficiently so that we can now choose what we believe. Many of us are turning away from the dogma of organised religion and seeking our own spiritual path. Sometimes it can feel like a long and treacherous road as we learn to navigate our way through the bewildering complexity of beliefs and different teachings, most of which we may end up rejecting as irrelevant to our needs.

Spiritual beings

What does it mean to be spiritual? For me, spirituality does not mean floating around on a cloud of saintly goodness. People often feel guilty and a failure when they try to 'be spiritual' and still end up yelling at the driver who just cut them up on the road, or they are mean to their spouse. Living in the real world means being human with all our frailties and strengths: one day you can feel calm, loving and wise, and then just as suddenly you feel irritated, judgemental and petty.

Most people believe that we have to 'do' or 'be' something special to be spiritual. We compare ourselves with others whom we regard as more qualified to be spiritual, while we could never be 'good enough'. This is programmed conditioning due to centuries of beliefs passed down from one generation to the next. We have lost touch with our own soul, burying it under layers of insecurity and low self-esteem.

Jerry believed that he wasn't a likeable kind of guy. His self-worth was based on how hard he worked at his job. He had a constant need to prove himself as worthy. On the other hand, his friend Helen was a 'spiritual' person because she was 'so good'. She only ever thought of others, had true compassion for everyone, and sacrificed her own needs so that everyone else would be happy. That she felt permanently depressed didn't detract from Jerry's belief that he was a non-spiritual person while Helen was truly spiritual.

In time, Jerry came to value his own uniqueness. He learned to love and accept himself just the way he was. When he realised that, as a spirit in human form he had nothing to prove, he found that just being himself was enough to inspire others who were attracted to his authentic energy. He saw that we are all made up of strengths and weaknesses. As he helped Helen through her depression he felt his heart open to her suffering, and in that moment he began to truly understand the meaning of spirituality.

Spirituality is the acknowledgement of Spirit as an essential component of human nature, and is linked to our sense of magic and mysticism. There is something in most of us that seeks the spiritual. If we believe the sages and spiritual teachers, then we already are spiritual beings just by being here on planet Earth. This should come as a relief. We are here in physical body because, at a soul level, we chose this existence to learn and create. Some of us are more evolved along the path towards love and wisdom than others when we arrive here. These may be the older souls. Others, younger souls, may have a few more lifetimes to catch up.

Most of us resist the possibility that we already 'know' everything we need to know and that what we seek is already within us: we have just for-gotten how to connect with the wise or authentic part of ourselves. While we are busy looking 'out there' for the answers, we miss the wisdom that is waiting within. Once we get past our mind's programmed conditioning and listen to the whispers, we become aware that we have a soul. It can feel like the 'real me', a wiser, more patient version of the 'me'. This wise self smiles lovingly while we flounder around in this human existence. She speaks to us but we can't hear her, because we have learned to tune her out. We have been taught to seek the expertise of others who are usually just as confused as we are.

When we tune into our own spirituality, we feel it as a deep sense of peace, love and interconnectedness. It is an inner sense of being a part of something greater than our ego personality. We feel the pull of Spirit towards something more meaningful. Many have a 'knowing' that they are here for a reason, although it is often not clear what that might mean.

Ordinary people want to live from a place of love and joy, in touch with their innate spiritual selves, but don't always know how to achieve it. Many are hearing the cry from their soul. They come from all walks of life and they are all hungering for 'something more'. I have had amazing conversations with all kinds of people, including waiters, taxi drivers, hairdressers and strangers on trains who, once they realise that they won't be laughed at, start talking about their dreams, their psychic experiences, and their yearning for magic and mysticism.

For a long time, religion and science ridiculed the concepts of magic and mysticism, but now we are hearing more about quantum physics, a branch of science that is showing us that there may be an explanation for scientific anomalies. They tell us that protons really can be in two places at the same time, that time and space are not linear, and that the human mind has powers of creation and healing way beyond the five senses. It may take a while for the conventional scientific community to catch up with these ideas but, in the meantime, we can seek our own truth by keeping up-to-date with the pioneers who are already pushing the boundaries of scientific research.

Doing and being

In the industrialised world, most of us are so focused on the external world of DOING that we have neglected our internal world of BEING, to the detriment of our mental, physical and emotional health. When I was a kid, we sang a skipping song: *"Keep the kettle boiling, miss a loop you're out."* The game was that two people held the skipping rope and kept it turning while we queued up to jump in and out of the rope without stopping it. I remember the fear and shame of catching my foot on the rope and being the one to bring the game to a halt.

Too many of us live as though we must 'keep the kettle boiling' because if we miss a loop our world will come crashing down around us. Ironic really, because I also remember the image of the brave new world being painted in the 1970s, one in which, as technology got more sophisticated, we would have more leisure time. All these years later that optimistic vision for our future clearly hasn't happened. While some people cannot find work, others are working harder and often doing the job of two or three people. On top of that, they may be trying to bring up families, be loving partners, good friends and family members, and manage with less money to pay ever-increasing living costs. The pressure is enormous. It can feel like constantly juggling plates in the air. Making enough time to just relax and do nothing seems like a luxury. Even when there is time to relax, some people feel so guilty that they aren't 'doing something' that they can't enjoy the moment. The inability to relax is endemic and can lead to exhaustion, burnout and ill health.

With most working practice based on left-brained thinking, when we walk through the door of our workplace it is easy to feel like a brain on a chair, as if we cut have ourselves off at the neck. We are actively discouraged from being emotional or from making decisions based on emotion. Being unwell, overwhelmed, or spiritually and emotionally drained are all seen as a sign of weakness. We ignore our inner self and the need for peace, harmony and tranquillity at the risk for our physical and mental health.

While having too much to do is a fact of life for many people, for some it is a way of filling a void. Busyness keeps the fears at bay. Keeping busy also prevents us from turning inwards and being in stillness with ourselves. The fear is that we may not like what we find there. Yet when we make friends with ourselves we can relax as we have one less person with whom we think we have to do battle.

Accessing our inner world can feel scary. We know so much about life 'out there', but nothing about who we really are. Going inwards is something that those on their spiritual path have been doing for thousands of years. Organised religion took over the wellbeing of our soul and discouraged us from seeking connections to our spiritual selves and the Divine unless it was through the conduit of a priest or holy man. Healers and those in tune with their multi-sensory abilities were actively discouraged through ridicule, exclusion, torture and death. We learned to mistrust ourselves. This left a spiritual void which we have tried to fill by turning outwards, focusing on what we can experience with our five senses. We try to satisfy that internal longing through constant busyness, for power over others, status, needy relationships, and the acquisition of material possessions.

Taking quiet time for ourselves helps us reconnect with our inner world. It is a process of reintegration of the external world of doing and the internal world of being to find that elusive inner peace that so many people desire.

Reconnecting with our divine self
Because we are stuck in rational brain, 'focus on the here and now' mode, it can seem like a real challenge to get in touch with our own

soul. Until we do we will not be able to integrate every bit of ourselves and feel whole again. Our life may seem unfulfilled. We can't shake off the anxiety that there must be more to life than this. When we are able to connect with our true nature on all levels: the mental, physical, emotional and spiritual, then we can start to walk with a foot balanced in both worlds instead of with a lopsided limp.

The different methods that mankind has employed throughout history to reconnect with his gods or divine self can seem rather complicated and a bit random. They have involved the use of magic herbs and mushrooms; living in the wilderness alone; fasting; sitting cross-legged on mountain tops; walking on hot coals; self-flagellation; hair shirts; sexual abstinence; living in silence or isolation from society; wandering alone in the wilderness; sweat lodges; years spent in meditation or prayer; self-deprivation; self-denial; denying others fun and laughter; avoiding certain foods; sleep deprivation; walking miles barefoot on pilgrimage; and animal and human sacrifice. The more joyful methods include chanting, drumming, dancing and singing (with or without those magic mushrooms).

Some folk need to challenge their human endurance to the limit in order to feel the connection to their God or spiritual self. Perhaps they chose to come here to experience extreme human conditions and emotions. These are the people who seek to reach an altered state of consciousness through shamanic vision quests (isolating themselves on a mountain top with no food for five days), white water rafting, bungee jumping, walking a tightrope between skyscrapers, or climbing high mountains without oxygen. For them fear and excitement, which have the same stimulating effect on the mind and body, allow them to transcend the mind and all its inane chitter chatter.

To the fainthearted, most spiritual practice can seem like really hard work and involve an awful lot of pain or suffering. If we are spiritual beings having a human experience, then to my way of thinking, we should be able to access our spiritual self through our human self with joy and in comfort.

Stillness

There is one universal spiritual practice that can be learned and practised by everyone, and that is stillness. Stillness is a detachment from our mind that allows us to achieve a peaceful state of being. It is a space within our mind where there is nothing, no thinking, no drama, just peace. Through stillness, we replace noisy mind chatter with silence, which allows us to hear the whispers from our soul. We connect to 'other' and suddenly our life starts to make some sense. Eckhart Tolle tells us in *A New Earth*:

> *"Stillness has no form – that is why through thinking we cannot become aware of it … You are never more essentially, more deeply, yourself than when you are still … When you are still, you are who you are beyond your temporal existence: consciousness – unconditioned, formless, eternal."*

To reconnect with our soul self, it is vital to have enough quiet time to just be with ourselves, undistracted by others or by activity of any kind. This represents quite a challenge for those who are so wound up with busyness that they feel anxious when they stop. Most people feel very uncomfortable at the prospect of doing absolutely nothing: no reading, no listening to music, no fiddling with smart phones or i-thingies, and no chatting with anyone. Yet we can all find a few minutes somewhere in our busy day to consciously sit quietly, not focused on anything, letting our mind wander through daydreaming, contemplation and meditation.

Daydreaming

As children most of us were quite naturally able to daydream: detaching the mind from current everydayness and going into dreamlike thoughts and fantasies while still awake. Yet if we were caught daydreaming at school, we were admonished for 'not paying attention'. This is a shame because time spent letting our mind wonder in a daydream helps us reconnect to our creative right brain and our intuition. Through daydreaming we may tune into the whispers from our soul and our unseen guides.

Our daydreams are a form of visualisation. When we daydream we connect with our imagination and see ourselves living our dreams, recreating a reality where we reach our potential. Some studies show that people who allow themselves to daydream tend to be more creative and are more able to think outside the box than non-daydreamers.

Contemplation

Contemplation is a form of daydreaming where we start with a concept or thought and immerse ourselves in it, following the images, ideas and trains of thought until a truth reveals itself. For example, letting the mind wander around the concept of walking with a foot in both worlds may reveal an insight or a sense of true understanding: that 'aha' moment as we understand something at both a heart and mind level.

During contemplation you should start to relax and feel more connected. If you feel more anxious that is a sign that your ego is in control. You find yourself going over and over a situation that makes you feel resentful, guilty, ashamed or anxious. This is not contemplation. This is 'going nowhere' thinking and getting stuck. The moment you realise you are in ego stories about right and wrong, good and bad, them and us, who did what to whom and how bad somebody or something is, it is time to stop. Breathe and see if you can get back to a daydreaming or contemplative state.

Meditation

Contemplation where you mull over a train of thought to see where it will lead is different to meditation. Learning to meditate helps to quiet a busy mind. The object is to let go of organised thinking and let your mind wander while you focus on your breathing, an object or a mantra. The aim is not to stop all mind activity, but rather to detach from any thinking and allow it to pass by without your need to take part in it.

Meditation certainly relaxes the mind and body. Research on the brain during meditation shows a slowing of brain waves from beta waves, when the brain is in active thinking mode, to the slower alpha waves which characterise wakeful rest. Experienced meditators are able to move into theta waves indicating deep relaxation which is different to the delta waves of sleep. Elizabeth Gilbert describes her own experience of moving into theta waves in her book, *Eat, Pray, Love*. She tells us:

"Mystics across time and cultures have all described a stilling of the brain during meditation and say that the ultimate union with God is a blue light radiating from the center of their skulls ... and which Yogis call the 'blue pearl'."

She goes on to tell us about neurologists who scanned the brain of a Tibetan monk during meditation. They were able to see clearly how his brain stilled so completely that all his neurological energy pooled into the centre of his brain into a small, cool, blue pearl of light, as described by Yogis.

I tried a meditation class a couple of times but with my overactive Western mind I had real problems detaching from my thinking. I would start to meditate and then, absolutely convinced I had sat there for thirty minutes, I would check my watch to discover that a mere five minutes had passed. Then one day my daughter gave me a meditation CD that really calmed my active brain. I started to meditate on my own to this music and, after what I thought was five minutes passing, I would check my watch to find a whole thirty minutes had gone by. I felt relaxed and at peace with myself. With subsequent practice, I am now often able to sit quietly without music and move into what feels like a 'settled place' where I am at one with the Universe.

If you have tried meditation and found it too hard, play some meditation music that resonates with you at a heart level. Sit quietly and comfortably with your eyes closed and just focus on the music and the relaxing effect it has on your mind and body. If images come to mind through the music, allow your mind to wander around the images. If you start getting into thinking and mind chatter mode, see if you can just let the thinking go. Imagine balloons around the thoughts, see yourself letting go of the string and watching your thought balloons float up and away. You do not have to attach to your thinking.

Mindfulness

To live a conscious life means being mindful. When we are mindful we are completely in the moment, free from the mind's worries about the past and the future. Mindfulness is a form of daily, minute by minute meditation where we tune into our chattering mind and consciously let it go. We keep bringing ourselves right back to the moment and a sense of calm.

Mindfulness means being able to observe how our mind's programming can keep us stuck in external reality and noisy, chattering, busyness. For spiritual intellectuals, understanding how the mind works is an important step towards taking back control of our mind instead of it controlling us. Eckhart Tolle in *A New Earth* tells us:

"Unless you know the basic mechanics behind the workings of the ego (mind), you won't recognise it, and it will trick you into identifying with it again and again. It takes you over, an impostor pretending to be you. The act of recognition itself is one of the ways in which awakening happens."

Mindfulness starts with becoming the Observer of our mind, a process of conscious observation which raises self-awareness. When we understand the part our mind plays in our thoughts, feelings and behaviours we can begin to let go of some of the deeply embedded programmed conditioning that causes us to self-sabotage. Finally we find some relief, a sense of peace and connection with our soul. Eckhart Tolle again:

"At the heart of the new consciousness lies the transcendence of thought, the newfound ability of rising above thought, of realising a dimension within yourself that is infinitely more vast than thought. You no longer derive your identity, your sense of who you are, from the incessant stream of thinking ... What a liberation to realise that the 'voice in my head' is not who I am."

Because we chose to come to this beautiful planet to experience the joy of living with Mother Earth, being in nature helps us to connect to our innate spiritual self. Walking with bare feet in the earth, on dew drenched grass or feet paddling in the ocean, can bring a sense of peace and connection to ourselves and everything around us.

Most human activity, when done from a place of peaceful and relaxed enjoyment, can connect us to our spiritual self. We may experience it when absorbed in any form of creative self-expression such as dancing, painting or sewing; making love; listening to or making music; hugging another person; being around animals; playing with children; being immersed in work that inspires us; connecting with love to other people; spending time in quiet contemplation or meditation. Anything that comes from the creative right brain connects us to our spiritual self. The more able we are to make that connection at will, the more free and peaceful we feel.

Intuition

Our soul tries to bring to our awareness that we are more than an ego personality, that we have powers beyond our mind's imagination. The messages may take the form of intuition, which is a form of 'knowing' without any conscious thought or rationale behind it. Intuition is a voice from the right brain wherein lies our connection to our soul or wise self, to a collective consciousness, our spirit helpers and guides, and to a higher power, whatever we perceive that to be.

Intuition may come in the form of dreams, hunches and synchronicity (often brushed off as 'mere coincidence' or 'luck') that seem to defy logic. It can occur as 'chance' encounters or random but meaningful conversations with friends and strangers. Intuition is usually accompanied by a feeling in the body, often referred to as a 'gut feeling', or a flutter in the solar plexus.

As intuition is so hard to define in mainstream scientific terms, we are pretty much taught to ignore it. Instead we are trained to think only with our rational, logical left brain. It then becomes even harder for us to hear our intuitive voice because it is drowned out by our noisy mind chatter.

As we become more comfortable with listening to our intuition, following the sudden 'whim' to do or not do something, decision-making becomes much easier. We learn to trust that we are being guided and the messages become clearer. When I ask for guidance, I sometimes hear words quite clearly in my head as though they are being spoken by someone. I don't hear long sentences, usually a phrase which is clear and concise. It tells me exactly what I need to hear even though it may not have been what I was expecting to hear.

So how do you recognise when you are being guided by your intuition towards integrity or being directed by your ego to resist change? You can start by noticing how you feel. Do you feel stressed or anxious? Are the voices nagging, loud or critical? Or do they sound like a whisper from the depths of your heart and soul accompanied by a flutter of anticipation like butterfly wings? Maybe you feel a surge of positive energy? With practice you will know when your intuition is guiding you to successful creation, and when your ego is trying to keep you stuck in your story.

Guided visualisations

I use guided visualisations in my work for relaxation, for unblocking deep-seated subconscious beliefs and behaviours, and for helping people to move forward when they feel stuck. Guided visualisations harness the power of an overactive Western mind by allowing the mind to conjure up images and then guide them to achieve a specific objective. They help open our heart, connect to our soul self, create a sense of peace, and can help with healing from physical health problems. They even work for people who aren't particularly visual because they involve all the senses, including auditory and feelings. The person experiencing a guided visualisation stays in control at all times.

All ancient healing and spiritual traditions use guided visualisations as a form of inner journey to ask for guidance, by connecting with our innate wisdom, our soul or higher self, our intuition and our invisible helpers: our angels, guides or Spirit. Because we have been brainwashed to discount anything magical, mystical, spiritual or paranormal, it is too easy for many of us to dismiss the messages from our guides as just our imagination. I don't think it matters where the guidance originates, whether within the circuitry of our brains (the mainstream scientific view) or from external sources (the spiritual perspective). If the messages we receive help us to move forward from where we are stuck, then it doesn't really matter from whence they came.

Deirdre had a great life, good job, excellent health and a kind, if rather emotionally-distant, husband. But she felt empty and restless, and said, *"I want to know my mission in life"*. I suggested that she ask for guidance in a guided visualisation. Deirdre was sceptical but agreed. When she was relaxed and her mind had taken her to a peaceful place in nature, I suggested she invite her unseen helpers to join her. She could then ask them about her mission in life. Deirdre was surprised to find that she was joined by a group of angels who lifted her up and took her on a tour around planet Earth, showing her how people lived in different parts of the world, both rich and very poor. With great kindness and love they told her that this lesson was about feeling humility and gratitude for what she had. She had no need to be anxious, she would always be safe. When they set her back down in her favourite place they told her that when she was ready, they would give her the next lesson. At first Deirdre was awestruck, but then her ego stepped in and dismissed the vision as a figment of her imagination. Confused, she chose, at least for the time being, to stay stuck in her feelings of restlessness and lack of meaning to her life.

The Shamanistic and Pagan traditions also connect with animal and nature spirits and they often show up to guide those who need help.

Martine had just started on an anti-candida diet to help with some health issues. It was a big change to the way she normally ate, and she was feeling emotional, lonely and hopeless. During the inner journey she described standing on a high outcrop of rock at the edge of a large forest. In her words: "I am looking down into a gorge with a river flowing at the bottom, and out to forested hills and mountains in the distance. I am floating, but I can't 'see' myself, so I am not sure what my physical form is. I see a large cloud coming towards me in the shape of a lion's head and it goes right through me. It is like a mist lifting. On another outcrop I see a rearing horse and further away still a bison. I sense that the forest is full of life. I feel the power of the forest and the mountains, overwhelming but not threatening. From the corner of my eye I see a stag coming out of the woods. He stays at a distance at the edge of the trees and looks at me. The word 'patience' resounds loudly in my head. Still feeling hopeless I ask 'how long?' 'Just patience' comes the reply. Then the vision fades and I feel reassured and supported."

According to Stephen D. Farmer, in his book: *Animal Spirit Guides*, stag spirit shows up to *"help us release something that no longer fits in your life so that room will be made for the new that's ready to be birthed"*. It provides protection and lets us explore new beginnings without fear of losing ourselves. Stag energy can give us confidence and may indicate a leap of faith towards spiritual awakening. Those with the stag as their animal spirit usually have a high level of intuition, which was very appropriate for Martine.

Danielle was a shy and sensitive person. Over the years she had successfully changed much of her old programmed conditioning and was ready to take the next step towards embracing her authentic self. She saw herself sitting cross-legged in the bluebell wood (a safe haven to which she had gone in previous inner journeys). She said: "It occurred to me that it was a very safe place where I could shut myself off from the world, protected by the trees. Then a doe with big eyes came towards me and let me reach out and stroke her. I thought to myself that this was silly, it was too much like a Disney movie. I half expected there to be cartoon animals singing and dancing all around me, but that didn't happen. The doe was real, not a cartoon, and she stayed. Then suddenly I was no longer in the wood but on top of Glastonbury Tor (an ancient sacred site in Somerset, UK). Although I was totally exposed as I looked down on the countryside all around me, I felt safe."

The Doe spirit comes to help us walk the path of consciousness and unconditional love. It teaches us the power of being gentle with ourselves and to honour the child's innocence within. It also reminds us that we can touch the hearts and minds of others through the power of love and compassion. Danielle identified with the message to be gentle with herself, and that it was safe to love and be loved.

Some people connect to a different kind of nature spirit, 'elementals' that include fairies and gnomes. The vocabulary used to describe these ethereal beings varies depending on the language and tradition. In Irish Celtic tradition they are referred to as 'the little people'. Organised religion and science have pooh-poohed nature spirits as childish nonsense. As a result, we have disconnected from Mother Earth and continue to exploit and plunder her without regard for the future of her health or survival. Tanja's experience shows that 'the little people' can show up at just the right time to guide and support us.

Tanja was suffering from self-doubt both as a wife and a parent. She hated that she became easily reactive towards her husband and two small children, and rarely felt truly at peace with herself. During a guided visualisation she found herself on a high plateau. She described it as: "a bit higher than the hilly, woody area around me. I had struggled with deciding whether I wanted to be more down and protected by the woods or up high on the plateau. In the end, I chose the plateau, so I could see everything and feel the power of the wind, the sun and the land below me. I sat there in a yoga position, open to whatever came to me. I asked for guidance on what to do about my current situation. Then a group of about six small, hairy, gnome-like creatures with big noses came running around me (this was not the first time that Tanja had been guided by elementals, particularly gnomes). They were chatting, and settled down next to me around my feet. I could not understand what they were saying but their intention and my understanding was their presence was to support me. As we looked down from our plateau at the landscape, I experienced a warm, calming power that felt like a blanket enveloping me. I had an insight that

I have all the necessary tools and all the knowledge to cope. I understood that I have done really well so far and I will be able to continue. Then I found myself walking through a jungle-like forest on a meandering foot path. The small creatures were no longer with me, but the warm awareness and feeling of strength stayed with me. I heard an inner voice telling me to go on, that I am on the right path. I was surprised and reassured by the strength and clarity of the message: 'You have all the tools and all experience you need to continue. You will be fine.' I still have this warm and calm feeling and it is great."

Leap of faith

As a truth-seeker you may have to take a blind leap of faith. Most of us are taught that 'seeing is believing', in other words, we will not allow ourselves to believe anything until it has been proved to be of value. This way of thinking stops most of us even trying, because we need to know in advance that we will succeed. Our ego demands proof or some way of measuring success: *I need to see results before I can continue with this. How do I know this will work? I can't fail again, I must know that I will succeed this time.*

We cannot know the outcome of our voyage of self-discovery. There is an element of trust that whatever happens is all part of the journey and that we will grow from the experience.

In the movie, *Indiana Jones and the Last Crusade,* in his search for the Holy Grail that will cure his dying father, Indiana Jones arrives on the edge of an abyss. He must get to the other side but there is no way he can jump. He must take a leap of faith. The ancient writings tell him that the bridge of faith will appear to support him and take him across the abyss to the other side. It is a heart-stopping moment as he takes his first step out into nothing. The bridge appears and he crosses safely.

Many people feel stuck and afraid to move forward. They want to take the leap of faith but continue driving along through life with one foot on the accelerator and the other on the brake. When we are willing to tune into the whispers from our soul self, we can start walking with a foot in both worlds: the here and now, everyday, clunky, three-dimensional world of our physical selves, and the higher state of connection with 'something else' and our creative self-expression.

Some are afraid to take the leap because they are afraid of failure. This is ego-programmed conditioning: *I won't take the risk because failure is painful.* On our personal journey of self-discovery we cannot fail. We can stumble, fall, pick ourselves up, lick our wounded pride and figure out how to keep going. We can never be a failure in the internal world of personal and spiritual growth. We can only learn whatever it is we need to learn to reach our potential for health, happiness and unconditional love.

The only thing we need to believe in is ourselves. We take a leap of faith and believe that our higher, wise or authentic self already 'knows' exactly what we need to do to regain wholeness. In these terms, wholeness is the integration of every bit of ourselves, even the bits we don't like. When we reconnect our mind, body, emotions and spirit, we regain integrity.

Finding the balance

Walking with a foot in both worlds can be very challenging. Liz, a PR assistant in her mid-forties was very sensitive to the harsh reality of living in the twenty-first century. She was aware of a connection to something deep inside that was not being nurtured by her career, relationships, healthy income or global travel. In the search for this connection, she spent most of her vacation time and weekends on retreats learning about energy healing. Each time she returned from a course she felt uplifted, for about five minutes. Then she would return to earth with a bump on Monday morning, sat in a traffic jam, and spending ten hours a day coping with problems at work.

Liz had a really hard time dealing with everyday life when her heart just wasn't in it. She heard the call from her heart and soul but had no idea how to respond while living in the external world of doing. In her mind it was all or nothing: she either had to leave her job for something vague and be unable to pay her bills, or she had to suffer the next twenty years at her desk until she could take retirement.

The strain of living with inner conflict eventually burnt her out. She collapsed, had to take sick leave and it was months before she was well enough to return to her job. She decided enough was enough. To avoid further emotional turmoil, she would just focus on living day to day and ignore her soul's yearning.

This decision didn't make her feel any happier. Every waking moment, and even in her dreams, Liz had a very powerful sense of being here to help others. She became restless and agitated, but afraid to attempt her soul searching again because she didn't want to risk having another breakdown.

When she started learning to walk with a foot in both worlds, Liz realised that there was a middle way. Her black and white thinking was the root cause of her distress. She was able to find balance in her life, both the external world of doing and her inner world of connection to soul self. Eventually she learned to ask her unseen helpers, her angels and spirit guides, for guidance, and to trust that she would recognise the guidance when it came. She was able to do this while still going to work, paying bills and living her daily life, all without all her usual stress.

From a practical perspective, Liz realised that she didn't have to give up the job that provided financial security. Instead she decided to start a women's group to provide an opportunity for women who felt torn like she did. They could bring their skills and experiences, and support each other in the process of walking with a foot in both worlds. The women's group initially met once a week but soon developed into weekend retreats with Liz organising facilitators and the admin side of things. Within a couple of years, Liz was doing so well that she was able to reduce her full-time job to part-time and run her retreat business from home. She was fulfilling her soul's purpose by helping women, and she was having a lot of fun in the process.

Acceptance

There is still a wistful hope in the human psyche that if we work hard enough at this spiritual thing, we will reach a magical moment in life when everything is fixed and we will live happily ever after. Indeed, our childhood is full of stories that start with 'once upon a time' and finish with 'and they lived happily ever after'. So there we are, we have worked at this walking with a foot in both worlds and had glimpses of what it feels like to be an evolved spirit in human form. We have finally found our balance, are on the right track, got it all sorted and have a smug sense of 'I've nailed it!' Then all of a sudden life throws us a cow pat or several: we lose our job, our partner leaves us, we can't afford the car repairs, our fifteen-year-old son is going off the rails, our very best friend from childhood dies unexpectedly, or we have just been diagnosed with a hard-to-treat health problem. Our world is falling apart. This is not what we signed up for.

Life falling apart triggers strong feelings of anxiety, fear, grief, guilt, loneliness, shame, anger, powerlessness and helplessness. It doesn't matter how much we intellectually know that horrible things happen, we still continue to resist this simple fact of life. Try as we may, it is hard for most of us to completely accept that life involves feeling pain and suffering, along with the moments of fulfilment and joy. When we are experiencing shock and pain, how do we handle this apparent discrepancy between spiritual and human life without going completely crazy? Unless we are willing to withdraw to an ashram or monastery, we are stuck here bumbling along trying to make sense of it all. I talk more about falling apart in Chapter 11.

It doesn't matter how spiritually evolved we think we are, most of us have a tendency to run away from the pain, to try and suppress it, to 'get over it' as quickly as possible and 'move on'. We turn to our habitual addictions to distract us: food, chocolate, alcohol, smoking, never being alone, busyness, the latest gadgets, prescribed medications, shopping, excessive exercise. We are good at pushing away our feelings which causes them to get blocked as emotional energy in the body. We can end up carrying around a lifetime of heavy emotional baggage because most of us are not taught to be comfortable with our feelings, to just allow them to flow through us without resistance. Rather than running away from them we can learn to be at ease with them. Pema Chödrön calls them the *"sharp points"* and tells us:

> *"Lean into the sharp points and fully experience them. The essence of bravery is being without self-deception. Wisdom is inherent in (understanding) emotions."*

Learning to lean into the sharp points of painful emotions releases blocked energy and can have a dramatic effect on our physical and mental health. We begin to experience acceptance, which is not an easy concept for the Western mind. Acceptance doesn't mean 'putting up' with anything that goes against our values, nor does it mean 'being resigned' to something that hurts us. While we may care deeply that someone we love has died or that our dreams have been shattered, acceptance means finding that sense of peace in the middle of chaos because, at some level, we may sense that whatever is happening right now is happening for a reason. It may not yet be clear what that reason might be.

Walking with a foot in both worlds is observing ourselves handling life as a human being, doing the best we can, dealing with the joys and the crises because this is what we chose at a soul level. If we believe in reincarnation, then we chose to come here and have these experiences to help with our spiritual evolution. How we deal with life's challenges is the test. Can we allow ourselves to feel whatever we feel, without resistance? Can we then deal with the situation in a calm and rational way, aided by our intuition guiding us through the mire?

Acceptance is the opposite of fighting reality. It is being with reality, allowing ourselves to feel what we feel with loving kindness and compassion towards ourselves. If we cannot change external circumstances, acceptance means that perhaps we can go inwards, examine our thinking and even turn adversity into an opportunity to help others in a similar predicament. When we suffer, we find our compassion for those who are also suffering, and through helping others we may find our own path.

When we learn to walk with a foot in both worlds, life changes in ways we hadn't imagined. We start to experience a sense of freedom that has nothing to do with where we are, what we are doing or who we are with, but is an internal state of being. We can feel devastated, anxious, grief stricken, or enraged, but have a sense of calm at our centre, a place to which we know can return when the storm has died down. It is already in every one of us just waiting for us to connect to it.

Chapter 4

Fear and love

"There are two basic motivating forces: fear and love. When we are afraid, we pull back from life. When we are in love, we open to all that life has to offer with passion, excitement and acceptance." John Lennon

What stops us from seeking our own truth and living a conscious life? If walking with a foot in both worlds brings so much peace and serenity, why aren't we all doing it? Probably because it is just too easy to make excuses that sound perfectly rational and logical: *I don't have time. It doesn't fit with my schedule. I can't afford to give up what I have now. My family and friends wouldn't approve. My spouse would think I had gone crazy. What if I fail? People will think I am weird. I don't want to be different. How can I know for sure this is right for me? What if I lose everything? Better to stay with what I know than to take a risk. It's not the right time.*

While timing is an important part of when and how we start making changes, behind many of our excuses is the primal driving force of fear. Fear is what stops us in our tracks, often before we have even taken the first step. Fear causes us to hold ourselves back through lack of self-belief and self-trust. Fear and the ego block the whispers from our soul.

Elizabeth Kübler-Ross, psychiatrist and pioneer in near-death studies, said: *"There are only two emotions: love and fear."* All other emotions are shades and tones of these two primary emotions. Human beings are designed to live mostly in a state of love, and keep a small amount of space for healthy fear, the kind of fear that protects us from injury and death.

Love is our natural state of being, yet as a species, we have learned to live mostly from a state of fear. It is so pervasive that we no longer recognise that most of our thinking and behaviours stem from fear instead of love. This has had a disastrous effect on humankind at both a personal and a global level.

Fear is hardwired into the primitive part of our brain (also called the 'old' or 'reptilian' brain) for safety and survival, which are the sole purposes of fear. We do not have to fear events, other people, and especially ourselves, unless they, or we, present a direct threat to our safety or survival.

As a species we have learned to live in fear of many things that have nothing to do with threat or danger. We fear others, what they might think of us, what they might do to us, how they might make us feel. We have learned to fear ourselves. We fear that we are not good enough, that we must prove ourselves, that we don't belong, and that we are not lovable or deserving. We fear success and failure, rejection, disapproval and being outcast. Because we don't feel safe in our own self-worth, we are more sensitive to the opinions and actions of others. Fear of our own lack of self-worth is usually the root cause of self-sabotaging or self-limiting behaviour.

Many people spend their lives with low-level background anxiety (which is a shade of fear) never really understanding its origin. I thought I had understood and overcome most of my fears until I had a burnout. Then I started to recognise the subliminal anxiety that accompanied me through life. With anxiety the adrenals produce the hormones cortisol and adrenaline to create a state of fight or flight. This is the body's primitive survival technique for either removing us from danger, or giving us the energy and strength to fight it. If cortisol and adrenaline don't get switched off after the danger has past, they start causing problems with health. In particular, cortisol, constantly circulating in the blood, damages the central nervous system (the brain), the immune system, and the adrenal glands themselves. It can even damage bone endings and many enzyme systems in the body.

As I tuned into my body, I suddenly realised that a simple thought about my day's schedule triggered an adrenal rush of fight or flight hormones. I experimented by deliberately thinking thoughts and bringing up memories, and noticed how my adrenals responded instantly to even the most innocuous of thoughts. This was crazy! No wonder I had burnt out. Even though, at a conscious level, I was dealing well with the stresses in my life, my biological coping mechanisms had been worn down by the ever-present overstimulation of subconscious anxiety. I realised that I had probably been anxious since early childhood. In my coaching practice, I see the presence of constant low-level anxiety in many of my clients, especially those who are HSP (highly sensitive people). HSPs seem to absorb more nervous energy and anxiety than the mainstream population, and are therefore more prone to anxiety-related disorders and burnout.

Much of our fear is habitual and imagined. For most of us actually going through a crisis is often easier than living daily with our imagined fears. As Mark Twain so appropriately put it:

"I have been through some terrible things in my life, some of which actually happened."

Fear is the antagonist of peace. There can be no peace with fear, only more fear. We hand our fear on from one generation to the next, each generation unconsciously picking it up and carrying it for all the generations that have gone before. We usually don't understand its origin, we just recognise that it holds us back, and yet we are afraid to confront our fear and let it go. We fear our own fear.

Tribal influence
Our fear-driven programmed conditioning comes from the tribe, meaning our family, social groups, our peers, schools, culture, religion and national identity. Those who have had a religious upbringing know all too well the feelings of guilt and fear generated by religious indoctrination.

Whether or not we have consciously embraced its teachings, organised religion has been part of our tribal roots for the last two thousand years or more and has a huge influence on all of us. The Judeo-Christian tradition long ago removed magic and mysticism from our lives, telling us it was sinful and against God's wishes. We were discouraged from listening to our intuition because we are prey to destructive impulses and, without external control, we cannot be trusted to make wise decisions, or to live a good life. Our ancestors learned to conform for survival by not trusting themselves and always looking for guidance from the chosen few. We continue these patterns today even when we don't want to.

Tribal influences are intimately woven throughout mankind's history. It can be hard for even the most sceptical of us to shake off the deeply-held beliefs of the collective psyche. Our hunter-gatherer ancestors lived in groups that needed to stick together for basic survival. They often moved from one location to the next seeking out the best sources of food. Cohesion was important, with survival being dependent on shared beliefs, habits and strengths of the tribe. The instinct to conform to tribal beliefs continues now.

These affiliations are deeply embedded in our subconscious. Family ties can be uplifting and supporting, but they can also be neurotic and destructive, depending on how much fear has been passed down through the generations. You may be familiar with some variation of these truisms: *Blood is thicker than water. United we stand. Don't air our dirty laundry in public. We have always done it this way. What will people think?!* Their veracity is rarely questioned unless we become conscious of our thinking. They can keep us stuck forever in family patterns that act like unbreakable chains. Key figures may control with an iron rod to keep family members pandering to their neuroses and psychoses. Children are afraid to stand up to their belligerent parents, or vice versa, because of a deep-seated fear of being different to the tribal beliefs and expectations, no matter how crazy they may be.

As children we learned to suppress our own emotions and desires, to try to be good and perfect in the vain hope of earning love and approval. We learned to conform and to hide behind roles, to do what was expected, and to jump through hoops to please others. When we were told that Santa doesn't visit naughty children, that we wouldn't have the promised birthday party if we didn't perform in the exams, or we would be punished if we were bad, we soon got the message that we would never measure up to expectation. We could never be good or lovable enough. You may have grown up hearing at least some of these, usually delivered in a scolding tone of voice designed to belittle or humiliate: *Don't you argue with me! Don't answer back! Bad boy/girl! What on earth is the matter with you?! Why can't you be like … (brother, sister, neighbour's child)?! You should be ashamed of yourself! Don't be selfish. Don't be lazy! Who do you think you are?! Don't boast! Don't try to be better than you are! Don't stand out from the crowd.*

This negative conditioning is based on fear, but is so common that we don't even recognise that our beliefs and thoughts are fear-driven. Even those brought up in an environment full of love and nurturing may have received some of these fearful messages about life: *It's a dog eat dog world out there. You don't get anything for nothing. You have to work hard to survive. Laugh and the world laughs with you, weep and you weep alone. Failure isn't* an option. *There's no gain without pain. Those who ask don't get. Don't expect anything from anyone, you are on your own out there. You've made your bed, now you have to lie in it. The rich get richer and the poor get poorer. There's no such thing as a free lunch. Life's a bitch and then you die* (or as they say in California,'life's a beach and then you die', which I much prefer).

Few of us have reached adulthood escaping the power of disempowering beliefs which make up our negative programmed conditioning. They are deeply embedded in the subconscious and they have the power to control us. For example, if you learned that you were lazy if you weren't seen to be working hard, when you do try to relax you feel anxious and stressed. Deep down in your subconscious lies the belief that you must keep proving your worthiness by working hard all the time.

As adults we live in fear and insecurity because we have learned that love is conditional on being good, getting things right, and on being what others expect us to be. If we believe that nobody can love us for just being who we are, we are forever giving away our power to please others in the hope of feeling loved. The harsh authoritarian voices continue to live in our head, they keep nagging, scolding and judging us, usually more severely than anyone else would.

How can we ever truly relax and enjoy life? We may want joy and inner peace, but our internal emotional environment is in turmoil, struggle, conflict and disharmony. When we attempt to adhere to the rules of others, we cannot be true to ourselves. We cannot love ourselves for our inherent goodness, perfection and wisdom: we don't even believe we are inherently good, perfect or wise. We feel split and fragmented. We limit and sabotage ourselves in an attempt to suppress the clamour of our soul to throw off the shackles of fear and set ourselves free to be our authentic self.

It is exhausting to live like this. Unless we make a decision to the contrary, we are destined to continue to carry the burden of fear, purely because we don't recognise that is what we are doing. When we do become conscious of this process, we are afraid to drop our fear because we have deeper fears about being rejected or abandoned if we go against our 'tribal' beliefs.

Sterile science
Besides tribal and religious influences, we are also conditioned by the sterile view of mainstream science. Despite decades of published research

to the contrary, the popular view is still that there is nothing outside of our five senses. There are no such things as the soul, intuition, telepathy, sixth sense, psychics, near-death experience, mediums, channelling, magic, mysticism, nature spirits, astral projection, spirit guides, angels, miracles, faith healing or reincarnation.

Over the centuries people have suffered for deviating from religious doctrine and following their own metaphysical beliefs and abilities. Over a much shorter period of time, mainstream science has managed to achieve further suppression of our innate powers by telling us that these things do not exist, marginalising all those who say that they do. For many people, science has taken the place of religion. The left-brained, five-sensory folk staunchly defend their scientific views as absolute fact, dictating what we should believe and denying all of us who experience life in more subtle ways.

Mainstream science gives us a mechanical explanation of life based on what can be observed, measured, theorised and calculated with the left brain, the rational part of the mind. The conclusion seems to be that life is random and that we are victims of luck, coincidence, health problems, accidents and death. God can't be disproved, nor can 'He' be proved, so the scientific jury is still out on that one. There is no room for the idea that life may not be so random, and that we may have a soul plan or a purpose for the things that happen to us. Cutting ourselves off from the spiritual means that we feel alone and insecure in a random Universe. This sterile and random view of life tends to play into our basic survival fears. We fear change and avoid taking risks. We suffer because we cannot eliminate life's uncertainties, no matter how hard we try. We anxiously try to control external circumstances to make our lives safe and secure. If only we had enough money, the right insurance, the right relationships, material possessions, status, or enough people around us who share our fear-driven beliefs, then we might just feel safe, at least for a while.

Our vulnerability means that we dare not trust happiness because it never lasts long. Some more maxims: *Don't get too excited, it might all go wrong. It will all end in tears (or there will be tears before bedtime). Better play it safe, you never know what might happen. Look before you leap. Better the devil you know (than the devil you don't know). Don't jump from the frying pan into the fire. Don't go there, it might be dangerous. Be careful! Don't stick your neck out.*

Being comfortable with uncertainty is the route to freedom and peace of mind. Pema Chödrön, Buddhist teacher and author of *When Things Fall Apart*, tells us:

> *"If we're willing to give up hope that insecurity and pain be exterminated, then we can have the courage to relax with the groundlessness of our situation."*

When we are influenced by fear, we feel trapped or driven. When we can relax with uncertainty and death, then we open ourselves to love and a fulfilling life.

Fear disconnects

Fear creates feelings of separateness, disconnection, anxiety and an inability to function from our wise or soul self. It distorts our thinking and is disempowering. We feel vulnerable, unsafe and insecure, which are all shades of fear. Fear is a state of contraction where we close in on ourselves: we can no longer open our hearts to our own needs or those of others. Relationship conflict results from fear: the fear of being controlled or manipulated, of being unloved, of not being good enough, of not being seen or understood, of being treated unkindly or unjustly, of betrayal and abandonment, or of not getting our emotional needs met.

When we live in fear we turn to others to provide the solutions. We look to governments, corporations, institutions, tribal leaders, the church and experts to know how to live. Thus we give away our personal power and stay stuck in fear.

All wars and conflict are caused by fear. Fear drives us to be right at all costs. Its disconnection pushes us to hate and to make wrong the other person, group, religion or nation.

I gave a talk to a group of about thirty people on the subject of fear and how fear is usually the cause of aggression in the world. One of the men in the audience angrily interjected with a comment that: *"Of course we aggress others. There is a lack of resources and we have the right to invade other countries and take what we want!"* So there it was, clearly articulated, the belief that we have the right to cause suffering to others to assuage our own fear of not having enough. No doubt there are enough resources for everyone if only we were willing to live from a place of love and sharing, instead of from fear. Over-consumption and waste in industrialised countries would more than meet the basic needs of those still struggling in other parts of the world. The attitude of entitlement is arrogant and causes a perpetuation of suffering and fear. This is mankind's craziness.

We are fed a steady diet about all the negativity in the world. We focus on the fear-driven violent behaviours of the few rather than the loving, courageous actions of the majority. I have often wondered, what if we were to focus only on the loving acts of kindness and goodness in people, would we eventually create a cultural climate of aspiration and hope? Being loving and kind would be the example that would be shown to the world. Violence and selfishness would be viewed as deviant behaviour and would eventually die out, starved of the attention that feeds it today.

Things are changing. We are moving towards more genuine 'people power' thanks to the internet. Online campaigning organisations, started by inspired individuals, give millions of us all around the globe a powerful platform from which to express our opinions about the kind of world we want to live in. At a grassroots and a personal level, we can change the status quo of fearmongering, and take back our power to protect human rights and the health of the planet.

Understanding fear
To live a conscious life we can become aware of our fear and understand it. Once we have identified our fear, we can decide if it is rational or irrational. If the car suddenly swerves out of control you will definitely feel rational fear for your safety and will do your best not to have an accident.

Irrational fear is a message from the subconscious that an old programme from our formative years is being triggered. The trigger for fear could be anything, depending on your programming: you have decided to confront the bullying colleague at work, to stand up to your overbearing father, to ask for a pay rise, to enrol in singing classes, to offer backstage help at your local dramatic society, or to start a blog. From the minor to the major, certain events or people may provoke irrational fear in you. Once we recognise the patterns, then we can gently move them out of the way and let them go. Understanding fear is the key to overcoming it. It allows us to take back our power so that we are no longer a slave to irrational fear.

The different levels of fear

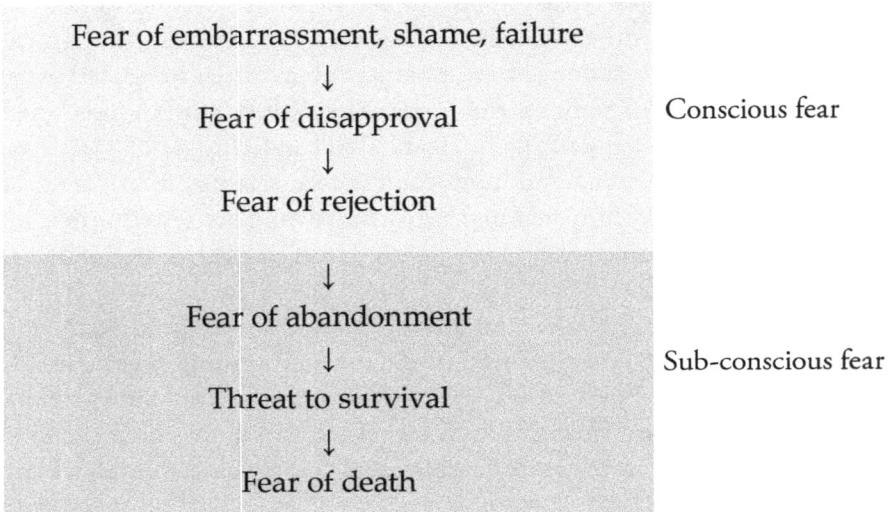

Fear of embarrassment, shame, failure
↓
Fear of disapproval   Conscious fear
↓
Fear of rejection

↓
Fear of abandonment
↓
Threat to survival   Sub-conscious fear
↓
Fear of death

There are different levels of fear, the conscious and the subconscious. At the conscious level, we are usually aware of the more obvious fears: the fear of embarrassment, shame or failure. We fear looking stupid or making a fool of ourselves. This fear is enough to stunt our development and stop us even trying to do the things we want to do. Fear of embarrassment, shame and failure stop people from speaking in public, starting a new project, asking for help, changing careers, studying for a qualification, leaving an unhappy marriage, learning a new skill, or confronting a difficult person.

Guilt

At the first level, accompanying embarrassment, shame and failure, is usually a good dose of guilt which, like fear, can be rational or irrational.

Rational guilt is like a warning signal that tells us we have not honoured our own highest potential by behaving badly or thoughtlessly towards others. We feel rational guilt when we have acted in conflict with our conscience or values by hurting someone or something. The fear we feel is shame about our behaviour and our self-worth. Rational guilt is aligned with conscience, and is an honest self-admission of wrongdoing. There isn't a person on the planet who hasn't screwed up at some time in their life. We have all done things or behaved in ways of which we are not proud. Getting it wrong, hurting ourselves and others, is all part of learning our life lessons. In an ideal world, we feel the guilt and listen to the message from our conscience. Then we take responsibility, apologise, make amends as best we can, learn from the experience, become wiser, forgive ourselves for being human, and finally let go of the guilt. Allowing ourselves to accept that we can't always be perfect, whatever being perfect might mean, is all part of our path through life.

Irrational guilt and shame are completely different. We learned irrational guilt and shame as a fear-driven response to the demands of our tribe. We learned to feel anxious and responsible for events outside of our control, or for how others feel, even when we have done nothing wrong. The perceived disapproval of tribe members causes us to feel shame just for being who we are. We flounder in a sea of low self-worth, shame and guilt.

Irrational guilt means we can feel guilty about anything: leaving a job (and letting people down), telling our parents that we want to organise our wedding our own way, eating a piece of cake, taking time out to read a book, leaving our spouse to go on a weekend retreat, being a working mum, or saying no to a family member or friend.

Irrational guilt and shame are a heavy burden. It is hard to move in any direction when whatever action we want to take brings up the fear of guilt and shame. Guilt is corrosive. It tears us down, reduces us to our smallest self, paralyses us and prevents us from being happy. It is a wasted emotion.

Carrying irrational guilt and shame around serves no purpose except to keep us disconnected from our authentic self, thus reinforcing the fear that we can never be quite good enough.

Disapproval and rejection
After embarrassment, shame, failure and guilt, the next level is the fear of disapproval: if I make a fool of myself people will laugh at me and disapprove of me.

Why do we fear disapproval so much? Because the next level of fear below disapproval is rejection: if others disapprove of me they may reject me. Often the fear of rejection is below the level of consciousness, deep in our subconscious, and is a powerful demotivator to striking out on our own spiritual path. We are social animals and need to belong to a community.

Diane wanted to solve a health problem. She was also overweight and had just recovered from adrenal exhaustion. She had a large cyst on an ovary which her doctor thought might need to be removed if it had grown any bigger at her next six-month check-up. Diane had read about natural healing and wanted to know what she could do to help her body to heal. She also wanted more energy and to lose about ten kilos. Right at the beginning of our session together, Diane put a caveat on any recommendations I might make. She was not willing to give up gluten or dairy products: she had already tried that for another health problem and it hadn't worked.

Diane was a self-confessed sugar addict and drank two to three glasses of wine every evening, as well as three or four sugary coffees throughout the day. When I talked about detoxing from sugar, alcohol and caffeine as a first step towards health, she immediately went into resistance. She insisted that she couldn't possibly give up sugar and wine, not even for a month. When I asked her why, she answered that she didn't want to feel different to other people. As an adolescent she had been bullied and all her life she had felt as though she didn't belong. She was not prepared to feel different to other people now, even if it meant her cyst might grow. For Diane, the fear of disapproval and rejection were a stronger motivating force than the possibility of working with her body to be healthy. It took some time before she was able to disassociate her eating habits from social approval. It took even more time before she realised that, not only did she not need social approval, but that most people really weren't that interested in what she was eating or drinking.

Abandonment and death
The fear of rejection leads to the next level of fear which is abandonment. This represents a threat to our very survival, at least in the mind of the baby and child. Generally, once people reach adulthood, most are able to fend for themselves. They don't need to fear being abandoned, yet this is the primal fear hardwired into our brain, because to be abandoned as a small and helpless baby means certain death.

Death is the ultimate fear. This means that our fear of embarrassment is linked to the fear of death. We even say, *"I could have died of embarrassment"*.

Actors who forget their lines, or break character by laughing, use the expression 'corpsing' to describe the experience. When we won't allow ourselves to stand up and speak in public because we fear embarrassment, shame or failure, we are being driven by our primal fear of abandonment and death. I once heard the expression, '*embarrassment is the route to freedom*'. It means that if you can allow yourself to feel embarrassed or ashamed without it destroying your sense of self, then you will be free to do or be whatever you want. I am a blushy kind of person, and for years I wouldn't talk in public because I hated the feeling of a hot flush spreading all over my face and down my neck. It announced to the world how vulnerable and anxious I felt. Then one day I realised that the need to speak my message was more important than whether or not I looked foolish. I decided to just brazen out the blushing and carry on as though it was nothing to do with me. 'Embarrassment is the route to freedom' became my mantra. Gradually I noticed that I cared less about the blushing and being embarrassed, the result being that I found I was blushing far less frequently. Having removed one obstacle of fear from my path, my confidence grew.

Most of us have conscious awareness of the fears of embarrassment, shame, failure, disapproval and rejection. Few link them to the subconscious fears of abandonment, threat to survival and death. If death and dying are our ultimate fear, then being at peace with our own mortality banishes fear. When we understand who we really are, embodied spirits having a human experience, the fear of death becomes meaningless. Each of us has to find our own truth so we can live life to the full and be at peace with our own dying.

Love

Most people know what love feels like. While growing up, they have experienced some form of love from family, friends and community. Even if abuse or neglect were thrown into the mix, the fact that someone reaches adulthood, albeit psychologically scarred, means that someone somewhere showed them sufficient love to survive. We know this because research in the 1970s showed that babies in Soviet orphanages died from lack of love. They were fed, changed and kept clean, but had no stimulation and no loving physical contact from their minders. Physical affection is needed to stimulate the production of growth hormone and the immune system. A human baby must receive love to survive, without it their body shuts down.

Once we are adults, love is a state of being that starts and ends with us. It is not dependent on situations or people. Unfortunately, most of us learned that love is conditional, that it can be switched on and off, depending on the person who is giving the love. As children we learned to survive by tuning into the state of mind of our primary caregivers and the cultural psyche of the society in which we were raised. We got the message: *Please me, please others and be good (whatever I decide 'good' to be)*, with the stated or implicit understanding that we were not lovable unless we complied. Some people learned to comply and some learned to rebel. Both reactions are a compromise on heartfelt love.

We learned different ways of loving, depending on whether someone 'belongs' to our tribal or social group, and whether they share the same beliefs about how to live. If they are perceived as different then we may be judgemental, resentful, unforgiving, cruel, hostile, bullying and even violent towards them. In this case tribal allegiances are more important than showing love and compassion towards all people, no matter who they are or what they believe. Human beings carry out the most appalling atrocities against each other because we perceive the other as different.

Some of the worst conflicts between individuals are caused by the myth of romantic love which pervades our culture and our subconscious from an early age. We are taught to believe that if only we find the right person to love us, and whom we can love, then we will feel whole and at peace with ourselves. Yet it hardly ever works out that way. Once the first flush of romance and sexual attraction diminishes, each partner can withdraw their love if the other does not fulfil their emotional needs, or behave according to their world view.

Love is unconditional
Love is unconditional. It allows us to live in a state of interconnectedness with ourselves, each other, every living thing on the planet, and a Divine Source or God, whatever we each perceive that to be. Love is a state of expansion and trust. You don't have to 'measure up' to someone else's definition of perfection or acceptability to feel love. When you live from a place of love, you can trust your emotions and your intuition. You live life with courage and joy.

Conditional love is an oxymoron. Love is never conditional. It is not dependent on another indulging our emotional or psychological needs.

Conditional love is fear in disguise: the fear of not getting what we want, even if what we want causes suffering to someone else.

Unconditional love is about wanting the best for others as well as ourselves. If your parents want to split up, your partner wants to leave you, or your kids want to live a life that is totally contrary to what you had planned for them, love is letting them go to follow their own path, no matter how hurt or disappointed you might feel. Letting someone go with love is one of the greatest gifts we can give in all our relationships. Ultimately it is a great gift to ourselves because, once we have got through the pain of loss, love helps us to keep growing. Those that we set free with love may remember how supported and understood we made them feel. They will have learned a valuable lesson in unconditional love, which hopefully they then pass on to others. Love really does make the world go round.

Nobody's doormat

Love isn't always an easy option. Jesus said: *"Love your enemies and pray for those who persecute you."* He didn't say let those who persecute you continue to do so. Opening your heart, and feeling love and compassion for all is not a namby-pamby approach to life that lets people walk all over you. You are nobody's doormat. Love is not self-deprecating. It is always honourable and respectful. Love does not indulge in dishonourable or disrespectful behaviour towards others.

Love can be determined and tough. Mahatma Gandhi used peace and love to gain independence for India. No mean achievement. Loving parents get their delinquent or drug-addicted children into rehab, depriving them of their freedom in the hope that the shock will bring them back to a state of balance. Caring spouses can withdraw their support from partners who are in the process of self-destructive behaviour, hoping this will help them save themselves. Adults can kindly but firmly insist that their parents treat them with respect and refuse to be drawn into the mind power games of their childhood.

Love is firm and kind. It sets boundaries and creates a safe environment for personal and spiritual growth. Love does not hurt. People hurt. Love sustains life. Fear stunts and distorts. Love shines light into our hearts and our lives. Fear shuts us down and locks us in dark places. This passage from 1 Corinthians 13 describes pure, unconditional love:

"Love is patient and kind. It is not jealous or boastful, arrogant or rude. Love does not dishonour others nor does it insist on its own way. It is not irritable or resentful. Love does not delight in evil but rather rejoices in the truth. Love bears all things, believes all things, hopes all things and endures all things. Love never fails."

We are so far from the experience of unconditional love that it often takes a momentous event in our lives to understand its true meaning. Sometimes it is only when someone dies that we realise how much love we felt for them. Sometimes it is new life that brings the experience of love. I didn't really understand the meaning of unconditional love until my children were born. My heart opened and feelings of love and protection flowed through me. Call it biology or hormones, but I would have laid down my life for my children. Parents all over the world make huge sacrifices because of absolute love for their children's happiness, safety and survival.

Love is a powerful emotion that brings out the best in the human spirit. Love helps people rise above petty grievances and self-interest, and reach out to help their fellow man, woman and child. The ability to empathise with the suffering of others makes the world a kind and compassionate place. Love is the glue that keeps us connected. The Dalai Lama XIV tells us:

"Love and compassion are necessities, not luxuries. Without them humanity cannot survive."

Love makes us human. Even in the midst of atrocities, the human spirit's ability to love and keep on reaching out rises above all the selfishness and violence perpetuated by the few. Seemingly ordinary people like you and me lay down their lives in amazing acts of heroism so that others might live. When the media focuses our attention on so much negativity, it is good to be reminded of the power of love and the human spirit.

Love drives out fear
Fear keeps us trapped in cycles of resentment, hatred, revenge, hostility, aggression and violence. We drive out fear when we learn to open our hearts and keep on loving. In the words of Martin Luther King:

Fear and love

"Hate begets hate; violence begets violence; toughness begets a greater toughness. We must meet the forces of hate with the power of love."

Learning to open our hearts and let go of fear really does change lives. Jack initially came to me for weight loss. He was also attracted to my *Live a conscious life* coaching to help him release his constant anxiety. In his words: *"I live in fear every day of my life."* He was afraid of losing his wife and children whom he loved dearly. He had worked with a therapist trained in past life regression therapy and discovered that indeed he had lost his family in a previous incarnation.

Despite knowing why he felt afraid, it didn't dispel his fear in this life. His constant anxiety led him to comfort eat and he had gained twelve kilos. He was sick of eating for all the wrong reasons. *"I do not want to pass my irrational fears on to my children,"* he said. As we explored his fears, Jack suddenly 'got it'. He was able to connect his mind to his heart and soul: he felt pure love surge through him as his fears dropped away. I had tears in my eyes as he said to me, *"I now realise that I AM love. There is nothing but love, everything else is an illusion".*

Jack saw how when he lived with his heart open, everyone around him changed. His relationship with his wife and children improved dramatically because he was no longer afraid of losing them. He no longer held back in showing them his love. Living from a state of love brought out the best in Jack and all those who came into contact with him, including his colleagues and friends. He said he felt like a beacon of light in people's lives, just by being himself. This from a down-to-earth computer software designer!

No longer comfort eating, Jack discovered that he could continue enjoying food without overeating. He easily lost the twelve kilos and decided to join a health club where he discovered that, through regular exercise, he really liked the feeling of connecting his mind and emotions with his body.

When we see the world as based on unconditional love, there is no more fear, guilt, shame or insecurity. Love is a powerful tool for self-liberation. There are no mistakes. Life is forever unfolding. If we make choices that don't work out, we make new choices. The fear of failure, of not being good enough, or of never reaching perfection, all melt away. Unconditional love means we are all loved and perfect just as we are. We have nothing to prove. Our goodness and worthiness are not in question. We reconnect to our own heart and soul.

During a guided visualisation on love, I asked the group to visualise their hearts. Pauline saw her heart as a big, full, perfectly shaped heart wrapped in shiny red foil, just like a chocolate heart. It was very big in proportion to her. When she looked closer she could see that there were little cracks in the red foil. When she removed the foil, the heart inside was perfect. The heart reminded her of love and she felt very warm, comforted and serene.

When she came out of the visualisation, she realised that her heart was already perfect and whole, and that she didn't need the damaged protection (the red foil) any more. It no longer served any purpose. What stayed most with Pauline were the feelings of intense purity, peace and happiness. Just like Jack, she understood that she already IS love. In an email sent to the group after the session she wrote, *"I have had an epiphany!! I am love!! Love means I can do anything and no matter what happens, I can always come back to a state of love. In the car I just kept thinking of all the times I heard spiritual teachers say 'you are love, you are whole' and I never got it, but now I feel so happy and amazed"*. She felt moved that she didn't have to find love, work hard for it, or be approved of by others or herself to feel it.

When we all realise that we are love, pure and simple, then our fears can no longer hold us back and the world is a brighter, more vibrant place in which to live. Marianne Williamson, spiritual teacher and author of *Return to Love*, tells us:

> *"Love is what we were born with. Fear is what we learned here. The spiritual journey is the relinquishment or unlearning of fear, and the acceptance of love back into our hearts. Love is the essential existential fact. It is our ultimate reality and our purpose on earth."*

The language of fear and love
Moving from a state of fear into love is part of our spiritual journey and our soul's purpose. We can start by recognising when we are in fear. This means doing something that we are not taught to do, which is to check in with our emotional state many times a day. This is especially important if our emotions are running high, or we feel stressed. It doesn't really matter what the trigger might be. What is important is tuning into the feelings and identifying from which state they originate: love or fear.

The first thing is to notice your body and general energy. Contracting inwards, closing down, feeling protective, breathing shallowly or holding your breath, shoulders stiff, jaw tense, head down, arms crossed, all indicate that you are in a state of fear.

Notice the language you use when describing how you feel. All these words mean that you are feeling some shade of fear:

Abandoned, afraid, agitated, alarmed, angry, anxious, apprehensive, ashamed, blaming, cautious, closed down, concerned, controlling, controlled, cowed, cowardly, daunted, deceitful, depressed, despairing, destructive, disconnected, dismayed, disquieted, distressed, doubtful, in dread, in a cold sweat, excluded, fainthearted, fearful, guilty, hesitant, horrified, impatient, irritable, jittery, jumpy, manipulated, mind-chattering, needy, negative, nervous, panicky, paralysed, pessimistic, petrified, phobic, pressurised, quaking, quivering, rejected, repulsed, resentful, rigid, scared, self-limiting, self-sabotaging, shocked, spooked, stagnating, strung out, suffocated, suspicious, tense, terrified, timid, trembling, twitchy, uneasy, unhealthy, vulnerable, worried.

When you are in a state of love, your heart is open and your mind is at peace. You feel expansive, breathe easily and your body feels flexible and free. You might use words like:

Accepting, affectionate, alive, appreciative, aware, blessed, calm, capable, carefree, cherished, contented, compassionate, connected, courageous, creative, determined, dreamy, empathic, empowered, enchanted, energetic, enduring, excited, expansive, fearless, flexible, forgiving, free, grateful, growing, happy, harmonious, healing, healthy, heartfelt, honest, honourable, hopeful, inclusive, infinite, inspired, integrated, in the flow, joyful, kind, liberated, lighter, loved, loving, magical, motivated, optimistic, passionate, patient, playful, peaceful, positive, radiant, respectful, safe, serene, self-loving, spiritual, still, strong, tender, trusting, timeless, tranquil, understanding, warm, wise.

Perhaps you identified *resentful, pessimistic* and *mind-chattering* as fairly consistent emotional states for you. How does this mean that you are in a state of fear rather than love?

When we are in a state of love, we don't waste time feeling resentful. We recognise when somebody has been disrespectful towards us, when they have crossed our boundaries, and we make a heartfelt decision whether or not it is worth confronting them. With an open heart we can see clearly how other people make mistakes and sometimes get it wrong, and then decide if we would rather let the incident go. Or we may see a pattern of disrespect emerging and realise that we want to confront the person and their behaviour in a firm but kind manner. In any case, we let go of resentment which keeps us stuck in fear of others.

Pessimism is a belief that if something can go wrong, then it will go wrong. This can only be coming from a state of fear. Conversely, optimism sees the good in everything and believes that there is always a solution to every difficulty. And if there isn't, well, we can accept what is and trust that our wise or higher self knows why we are experiencing these challenges.

Mind chatter can be positive and loving for those who are at peace with themselves. It can be a dynamic conversation going on between the creative right brain and the doing left brain. For most people their mind chatter is usually nagging, busy and distracting. It keeps them from feeling love in their heart and peace in their mind. If our mind chatter feels stressful, draining and critical, then we are in fear.

When we recognise that we are into our fear-driven thinking and reactions, we can switch our thinking. This is not about suppressing feelings that originate in fear, but is a process of observing, recognising and acknowledging the fear. We then decide if it is a warning about a threat to safety, or if it stems from irrational fear. Then we can gently detach from the fear and our reactions because they no longer serve a purpose.

Self-love

Living a conscious life means that we can consciously choose to live from a place of love instead of fear. When we are locked into our habitual negative patterns it may come as a surprise to learn that everything is a choice. It takes practice. As we switch our focus from trying to measure up in the external world of doing, we embark on an inner journey of self-discovery. We learn that living from love instead of fear starts with developing a loving relationship with ourselves, the one person with whom we will spend our entire life. This is already a huge step to take. Self-love is something that most of us have been taught to run away from.

Summoning up the courage to step onto our own path and follow it wherever it leads may take us away from tribal lore and beliefs. Many people feel the tribe's resistance to their changing: *Why would you want to follow all that spiritual nonsense? Don't tell me you have given up sugar, what on earth for?! We've always done it this way, why do you want to be different?! We know you better than you know yourself, this isn't how you really are.*

The implication being that, to keep everyone else happy, we must not change but instead continue to play the role we were assigned when we were younger.

Nobody is going to give us permission to break away from the chains that bind us. Only we can do that. Love is about letting others believe what they like. They may not want to follow us. They may certainly not understand us. Forget trying to explain because they usually can't hear what we are saying. Instead focus on understanding them. They are as they are: it is not our job to change them. The only person we can change is ourselves. We can lovingly let go of the patterns that hide our authentic self.

As a spiritual being in human form, we no longer have to hold ourselves back, deny our dreams or suppress our emotions. People can spend a whole lifetime wanting to be truly free and happy, but afraid to break with the tribal beliefs that keep them stuck. Living with peace of mind means choosing to stop living from a place of fear and instead choosing love every time. As Albert Einstein, one of the greatest scientific minds of the twentieth century said:

"There are two ways to live your life: one is as though nothing is a miracle, the other is as though everything is a miracle."

It is time to believe in the miracle of love. You can decide right now to put down your burden of fear and live from a place of love and peace. You don't have to have all the answers straight away. You don't even have to believe that you can do it. The important thing is to believe that it is possible.

Chapter 5

Unravelling the mind

"The mind is everything. What you think you become." Buddha

I tend to think a lot. I never thought it was a problem until I came up against alternative practitioners who told me that I was *"too much in my mind"*, making it sound as though I was suffering from a design fault. I felt confused and resentful at being judged for something that I believed was an important part of being me. While coaching others, it became obvious that most of us brought up in a Western-style culture are taught to be in our minds, which is why the mind is a very good place to start the journey of personal and spiritual growth. It is at the level of our thoughts, beliefs and emotions that we start to take back control of our habitual reactions and behaviours.

In the developed world we are very left-brain orientated. We have developed the left brain, the rational and thinking part of the mind, out of all proportion to the rest of us. This has left us very asymmetrical and disconnected from all the other aspects of being human. We are out of balance.

Most of us learned from a very young age that thinking and doing are more important than exploring our internal world of creative self-expression, spirituality and who we really are. While attitudes are changing, I still hear left-brained people deriding any sort of contemplative self-enquiry as 'self-indulgent nonsense', 'only for the feeble minded', or 'navel-gazing'. From an early age we are conditioned to ignore our physical and emotional needs: *Of course you are well enough to go to school. You can't go to the toilet right now, you must wait until lessons finish. Big boys don't cry. Put a smile on your face, nobody will like you if you look miserable. Don't frown, the wind will change and you will stay like that forever. Don't be sad, have an ice cream instead. You don't mean that.*

Around food, many of us learned to suppress our innate appetite regulatory systems: *Eat everything on your plate (even if you aren't hungry). Eat to please me (and others). It's rude to leave food on your plate.*

Do you ever remember being encouraged to daydream at school? How often were you told it was time to stop thinking and take time to just be still? How much support and praise did you receive for your creative thinking, even if you got the wrong answers to a problem? And who got the most attention or accolades, the dreamy, artistic types or the outgoing, aggressive, high achievers? The directive, *'Don't just stand there, DO something!'* says it all. What we should be teaching our children is 'don't do anything, take a minute to just stand there and smell the flowers, experience the glory of the moment or listen to the skylark'. Too many of us, especially HSPs (highly sensitive people), grew up feeling left out, lonely and anxious, our inner self crying out for recognition.

Children conditioned in this way grow into adults who feel disconnected from their body, emotions and spirit. They have no way of truthfully expressing themselves without fear of disapproval or reprisal for getting it wrong. They learn not to trust themselves. Many feel as though they are living a half-life. Others grow up feeling like they don't belong anywhere. We fill our minds with busyness to escape how we feel. One of the most common complaints of this century is an inability to switch off the mind. Our minds are full of noisy mind chatter, churning out thoughts at an estimated rate of between sixty and seventy thousand per day, most of them repetitive. Some thoughts are practical, organisational thoughts around our day-to-day existence. Some are insights and inspirational thoughts that move us forward in the direction we want to go. For too many of us, the majority of our thoughts are a stream of negative and nagging babble, full of self-doubt and even self-loathing. We feel stressed by having a mind that won't rest. It feels as though our mind controls us rather than the other way around. The average Western mind is not a very peaceful place to be.

Attachment to thoughts

Our mind is extraordinarily complex and is a powerful resource ready to be used to create the life and the health we want, yet we limit ourselves through our thinking and beliefs about ourselves. Thoughts are just energy created in our mind. They influence our emotional responses. They come and go, depending on the day we are having, yet we tend to give our thoughts and emotions great credibility. We believe that if we think and feel something, it must be true. We allow these transient energies of thought and emotion to create our reality in the moment, without any purposeful guidance as to what reality we want to create. We are conditioned to believe that we have no control over our thoughts and feelings. Consequently, we let them trigger the same reactions and behaviours, time and again, creating our suffering. Conflict and all kinds of self-destructive behaviours are based on people believing their thoughts. As Byron Katie, author of *Loving What Is* says:

> *"A thought is harmless unless we believe it. It is not our thoughts, but the attachment to our thoughts, that causes suffering."*

Most people are surprised that they do not have to attach to their thinking as their gospel truth.

Understanding how the mind and emotions work together to create our thoughts and beliefs gives us tools to stop the same old self-destructive or self-limiting thinking and behaviour patterns. Instead of being controlled by our thoughts we can learn to let them go.

The mind and personality

The mind is a concept that we know exists in the brain but is not identifiable in physical terms. There is no definable area of the brain that can be labelled 'the mind'. The mind is an expression of the personality, which also originates in the brain, yet has no physical location. It is the part of a person that thinks, reasons, feels and remembers. The mind is a way of describing processes that allow us to get perspective on how and why we think, believe and feel the way we do.

Our personality is made up of the characteristic patterns of thoughts, feelings and behaviours that make us unique. It is the expression of all the facets of an individual and remains fairly consistent throughout life. In Chapter 3, we met Daskalos, the late Cypriot spiritual healer, who tells us that we also have a 'permanent personality' that we carry from one lifetime to another. Therefore, the mind and personality are not exactly the same thing. When we start working with our mind to understand our habitual behaviours, we are not trying to change our basic personality, although some aspects of our personality may change in the process. For example, someone who reacts badly to stress may learn to respond more calmly to potentially stressful situations. An individual with low self-esteem that manifests as always pleasing others may become more confident and start asserting their true personality. An ambitious personality may remain ambitious but learn to temper their ambition with empathy for others.

The brain

I designed the brain diagrams on the following pages as a purely conceptual device to give a representative image of how I perceive the different parts of the mind function. They are not meant to show the brain in scientific detail, but rather act as an aid to help people visualise the workings of the mind and its connection to emotions and behaviours.

Neuroscience confirms that our brains are made up of two hemispheres: the left and the right brain. We can use both parts of the brain interchangeably, although some people are more left-brain dominant, while others are more right-brain dominant.

The left brain deals with day to day THINKING and DOING. It is the rational and intellectual part of the brain that allows us to plan, make choices, judge, analyse and interact with the external world, everything 'out there'. We use the left brain for information processing, scientific thinking and problem solving. It processes information in a linear fashion, taking details and arranging them in logical order. Without our left brain we wouldn't get anything done or make the myriad choices that we make daily. Our left brain is the side most developed in our schooling and the side we use most in our work. It focuses on the facts but does not see the bigger picture.

The right brain works in a different way. It sees the bigger picture first. It grasps concepts and knows intuitively without having all the details to begin with. The right brain is the KNOWING and BEING side of the brain and is the source of our creative self-expression. It is where our intuition and multi-sensory abilities originate, and is connected to our wise, higher or authentic self, to our soul and a Divine Source.

To our detriment, we have over-developed the left brain to the exclusion of the right brain. Albert Einstein never lost sight of Spirit in everything he researched:

> *"Everyone who is seriously involved in the pursuit of science becomes convinced that a spirit is manifest in the laws of the Universe."*

When talking about the mind, he said: *"We should take care not to make the intellect our god"*, and *"The intuitive mind is a sacred gift and the rational mind is a faithful servant."*

Ego as a concept

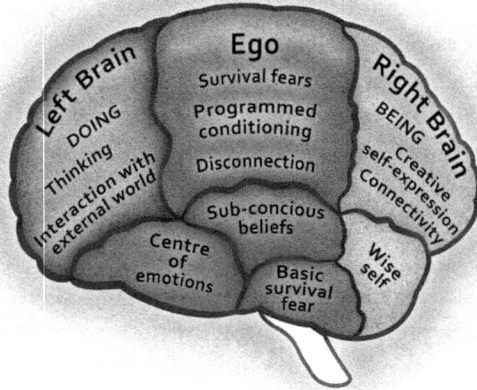

Brain diagram and ego 1

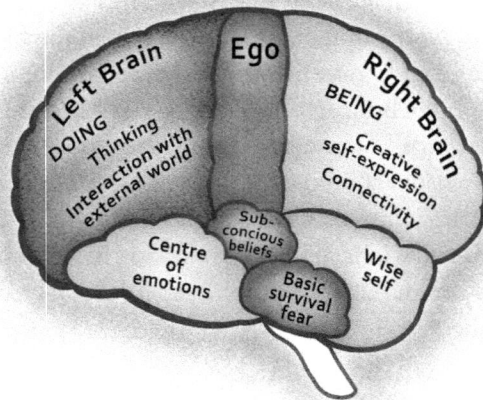

Brain diagram and ego 2

Just as the mind is a concept, so is the ego part of the mind. The English word 'ego' comes from Latin meaning 'I, myself'. In the nineteenth century, Sigmund Freud brought the word 'ego' into public consciousness as part of his structural model of the psyche.

In the diagrams above, I have placed the ego between the left and right brain to give a conceptual idea of its influence in our habitual thinking and behaviour patterns. In this model, the ego is a mind construct that deals with our basic survival fears. It is made up of all our thoughts and beliefs that are fuelled by fear. During our formative years, ego's job is to respond to the immediate, surrounding world and build up a 'mind map' to guide us through, help us adapt, fit in and generally survive until we can make it on our own. Its role is invaluable. Without an ego, the human species would probably never make it past childhood.

When we live from our authentic self, we live with an open heart, free from judgement, experiencing high self-esteem and peace of mind. We are completely aligned which radiates as a special energy that draws people to us. However, most of us do not feel safe enough to be real and authentic in our world. As we grow up, we receive negative messages from the adults around us. We compare ourselves to others, because our conditioning planted one major belief in our subconscious: *I am not enough as I am.* We spend our lives trying to prove to everyone and ourselves that we are enough.

Our ego teaches us the attitudes, beliefs and behaviours that get us approval or in some cases simply to survive, and we practise them even though they do not correspond to what we really want or who we really are. Because they become so entrenched and part of our self-identity, we continue to practise these behaviours in adulthood, long after their sell-by date. They are no longer appropriate in our adult life and act as obstacles to happiness as they lead us to replay the same self-limiting or self-sabotaging reactions and behaviours.

Our beliefs about who we are and our place in the world are based on our experiences growing up. As children we were not able to make adult judgements about conditional or unconditional love, about justice or injustice. We felt when something was wrong, but lacked the intellectual capacity to verbalise it. We also lacked the physical size or strength to demand what was right. We had no alternative but to see ourselves through the lens of our conditioning and identify with it. We learned to identify ourselves through our ego, even though it represents only a small part of who we really are. In ancient Chinese philosophy, the Tao (meaning 'the path' or 'the way') tells us:

> *"To serve your ego is to worship a false identify created by yourself. It is like someone suffering from amnesia reinventing herself because she had forgotten who she is."*

Ego remembers and is always working to correct the painful memories of our early experiences so we can feel better. It is the ego that creates the masks or personas behind which we hide, their purpose being to protect us and aid our survival in an apparently hostile world. In this process of adapting for survival, ego's link to fear creates a sense of disconnection from who we really are, our authentic self. We are cut off from our innate spirituality, and feel separate from others and from ourselves. We live in a way that feeds our fear. We are not true to ourselves but rather live to please others, paying the price in lost integrity. We don't live according to our own values, but instead adopt those of other people. We don't follow our dreams, heart or passion but stay stuck, restless and unfulfilled, living the life expected by family, partners, children, friends and colleagues. Then to distract ourselves from the pain of disconnection, we keep our mind busy so we don't have time to realise just how empty we feel. We have forgotten who we really are.

Exploring the diagrams

Diagram 1 shows the ego well in control. It has a direct link to basic survival fear and has developed plenty of subconscious beliefs about self, such as: *If I'm nice I may be acceptable. It's not safe to be angry. I have to rebel to get what I want. Nobody could love me the way I am. I was born a bad girl/ boy. I am stupid and can never succeed. I must be better than everyone else to succeed. I must not be rejected. I will never amount to anything. I have to fight for everything I want. Best to lash out first than be beaten. I must never look stupid. Better not get too close or I will get hurt. I need appreciation and approval to feel worthwhile.*

These subconscious beliefs are fuelled by the centre of emotions, which is usually churning out guilt, anxiety, shame, grief and fear. This in turn keeps the ego's belief that our survival is threatened and that we must hang on to our adaptive behaviours learned when we were younger. The owner of this mind stays disconnected from their creative self-expression and passion. They constantly self-sabotage even when they are tired of it.

People controlled by their ego live in a constant state of low level anxiety. Because the anxiety is such a normal part of their lives, they don't even recognise what is, in effect, a state of chronic stress. They just know they can't relax properly because their mind is always noisy and busy. All our neuroses, which are behaviours that manifest our underlying anxiety, come from a mind controlled by fear-driven programmed conditioning. These behaviours include all forms of self-sabotage in an attempt to assuage the anxiety of not being enough as we are.

I don't think our own mind wants to cause us suffering. The ego had a job to do, which was to protect us from perceived harm while growing up. It can't tell the difference between past and present. Everything that was a threat is still a threat: the demanding boss is the demanding father or headmaster who humiliated us, or the colleagues who gently tease us are the kids at school who tormented us and made our life a misery. Each time our ego perceives a threat, we go into our learned and adaptive survival behaviours: we sulk, get angry, defend ourselves, argue, rebel, act the fool, become forgetful, withdraw, cry, be extra nice, overeat or drink, take it out on our nearest and dearest, spend money, anything to hide our insecurity and hurt. Our adaptive behaviours are legion and none of them expresses the authentic self, hiding behind the behaviour.

In **diagram 2**, the ego part of the mind has taken its rightful role as the security guard for real threats to survival. If the bus is out of control and running straight at you, you want your mind to register the threat and connect immediately with your left brain to leap out of the way. If you are about to lose your job and you have a mortgage to pay, and a family to support, you will feel survival fear. At that moment you want your right brain to come up with some creative ideas about what to do, and your left brain to make them happen.

Here, the left and right brains have expanded because when we divest ourselves of our negative programmed conditioning, we become more effective at listening to our intuition guided by our centre of emotions, which is now focused more on contentment, joy and happiness, and less on fear. We then follow through with effective doing. Because the role of the ego construct has been diminished, we have less mind chatter. Our mind becomes a much more peaceful place.

The part of the brain devoted to the subconscious and often negative beliefs about self has diminished. Do we ever get rid of all our negative subconscious beliefs and programming? I honestly don't know. There are so many that we could spend a lifetime discovering them. Just as we think we must have dealt with them all by now, another one bobs up to the surface like a cork in water.

Moving from diagram 1 to 2

When we move from diagram 1 as our usual state of mind to diagram 2, we become connected to our right brain without the interference of ego's programmed conditioning. Life becomes easier as we feel guided towards certain ideas and actions and away from others, without the usual sense of struggle most of us experience. Once we learn to trust whatever messages we receive from our wise self and allow ourselves to be guided by them, we can start living a conscious life.

The big question is how do we move from diagram 1 to diagram 2? This is key to unlocking the door that reconnects the mind, body, heart and soul.

Some philosophies talk about 'death of the ego'. I think they mean that when we dissolve all our negative programmed conditioning, then we have a direct link to our soul self, so can live fearlessly and with passion. But does the ego ever really die? Does it really exist in the first place? When talking about the ego, we have moved from neuroscience into psychology and metaphysics. When the ego dies, then most probably so do we, but I am happy to leave that to others to research and debate.

My experience is that once we remove the inappropriate hold that ego has over our reactions and behaviours, we can set ourselves free to be a powerful, grown-up version of ourselves. This is the self that feels comfortable in its own skin, knows who it is and why it is here. As a fully integrated individual, we no longer need to involve ourselves in pointless dramas and self-sabotaging behaviours.

There are a number of ways to get from diagram 1 to diagram 2. The one thing to avoid is fighting with our ego because obviously we are fighting ourselves. As too many of us spend a lifetime fighting ourselves and struggling with our behaviours, beating ourselves up clearly doesn't work.

Making friends with the ego

A good first step is to make friends with the ego. This is an interesting exercise in detaching our identity from our ego and seeing it as a separate entity. It's as if a part of you can stand aside from the mind and look inwards to see its component parts. To make friends with the ego means being able to visualise it or, for those who are less visual, to hear or feel the ego's personality. The image that comes to mind is no doubt based on our childhood experiences. During a guided visualisation, Joanna saw her ego as a Michelin Man, benign and rather bouncy but with no clear identity. Anna said hers looked like a dragon breathing fire every time she 'stepped out of line'. Jan also saw her ego as a dragon, but a benign smiley one, whom she named Arnold. Sue heard her father's voice in her ego. I saw my ego as a very masculine, controlling genie. He looked like Yul Brynner, all muscles, shaved head, tattoos and a fiercely arrogant expression on his face. He definitely thought he knew what was right for me.

Once you have your image, you can now have a conversation with your ego. It goes something like this: *Thank you for wanting to protect me. I am grateful for everything you have done but I no longer want to behave or think in this way. I am all grown up now and it is time for me to change.* If this sounds totally weird that's because we are not taught to have conversations with the different parts of our minds.

Katie saw her ego as a stern, critical version of herself, reflecting her own father's strict approach to his teenage daughter. She called her 'Protector Katie' and, during a guided visualisation, thanked her for everything she had done to protect her from a dangerous world while she was growing up. But now she was in her sixties and wanted to free herself from the fears and old programming that were keeping her stuck. She wanted to return to the country of her birth and re-experience being in a place she loved, without the fear of travelling alone. Katie told Protector Katie all of this and explained what role she wanted her to play in her life from now on. Then she waited for the expected disapproval. She was surprised when Protector Katie turned to her with a smile and said: *"At last! I have been waiting a long time for you to ask me to let go."*

Katie felt a surge of relief and trepidation in equal measure. She could now let her fears go, if she chose to do so. It was all up to her. There was no monster holding her back, no protective parent figure keeping a tight rein on their adolescent daughter. It took a few more months of dialoguing with her ego before Katie book a trip alone back to the place she was born.

Recognising the role our ego plays in our self-limiting behaviours is the first step towards liberation from our old patterns of behaviour. The ego has been in control for a very long time, it won't just suddenly turn away and leave us alone. As we attempt to stop our habitual thinking and behaviour, it may become very insistent and demand that we react as we have always done to a perceived threatening situation. Its job, after all, is to protect us from attack and abandonment. This is when we get into that dispiriting cycle of wanting to change but find it impossible. An unseen obstacle seems to insert itself between us and our good intentions. You may want to stop eating chocolate for the sake of your waistline and your health, but the next time someone offers you chocolate, you find yourself guiltily giving in to what you perceive as temptation. You may want to stop being bad tempered around your children, but the moment they test the boundaries, you find yourself shouting at them yet again. Your ego has 'protected you' by keeping you stuck in your habitual behaviour to stop you having to deal with your real but subconscious fears of being 'not good, worthy or lovable enough'. Only when we allow ourselves to face our demons will we be free of the ego constructs.

When we have gone down the same old road yet again, most of us turn to some form of distraction, such as eating and drinking, starting an argument, getting irritable, or doing more busyness. The trick is to see if you can find another way of gently detaching from the nagging ego and its attempts to keep you stuck. Each time I was tempted to go into my usual reactive behaviours, such as being a victim, getting into an argument and feeling as though I had to defend myself, I gently detached from my habitual thinking. It took a lot of persistence. I noticed how sulky my genie would become when he realised that I meant it, I wasn't going down the same old behaviour track again. I handled his sulks by staying kind and grateful for everything he had done to help me survive and adapt to adulthood. Eventually he gave up and stopped trying to control me. I was then able to stop myself being hooked into other people's manipulation and mind games, and find a different way of dealing with difficult situations.

Sandra had grown up in a competitive male environment where she was not encouraged to be in touch with her natural femininity. Wearing pretty clothes or crying when upset were definitely frowned upon by her three brothers and her father. This made her feel afraid of her sexuality as a woman. When asked what her ego looked like, Sandra saw a monster who was trying to pull her back into the claggy bog of her old mind programming. Deciding to call him Joseph, Sandra tempted Joseph out of the bog by giving him something different to do other than keep dragging her back in. She sat with Joseph on the edge of the bog and talked kindly to him about his role in her life. She expressed gratitude for everything Joseph had done to help her be a successful, independent young woman. She told Joseph very specifically what she wanted his role to be from now on, which was to keep her safe from danger to her safety or survival. That was all.

Sandra had these kindly conversations with her ego many times over the next few months. Gradually she realised that as she felt less constrained by the fearful part of her mind, she was able to embrace and love all aspects of herself, including the 'unlovable' and rebellious girl who had shaped the passionate woman she had become.

Stuck in our stories

To understand how our ego keeps us stuck, we have to recognise the stories we tell ourselves about who we are and our place in the world. The ego is very happy to keep us trapped in our stories, because this is the familiar and therefore safe dis-comfort zone. We all have our stories, know all the details and run them often, either in our heads or in conversations with others.

Most people would say that they want peace of mind, yet their minds stick like glue to their stories, which they have absolutely no problem reliving constantly. We like telling ourselves stories along the lines of who did or said what to whom; who is right and who is wrong; and filling ourselves with anger, resentment, righteous indignation, guilt, shame, embarrassment and sadness. We conjure up the well-worn thought, fuel it with some emotion, and off we go, being our story. This is really easy for most of us. It's like replaying the same DVD without censoring it for truth or quality of content.

Joy, a woman in her fifties, came to see me about her weight, but her opening words were along the lines of *"I have had a tough life"*. She then told me about all the disasters in her life, mostly around an unhappy

85

marriage, divorce, being a single parent, moving continents, being short of money, losing her parents, the death of her ex-husband, and a daughter who spent a couple of years on drugs. She had clearly told her story many times in her head and in therapy. And yet her current circumstances were far from disastrous. She had created a life of relative ease and financial security with a loving second husband. Despite this, her story of a tough life had become her identity, even though it made her miserable and kept her stuck. I asked her to imagine for just a minute that she didn't have this story playing in her head anymore and that she could just switch it off. How did it feel? She closed her eyes, took a deep breath and visibly relaxed for a second or two and smiled. *"I feel relieved"*, she said. Then it all came flooding back and she was back into her stories again, this time about her weight, *"I can't stop drinking wine because my husband likes to have a glass of wine with dinner"*. *"I have so much responsibility for others that I have given up on myself."*

After talking it through she began to see the games her mind was playing and had been playing since childhood. She realised that her stories kept her in victim consciousness, which, as a strong woman who had coped with plenty of adversity and grief, was not how she really saw herself. Everything was in her mind and fuelled by strong emotion to create an on-going drama. She decided to stop following her ego into the stories of her past, and instead to focus on the present moment, reinforcing her thoughts with everything she had created right now.

Our stories are filled with limiting beliefs about ourselves. Brian had a successful career running a small IT company with long term contracts in multinational companies. It gave him a comfortable life. At the age of sixty the biggest of his contracts came to an end and he started telling his *'I'm not qualified enough'* story where nobody wants a man of his age working out of an office at home. He left school with no qualifications and *"everyone knows that you can't get on in blue chip companies without having all the right qualifications"*. Brian could validate every statement with 'facts' and would not budge from his storyline, despite all the evidence to show that he had an amazing career in blue chip companies, even without any formal qualifications.

When pressed for why he continued to think like this, he quoted a high school teacher telling him when he was sixteen years old, that without those precious qualifications he would hit a ceiling and never be able to go any higher. That teacher was probably dead by now (it was in the 1960s), or he might have changed his mind when he saw his bright students successfully making it in the world, despite their lack of formal qualifications. But like too many of us, what Brian heard at an impressionable age became his story for the rest of his life, despite all his experience to the contrary.

Track to nowhere
Our habitual thoughts are like railway tracks that go round and round arriving nowhere except back where we started. Also called looped thinking, these thought tracks run deep in our minds. With a brain scan, scientists are able to see our thought tracks. Repetitive thoughts form neural pathways that light up in the brain and they are reinforced each time we have a particular thought.

On your circular railway track you might start with a habitual thought: *There I go again, I have no will power,* which starts off a whole cascade of other thoughts that are part of the thought package, accompanied by strong emotion to keep those thoughts in place. As you arrive back where you started you realise that your negative habitual thinking literally is the track to nowhere. You are stuck like a hamster on a wheel, going around and around, all the while expecting the results to be different this time.

But you can change the points and get off that track onto a different track that leads somewhere, usually a sense of self-empowerment and a more peaceful state of mind. The trick is to recognise when you are stepping on to the track to nowhere and immediately change the points. You will know because strong emotion alerts you that you are in habitual, negative thinking. You will feel the iron fist grip your intestines; a tight band around your chest or head; maybe fluttering or a cannonball in your solar plexus; you start feeling hot and sweaty; or your throat constricts. Your body will give you ample warning that you are doing it again. Then you choose. You can choose to keep going nowhere, or you can change the points.

Carly and her husband, Dennis, would find themselves in the same tangled loop of arguments over trivial things. He would say something disrespectful and provocative to her like: *"Why can't you remember to get orange juice, you always forget something when you go shopping!".* She would feel attacked, unloved, disrespected, hurt and angry. She would immediately jump to her own self-defence, trying to reason with him. He would respond that she should have made a list because she should know by now that she can't trust her memory. They were off! The more she argued against his verbal abuse, the more upset she became, and the more Dennis threw himself into the game with escalating harsh words. It was demoralising, exhausting and completely destroyed trust. They were on the track to nowhere, except the divorce court.

Then one day Carly recognised what was happening right at the beginning of one of these arguments. She mentally saw them starting out on the same track, which she knew would ruin her day and leave her upset and disheartened. She immediately switched points and, seeing a new track open up before her, she took a deep breath, quietened her battered ego, and said: *"I am not going down this track anymore. It stops right here. You speak to me with respect or don't bother to speak to me at all. And by the way, you can do your own food shopping in future. I am not your housekeeper."* The look on her husband's face was a mixture of surprise and relief. She had called a halt to their destructive behaviour. It took many more months of practice to make sure she never got embroiled in pointless and heart-breaking arguments again. Dennis started to show renewed love and respect for her and their communication improved beyond expectation. He also took turns to do the weekly shop.

What we think and how we speak, even to or about ourselves, has the effect of reinforcing our negative thinking. Like Joy who 'had a tough life' or Brian who 'wasn't qualified enough', each time we talk about the negative things that we have experienced our mind believes that to be our reality now, even if it happened twenty-five years ago. This is because our ego does not know the difference between reality and fantasy. We can create a different more self-supporting reality by consciously choosing our thoughts. This means noticing everything we think, even when we are caught up in the daily drama of life.

Drama addiction
Human beings are addicted to drama. We love our own and we love other people's. The more negative the drama, the more we are attracted to it. Look at the popularity of soaps, reality TV and disaster movies. Watch the news or read a newspaper. They all focus on human drama, most of it negative. In our own lives, we not only get stuck on the circular railway track to nowhere, but we actively resist changing the points because our

ego is addicted to the drama of our story. People have even commented to me how boring a peaceful mind would be without their mind's dramas.

Margaret, a successful career woman in her forties, idolised her husband, Steve, and thought herself lucky to have attracted such a good-looking man. After all, he had been the centre of a lot of women's attention before they met. Steve was an inveterate flirt. In company, he would ignore Margaret and flirt outrageously with other women, even when it clearly upset his wife. When she confronted Steve with his behaviour, he told her she was making a fuss about nothing, it was all a bit of harmless fun. She ended up in screaming matches, throwing all kinds of breakables at him. Each time Margaret confronted him and demanded he stop his flirting, Steve stayed stuck in his own story of being determined not to be controlled by any woman. In his drama he was fighting to maintain his sense of identity, no matter what affect it had on his relationship.

Margaret thought there must be something fundamentally wrong with her for Steve to ignore her feelings. She felt powerless to change anything. In her frustration and grief, she would weep inconsolably for hours, but then she would get back onto the same track and around they would both go again.

I suggested that she stop the drama and find a different way to deal with her husband's behaviour, one that might actually lead to what she wanted, which was a grown-up relationship with a man who had feet of clay, not a demi-god. I suggested that she might be addicted to the drama of these interactions and, on reflection, she agreed. She said that without the drama of loud and violently expressed emotion, she would sink into boredom and despair. Her dramas allowed her to keep her focus on the external, blaming Steve for how she felt, which felt safer than going inwards and being alone with her thoughts and feelings. She thought that she needed the drama to feel alive. Yet the damage to her self-esteem kept her stuck in the belief that she was an uncontrollable and unlovable monster, one who didn't deserve the attention of this wonderful man to whom she was married.

Margaret chose to stay with her dramas because she wasn't ready to explore her internal world of self. She was too afraid to take back her power in the relationship and learn how to create something more nurturing. What she feared the most eventually happened, she and Steve separated. Both were broken-hearted but totally stuck in their need to stay as they were.

Our addiction to drama is damaging to self-esteem and to our mental, emotional and spiritual health. Our dramas keep us trapped in our ego's programmed conditioning, and they sabotage our efforts to become master of our thoughts and behaviours. We stay stuck and frustrated in our looped thinking.

Drama monster

We all have our own drama monster which I perceive as being part of the of the ego construct. As a small child in the 1980s, my son loved the He-Man stories. When I visualised my drama monster I immediately conjured up an image of the behemoth in my son's He-Man books. Actually the behemoth is a mythological beast mentioned in the Book of Job, but it will forever be the He-Man version who slumbers away quietly in his cave in my mind until woken up by the smell of food. Food in this case was me getting into my drama thinking: *I am, I should, they should, he ought, why can't they, I will never, I always, I can't bear it, this is impossible, it's making me ill, how can I live with this, I would rather be dead than ...* and every variation on the same themes of negativity. The more into my looped-thinking track I got, the more my drama monster woke up and grew. He got bigger and bigger until my whole being was taken up by my stories of being a victim in a world of injustice and unkindness. I felt terrible, but my behemoth was bright eyed, wide awake and very happy with this new influx of drama food.

Vicky was an artist and an author. Her drama monster fed off her constant stories about being excluded by her friends because there must be something wrong with her. *"I would never treat people like that,"* she declared with tears in her eyes at the hurt caused by the apparent rejections. Vicky drew a wonderful picture of her drama monster waking up from his sleep every time she got into her stories of imagined wrongdoings by others towards her. With each negative thought she drew a bigger version of him until he filled the page. He looked like a big cuddly teddy bear with a broad smile on his face. She laughed: it was all so silly. She decided to stop playing these mind games with herself and instead focused on understanding why she made herself suffer. Within months Vicky changed from an anxious young woman, always on the lookout for the next perceived snub, to a confident and contented woman whom people loved to be around.

Why we suffer

Drama isn't necessarily all bad. It can lead to change for the good. The real-life dramas that unfold on our television screens often provoke people to take action to change the injustice, inequalities and exploitation in our man-made systems. Through the power of our mind we create our life and have consciously created many wonderful achievements and happiness. Through our dramas we have also created our suffering, no doubt without realising that we were involved in the process. It is hard to imagine why we would do that. Perhaps we have something to learn or to come to terms with at a subconscious level about ourselves through the suffering. It may be that we don't get the message the first time, so our suffering continues to increase until, one day, we say to ourselves that we are sick of feeling this way and want to change. Byron Katie, author of Loving What Is tells us:

"I am the cause of my own suffering – but only all of it."

We suffer because we are afraid to acknowledge that we are the source of our pain. Everything begins and ends with us. We create the thoughts, feelings, beliefs and behaviour patterns that cause us to suffer. How can that be? Aren't others to blame for how we feel? Don't they provoke us into our reactions? Isn't it normal to feel hurt, angry or sad at the way we are treated?

Our reactions to a perceived provocation depend on our ego's programmed conditioning. If our programmed conditioning has created an expectation of the way people should treat us and they don't treat us that way, we feel justified in feeling what we consider to be an appropriate emotional response and then behave accordingly. If we believe that nobody should ever be rude or impolite to us, then we will react with anger or hurt when somebody inevitably does or says something that we perceive as rude. We may lash out verbally or even physically, or we may withdraw, saying nothing, but vowing never to speak to that person again. Usually our hurt and anger keep the story of their slight churning around endlessly in our mind. We feel powerless and anxious because we know our reaction has changed nothing. If only other people would live according to our requirements of them!

We can't change other people, but we can change how we respond to them, which in turn often makes them change their behaviour towards us. And if they don't, we soon find that we have less interest in them and start attracting more like-minded people.

Brenda was sick of relationships that started out well but then very quickly deteriorated. The men in her life would start out attentive, loving and giving, and within just a few months would begin making excuses not to be with her, preferring a night out with the boys instead. Brenda felt hurt and rejected. *"But I give them so much love and when I try to talk to them about how hurt I feel, they act like they don't know what I am talking about!"*, she exclaimed. In an attempt to get the love she thought she so desperately needed, Brenda ran after them with more love. Her expectation was that if she gave loving attention, then she should receive the same in return. Each time she felt rejected she became more despairing. Her feeling of abandonment overwhelmed her as she got stuck in her stories of being a victim of yet another uncaring man. She found it exhausting repeating the same old patterns of behaviour while nothing changed.

During coaching Brenda realised that her suffering was caused by her expectation that the more love she gave, the more she would receive in return. In time she learned to change her expectation of those she loved. She could be assertive and insist that she wouldn't put up with bad behaviour, but she couldn't make someone love her in the same way she loved them. How she loved them was her business. How they loved her was theirs. Her choice was whether she was prepared to accept what they were willing to give of themselves in a relationship. She also learned that her need to be loved was a deep-seated need from her childhood that only she could satisfy. To be able to love someone else in a healthy way meant loving herself first. As she grew in confidence and self-esteem, Brenda started attracting men who treated her in a loving and respectful way.

Revising the internal map
Most people who start the process of change do so because they no longer want to feel the way they do. M. Scott Peck, author of *The Road Less Travelled* says:

> *"Our finest moments are most likely to occur when we are feeling deeply uncomfortable, unhappy or unfulfilled. For it is only in such moments, propelled by our discomfort, that we are likely to step out of our ruts and start searching for different ways or truer answers."*

They then start challenging their thinking, which in turn begins the process of revising their internal 'self-map'. Also referred to as our 'life script', this is a concept developed by psychiatrist, Eric Berne in the 1950s as one aspect of his transactional analysis model of psychotherapy. I use the two terms interchangeably.

Our self-map is our blueprint of our world and our place in that world. It is the sum total of everything we have learned and absorbed through our formative years from those around us. It includes our beliefs about our worthiness and our capabilities. It also encompasses our abilities to survive or flourish in a world of doing and achievement, as well as everything we think, feel, believe and then manifest in our behaviour and in our health. Even the circumstances of our gestation, while we were still in utero, and our birth may leave a mark on our internal self-map.

This internal self-map may even have some imprinting pre-conceptually. We have probably come into this world with a rudimentary map in place from past lives and inherited from our ancestors. We are not born a 'blank slate' totally devoid of any kind of programming. If you have experience with children, you know already that each of us is born with our own unique characteristics and temperament.

It can be challenging to uncover and change the routes and landmarks that we have created or had imposed on our self-map. The benefit is that instead of feeling like someone with the wrong internal self-map that leads to misery, suffering and pain, we create a map that guides us towards ease, joy and light.

Eric Berne believed that if we were able to make the decisions that formed our life script when we were children, then we have the power to change it once we become aware of the script. Revising our internal self-map begins with a willingness to seek our own truth, no matter how painful if may be. For example, the person who clings to the child's belief that nobody must abandon them and that they are unlovable, may be reluctant to enter intimate relationships. If they do, they will eventually sabotage the relationship and push the other person away. They thus prove their story that they are not lovable and people always leave them. They keep their self-map intact, no matter how much it hurts. Because their negative beliefs generate a low vibrational energy around them, they attract other people with similar stories and self-maps, operating on an equally low vibrational energy. This combination is guaranteed to perpetuate situations that reinforce the internal self-map.

Human beings have an inbuilt tendency to avoid the truth at all costs if seeking it causes short-term pain. Families hang on to and pass on secrets and hurt down the generations. They bury anger, shame, fear, resentment, grief and sadness. This destroys the peace of mind of all who pick up the negative energy of that secret or hurt, usually having no idea of its origins. They just know that: *This is how we always behaved in our family. We never discussed that kind of thing. Difficult stuff always got swept under the carpet.*

Offspring pick up this negative energy and the distorted self-map that goes with it, and subconsciously agree to carry it, passing it on to each generation that follows. This creates untold unhappiness with no obvious cause in the here and now. We learn to be unhappy because that's what we were taught. And it's not even our unhappiness! It could have started with some hurt between our great-great-great-grandparents! Pema Chödrön tells us:

> *"The most fundamental harm we can do to ourselves is to remain ignorant by not having the courage and the respect to look at ourselves honestly and gently."*

We can only revise our self-map when we are willing to totally commit ourselves to a process of self-enquiry. This means wanting to uncover all our learned thoughts, feelings, values, beliefs and consequent behaviours, and expose them to the light of truth and authenticity. In the process of deep self-questioning we may end up rejecting many values passed on by parents and our tribe. This can be very scary because then we will start figuring out who we really are. It may involve rejecting some deeply-held beliefs and values that no longer serve us. We may also experience resistance from those close to us as we start to change. Separating from family and tribal truths, and following our own path, can feel painful at times, especially if we come from a culture that rejects those who do not follow its teachings.

It is up to each of us to decide how far we are prepared to go, if the cost of separation or rejection is worth it to liberate ourselves and our soul to follow our true path. We can decide that our journey begins with total dedication to the truth. From now on we will question absolutely everything and accept nothing without examination.

As we start changing our self-map, it can feel as though the foundation of our very existence is crumbling beneath us. We may feel as though we are wandering directionless in the desert with no exit strategy. This is frightening for people who are used to expecting to feel in control, dictated to by the ego. Part of the process is acknowledging that this is normal and allowing ourselves to be 'all at sea' for however long it takes.

We can turn the fear of uncovering the truth and change it into excitement at embarking on a voyage of self-discovery. The physical symptoms are the same and it is only our perception that dictates whether we are feeling fear or excitement. We have been conditioned to think that we can only learn through struggle. How much easier to learn through ease. Many of my clients have commented: *"I didn't know it could be so easy!"*. If you are struggling, you are on the wrong track going nowhere. Let go of control. Accept 'what is' and trust the process. Easier said than done, but ah, the blessed relief when you stop trying to control everything! This is the route to inner peace.

Chapter 6

Emotional guidance

"Your emotions are the slaves to your thoughts, and you are the slave to your emotions." Elizabeth Gilbert

How do you feel? Most people, when asked how they feel usually respond with 'good' or 'bad' to denote a whole range of feelings from contentment, through guilt to despair. Identifying how we actually feel is not something we are used to doing. I find that people often respond with what they *think* rather than what they feel: *I ought to change my diet. I can't handle the situation at work. I lie awake at night going over what's happened. I should be happy but I'm not.* This is because most of us have not learned the difference between our thoughts and our emotions.

Tuning into what we feel can be bewildering. Growing up we learned to suppress our feelings or to disregard them as unimportant. We were encouraged to subdue strong expression of emotion, even joyful exuberance, because it made others feel uncomfortable. So we became emotionally disabled, unable to harness the power of our emotions.

While some of us are naturally more emotional than others, we all have emotions that drive our behaviours. As a society we like to think that we make decisions and act based on logical and rational thought processes in the left brain. This is hardly ever the case. Strong emotions are attached to our thoughts, which in turn fuel the mind's stories and dramas so that they become real. Our reality is based on what we think, which in turn is fuelled by what we feel.

Thought plus emotion can guide us towards our dreams and our life purpose, or keep us stuck on the same old treadmill of self-limiting behaviour patterns. We have a thought and before we realise what is happening, our emotions can so completely overwhelm us we feel powerless to stop the thought and emotion cascade. Before we know it, we are being helplessly tossed around like a small ship in a gale force wind, often with the same sickening effect.

Feeling stuck and unable to move forward is a sign that we are either suppressing emotions, or letting them rule us without any guidance from our wise or higher self. We are more liable to self-sabotage, disengage from life, or create health problems when we don't know how to live in harmony with our emotions. Learning to identify them and then decide how we want to respond to our emotions is vital for all aspects of our mental and physical health.

When we begin to understand how emotions are linked to our thoughts, and our thoughts are fuelled by our emotions, we give ourselves the power to choose different emotions. This is a revelation to most people: just as we can choose our thoughts, we can also choose what we feel. Or at least we can choose not to get too attached to our emotions as our absolute reality.

Feelings and emotions

We tend to use the terms 'feelings' and 'emotions' interchangeably and, while they often do express the same thing, I think there are some differences.

Feelings encompass our connection between our physical self and the outside world, as in we feel with touch, or feel when we are physically touched. We can feel physically well or unwell, hungry or full, in pain or energised.

We have gut feelings that are connected to our intuition; we just feel that something is not right about a person or situation. We feel our emotions. Someone asks how we feel and our answer is our mind's interpretation of our emotions: *I feel sad, happy, angry, guilty, stuck.*

Emotions are energy that originate in the conscious or subconscious mind and are attached to our thoughts. Emotions are transient and impermanent, meaning that they come and they go. That is the nature of emotion: 'e-motion' is 'energy in motion'.

Before we teach them otherwise, children naturally feel their emotion, express it and then let it pass on through. Just watch a toddler in a supermarket being told he can't have a chocolate bar. His body goes rigid. His bottom lip quivers. You can see the emotional energy building up. It rushes through him and is catapulted out of him with tears and loud wailing, followed by shaking sobs as he deals with the dramatic energy that wracks his little body. It feels like the end of the world for all of five minutes because, a few minutes later, the energy safely released, the child calms down and gets on with the next thing, all upset forgotten.

Not that I am suggesting we all go around like tall two-year olds dramatically wailing and sobbing out our emotions whenever we feel like it. If we were lucky enough to have sensitive parenting, we learned to take responsibility for our emotions. As adults we can still learn how to deal with our strong feelings, how to express them in a constructive way, and then release them safely without inflicting them inappropriately on other people.

I return to the terrible twos. Standing in a long supermarket queue, I watched with admiration as a Belgian father, in response to his toddler son's demands for something, say a very firm *"Non!"* The child was rapidly consumed with a tsunami of a temper tantrum. He wailed at the top of his voice and thrashed himself around on the floor. His father calmly picked him, tucked him firmly under one arm and, ignoring the klaxon-like sounds emanating from his tiny toddler, continued to pay the cashier with his other hand. I noticed older Belgians standing in line smiling with understanding. Later I saw him in the car park cuddling and soothing his demented child. No admonishment, no yelling back or smacking, just understanding and strength that the child could rely on.

What a lucky child to have such a calm and caring father. Too many of us grew up learning to deny or suppress certain emotions, usually because the adults in our life couldn't cope with such an in-your-face expression of feelings. As small children we may have been punished or humiliated to shut us up. Our parents may have feared embarrassment about what others might think. A child's unfettered emotional outbursts can bring up their parents' own fears and vulnerability, and they have no idea how to deal with them.

Stoicism
Our upbringing may have taught us that we can only allow ourselves 'acceptable' feelings, denying others because we have learned to fear them. We may tell ourselves *I am never jealous, I never get angry or I'm not afraid of anything*, yet everybody feels something, even if they are not consciously aware of it. Suppressing our emotions strengthens and paralyses them. The effect is that the energy gets blocked, often leading to physical health problems, or a sensation of being mentally 'blocked'.

Many of us were brought up in a climate of self-restrained stoicism by adults who couldn't handle strong emotion in themselves triggered by the children in their care. Not that I'm knocking stoicism here. Historically it has got millions of people through world wars, deprivation, poverty, brutality, bereavement, natural disasters and many other tragic life happenings.

Stoicism (from the Greek philosophy of the third century BCE) is good training for dealing with life's ups and downs without expressing too much emotion. In dangerous times, keeping your feelings to yourself was an important survival strategy. Stoics are able to accept the way the world works without getting into a lather about everything. They tend to make the best of life and have an attitude that, no matter what is going wrong, you 'just get on with it', without complaining.

It doesn't mean that stoics don't feel anything, they have just learned to keep a lid on their emotions. They don't go around spilling their guts to anyone who will listen but rather choose who they will confide in. The drawback is that in order to stay strong and in control, they get so used to suppressing what they really feel that they may forget they have emotions at all. Or they end up with health problems related to blocked emotional energy.

People who are at the mercy of their emotions and complain a lot can become wearing, as they require others to continually bolster them up so they can make it through another day. Spending a few hours in the company of such a person can be energy draining. Stoics can have the opposite effect. While stoics are people you can always rely on in a crisis, they can come across as cool and unapproachable as they protect their vulnerability behind their 'I can manage' mask of strength and capability. Sometimes you wish they would display a bit of real emotion just to show they are still human under that calm exterior.

Human design
We can use our emotions to guide rather than limit us. They become our emotional guidance system (our EGS), acting as a warning system when we are emotionally blocked or out of balance. We can also use them to guide us towards making life-enhancing decisions.

When I was exploring the emotional causes of my chronic fatigue, I visited a shaman who asked me for my birth details. He then downloaded my *'Human Design'* chart, which looked like nothing I had ever seen before, and proceeded to tell me all about myself.

Human Design is a channelled system based on astrology and the I Ching (ancient Chinese wisdom for clarity and understanding). Human Design shows you who you really are and who you were born to be, rather than who you try to be. You discover that what you thought of as character faults, such as *I am too talkative, I'm such a geek, I'm a bit of a dreamer, I am far too impatient,* are how you are meant to be. It is an excellent tool for self-recognition and acceptance.

Human Design shows me that I have something called an 'Emotional Authority' meaning that I am governed by my emotions. Those of us with an emotional authority ride our emotions like a roller coaster, feeling something one day and then going completely the opposite way the next. We make self-supporting decisions when we allow ourselves to ride the emotional roller coaster and wait until it reaches a mid-point, neither up nor down. In this moment, the quietest point, we have emotional clarity and know what to do. If we make decisions while still on the roller coaster just to make powerful or unpleasant feelings go away, we can end up regretting it later.

As someone brought up in a conventional British culture of the 'stiff upper lip', this was news to me that my emotions could be my guide rather than my enemy. I had always understood that my emotional nature was just a nuisance, an obstacle to logical and rational thinking. Consequently, I mistrusted my feelings about many things.

I am grateful for my childhood training which showed me that I am able to be strong and self-reliant. The downside of relying too much on my strength, instead of listening to my 'emotional authority' and my intuition, was adrenal exhaustion and burnout in my mid-fifties.

The Observer
Learning to trust our emotions starts with becoming the Observer of our mind, a process of conscious observation without judgement or censor. The Observer notices when the mind is engaging in its habitual shenanigans: getting involved in its usual dramas, going around on the track to nowhere, telling the same stories, and staying with its internal self-map, no matter how painful it feels.

For example, you find yourself saying: *I have missed yet another session at the gym!* The Observer notices when you attach to that thought, how it then gets involved in a story of self-judgement and criticism that goes something like this: *It's costing me a fortune and now I am wasting my money. I will never get slim and fit if I don't commit. I am so bad at committing to anything. What's the matter with me? I have no willpower. I am useless. I will never attract a partner if I don't lose weight and get fit. What will my trainer think of me? I must be the worst client he has ever had. I am so bad with money. No wonder I can't afford to buy the things I want, I just waste everything I earn. What a failure I am! I need chocolate (wine, crisps, cake, ice cream, shopping, company ...) to make myself feel better.*

Turning to chocolate, or some other form of distraction, provides only a temporary relief from the mind's stories of how good or bad you are. You haven't dealt with the underlying problem which is the tyranny of the endless cycle of self-defeating thought patterns attached to strong emotional energy.

Loving detachment
The Observer is our conscious or wise self that notices how the mind and emotions drive subconscious habitual patterns of thought and behaviour, even when consciously we may want to change. It observes all of this without the need to judge, change, make it go away, deny or justify it. This is loving detachment from the anxiety-driven ego.

What you say and how you speak, even to yourself, has the effect of reinforcing your negative thinking. I used to deprecatingly call myself a 'technophobe' until I realised that this disempowered me. When I thought about it, it was clear that I wasn't really frightened of technology. My truth is that I am just not that interested in technology, unless I can see its immediate usefulness to me, then I will learn how to use it on an as-needed basis.

Pam would regularly admonish herself angrily with, *"You are so stupid!"* whenever she perceived that she had let herself down in some way or other. Her Observer noticed, without criticism, how she talked to herself. As Pam observed this phenomenon, she noticed how it made her sense of self-worth take a nosedive. Something shifted in her. She realised that she wouldn't talk to anyone else like that and she stopped talking to herself in derogatory terms.

The mind gets embroiled in its usual dramas, but the Observer stays lovingly detached. As you let go of the need to believe everything you think and feel, *this is how I feel, this must be real,* you realise that your thoughts are just thoughts and your feelings are just emotions created by your conscious and subconscious mind.

At a conscious level you can choose whether or not to attach to the thoughts and emotions, or just let them go. Detachment causes them to eventually lose power over you. As you observe and identify both your conscious thoughts and the emotions attached to them, you may find that, like Pam, you release some of your old patterns more easily than if you beat yourself up over them.

Being conscious comes from our wise or higher self. It is not ego driven. As you start observing your patterns of thought and behaviour, it is very easy for the ego to step in and either resist what you are doing: *I must be crazy to think I can change, I will always be unlovable/a failure/stupid*, or it will push you to change with deadlines: *I must stop this habit before the wedding/my holiday in July*, or *If I can't do it now I will never be able to do it*.

Either way, the ego sets you up to stay stuck because its thoughts are coming from a place of fear and resistance to change. When you tell yourself that you are just observing what the mind is doing and that you don't have to change anything, the ego can relax. Observing presents no danger to the ego's guard dog approach to our safety, so there is less resistance.

When you start detaching with love from your usual thinking, you will find other ways to perceive your so-called weaknesses or failures. For example, you might say: *I am finding this really challenging*, instead of *I am so useless. I am an empathic person* instead of *I am such a people pleaser. I am a perfectionist who knows when it's good enough* instead of *I am a perfectionist and it drives me mad. I believe myself to be worthy, no matter what my achievements* instead of *I must have recognition before I can think of myself as worthy*.

Supporting ourselves through changing our perspective on the truth lifts us up through the different layers of emotions. You don't have to even completely believe that the new statements are true. You just have to decide that speaking to yourself with compassion and kindness is a good first step towards reclaiming your lost self and your true power as a spirit in human form.

The range of emotions
I was inspired by the 'Emotional Ladder' in Gill Edwards' book, *Life is a Gift*, and have created my own version here. It shows the different levels of emotions that we are all capable of experiencing. It helps identify where you spend most of your emotional life.

There are no good or bad emotions. It's all just energy that we generate depending on our thoughts and beliefs. Living consciously allows us to be the Observer and notice how thinking and emotions are interlinked so that we can start detaching from our usual emotional state. When you next find yourself getting caught up in negative mind chatter and feeling 'bad', see if you can tune into and recognise the emotion(s) you are feeling.

Level 1	Elated, empowered, enthusiastic, excited, exhilarated, free, grateful, in the flow, intuitive knowing, joyful, optimistic, passionate, playful, unconditionally loving, timeless
Level 2	Accepting, appreciative, calm, compassionate, connected, contented, forgiving, having clarity, hopeful, inner peace, in the moment, open hearted, patient, relaxed, trusting
Level 3	Bored, frustrated, impatient, irritated, resentful
Level 4	Burdened, discouraged, disappointed, feel lost or stuck, overwhelmed, over-busy, resigned, sad, self-doubting, sense of loss, stoic, worried
Level 5	Angry, arrogant, blaming, enraged, full of hatred, jealous, judgemental, need to control, obsessive, pseudo-power, self-righteous, suspicious, vengeful
Level 6	Anxious, ashamed, controlled, guilty, insecure, lonely, martyr, pessimistic, rejected, self-sacrificing, trapped, unworthy, victim
Level 7	Abandoned, apathetic, depressed*, despairing, fearful, grief stricken, helpless, hopeless, powerless, suicidal thoughts* ** (Anyone who has long term depression with suicidal thoughts must seek professional help immediately)*

Levels 1 and 2 are emotions based around authenticity and love. It is hard to feel frustrated and insecure if you are living from a place of acceptance and gratitude. These are the emotions that have a higher vibrational energy. If you feel like this most of the time, you feel strong and confident about yourself and your world. The other five levels have a lower vibrational energy. When we are in balance and living from our authentic self we inhabit levels 1 and 2 most of the time.

This does not mean that we can inhabit levels 1 and 2 all the time. Human beings are designed to experience all levels of emotions, depending on their own innate emotional processes and life circumstances. If you lose your job or a loved one dies, you are hardly going to feel joyful and enthusiastic. We all move up and down the emotional ladder at various times in our lives.

It is quite normal to experience the emotions in **levels 3 and 4** from time to time, depending on how balanced you are feeling. If you spend most of your time in levels 3 and 4, it may be that you have too much busyness or demands on your time and energy, and this plunges you into feelings of resentment, irritation or discouragement. Paying attention to your Observer will help you discover why you push yourself beyond your limitations. Perhaps you are in a period of life when you absolutely have to keep going for financial reasons, career advancement and family life. Finding ways to deal with these demands on time and energy in a more balanced way is the challenge for most of us.

Levels 3 through to 7 are based on anxiety and fear. Boredom may be anxiety about having nothing to do and therefore being alone with self. Overwhelm may be anxiety about not being able to continue juggling plates in the air. Frustration may be anxiety at not having our needs met, such as the need for achievement or connection. Feeling lost or stuck may be fear of passing through life without knowing why we are here.

Fear keeps us stuck in victim consciousness. As a victim we feel powerless to change our thoughts, our circumstances or how we feel. Someone who feels angry and vengeful might find it difficult to relate to feeling like a victim. They are full of self-righteous anger which is an energetic emotion that keeps feelings of vulnerability and insecurity at bay. But when the anger levels drop, they again feel the fear of not getting their needs met, such as being heard and understood, or receiving the justice they believe they deserve.

Being stuck at **levels 5, 6 and 7** can indicate an underlying fear of many things: of change, of taking control of our life, of not having our needs or expectations met, of not living up to the expectations of others, of feeling disempowered, of financial insecurity, of failure, rejection, being unloved or unlovable, of being inherently bad, or never feeling good about self again.

You may be a people pleaser, dependent on the approval of others and not daring to live your life the way you want for fear of disapproval. People pleasers tend to have a low sense of self-worth. You may feel as if you are 'waiting for permission' from others to start living.

You may be keeping a tight control over either anger or sadness. Because you haven't learned how to express and deal with these strong emotions, you either turn them in on yourself, leading to apathy and depression, or you blame everyone else and turn your anger outwards, expressing it as hostility and aggression towards others.

Perhaps you have suppressed your passion and lack a sense of meaning or purpose to life. Or you can't accept your situation, even if it is based on choices you have made.

In his own words, Duncan was a 'Warrior'. His passion was teaching personal security. When he ran his self-defence classes and seminars he felt as though he was fulfilling his life purpose. After his children were born, Duncan found he could not support his family as a self-employed professional. He 'sold his soul' to a company doing IT work. Duncan got stuck in emotional levels 6 and 7: anxious, self-sacrificing, lonely, trapped, controlled, pessimistic, apathetic, despairing and powerless. He would move into levels 3 and 4: frustrated, impatient, resentful (especially towards his family), discouraged, resigned, sad and a great sense of loss. His physical health suffered as he became chronically fatigued.

Duncan had chosen to change his career for all sorts of practical reasons, at least temporarily until the kids had gone through higher education, but he couldn't accept his situation. His lack of acceptance was causing his discontent and chronic fatigue. He was also losing out on his relationship with his children because he was too busy feeling resentful to enjoy their childhood.

Learning to accept and surrender to his situation did not mean giving up on his dreams or true purpose. Duncan started to organise lunchtime self-defence classes at his place of work and was contracted by his company to help with their security. He used some of his free weekends to go on retreats and courses where he could be with other like-minded people to nurture his passion.

Duncan still needed his IT job for the foreseeable future, but by changing his thinking about his circumstances, he felt more at peace and energised. He gradually moved up the emotional ladder and started experiencing more of level 2 and occasionally level 1.

If you realise that you are blocked at any particular level between 3 and 7, this is usually an indication of where you are stuck in your thinking and beliefs about yourself and life. You may also be suffering from stress-related biochemical or lifestyle imbalances which can affect the brain and endocrine (hormone) system. This in turn can lead to emotional instability. Examples are lack of sleep and exercise, food intolerances, poor nutritional habits, blood sugar ups and downs, lack of key nutrients, chronic, long-term infection, and a stressful lifestyle. This is certainly something to take into account.

In the days when I ran nutrition and health courses, one of my students, Jeff, admitted that he was stuck at level 7, permanently depressed. He put it down to the fact that his wife had left him, taking their seven-year old daughter with her to another country. He found it unbearable that he only saw his daughter during school holidays. After the session about food allergies and intolerance, Jeff decided to experiment with giving up wheat and all gluten-containing grains. He was amazed how the fog of depression lifted despite nothing in his life changing. He was still sad about his marriage breaking up, but he no longer felt weighed down with black despairing thoughts about it. Jeff was finally able to allow himself to enjoy seeing his daughter when he was with her, instead of feeling depressed that she couldn't be around all the time.

While most people inhabit one or two levels most of the time, some people feel emotionally out of control, going up and down the emotional ladder constantly throughout the day. This is exhausting both for the sufferer and those around them. In this case, it is a good idea to investigate both psychological and biochemical imbalances.

Numbed down
If you don't feel anything at all, and don't identify with any of these emotional categories, then you are no doubt aware that you are numbed down. This is extreme self-protection and a sure sign of very tightly controlled emotions, usually anger, fear, sadness, shame, guilt or grief.

If the numbing down started in childhood, you may have been afraid to show extreme emotions like anger and sadness because they were not acceptable to the family in which you grew up. Now as an adult, you may be afraid of unleashing these emotions because if you start letting them out, *'they will never stop'*. The child within still fears the power of their emotions to harm themselves or others.

Becky's brother, died when she was nine years old and he was seven. They were out playing together when he chased a ball into the road and was hit by a car. While her parents never openly blamed her, Becky sensed their disappointment in her for not protecting her younger brother. She believed she had failed. She did not go to the funeral because in her culture funerals were for adults only, so she never had a chance to say goodbye to him.

Her parents were always loving and kind to her, but never talked of the dead child. Becky missed her little brother intensely, but was unable to talk to anyone about her grief because in her family this was a closed subject. She learned to suppress expression of any feelings and to all outward appearances was a compliant, pleasant, rather shy child.

In her thirties Becky developed colon cancer, from which she fortunately made a full recovery. However, she attributed the cancer to blocked energy from being emotionally numbed down. Getting in touch with her emotions became an important part of Becky's journey towards living a conscious life. She realised that her snappy, critical attitude towards her husband and children was because of stuck emotions trying to get her attention. To get in touch with her emotional guidance system, Becky first of all needed to acknowledge the anger she felt towards her little brother for dying and her parents for not allowing her to talk of her grief. *"But I can't feel angry towards them,"* she said, *"they didn't know how to do things differently"*.

Eventually she realised that it was safe to feel angry while not blaming her parents who were doing the best they could in a tragic situation. Feeling anger would not harm her parents or anyone else. It would help release blocked angry energy that was damaging her health and her self-confidence. Eventually, Becky was able to release her stored anger and replace it with compassion for her parents, her little brother and for herself.

If you learned that expressing any 'extreme' emotion was unsafe, even excitement, passion or joy, this may have led you into passivity, unable to express anything other than 'acceptable', non-threatening emotions such as patience, calmness and niceness. Like Becky, you may even be unconscious of the emotions seething below the surface, but they have to find an outlet, often through passive aggressive behaviour, self-sabotage, illness or burnout.

Anger

Anger is a difficult emotion for most of us to understand. We're either denying it or loudly acting it out because we have no idea how to use it for good. We just don't get that kind of training because most of the adults who brought us up had no idea what do to with anger either. Rarely are we taught to express our anger in a constructive or effective way.

Anger is a powerful signal that something is wrong. As an important biological mechanism for survival, anger protects and defends us against perceived threats or danger. It tells us that we are being compromised or hurt in some way. This means that there is nothing wrong with anger: it is natural and normal to feel it. It is what each of us does with our anger that makes the difference between self-empowerment and losing ourselves in levels 3 to 7 on the emotional ladder.

Of all the emotions, anger is the one that women generally have most difficulty expressing. If they do express their angry feelings, they do so ineffectively. Men aren't much better at it, either aggressively expressing their anger or bottling it up and letting it seep out in criticism and judgement. Most little girls' brains are hardwired for nurturing and peace-making. Their biology may be a disadvantage if they are brought up to please, protect and placate by denying their anger towards those who disrespect, neglect or attack them, physically or verbally.

Centuries of female suppression has taught us that to feel angry meant we were 'bad'. Being 'good' meant suppressing our true feelings and appeasing the person who controlled us. We learned to smile when we wanted to spit nails. We learned to shed tears when we wanted to scream and dig our claws in. We either became compliant, the good girl, or we became rebellious and really bad. Both strategies hurt us in the long run, and neither of them helped us be in touch with our anger or to use it effectively.

Afraid to express our anger, many of us learned to disguise it in tears, depression, disappointment, feeling hurt, guilt, angelic sweetness, being nice, procrastination, withdrawal, passivity, disasterising (always anticipating the worst), phobias, chronic anxiety, panic attacks, over-eating, and other acts of self-sabotage.

My favourite cover-up for anger were tears, being nice, withdrawal and eventually depression. I knew I was hopping mad, but I was afraid to express it so I suppressed it in the belief that I was strong and could handle it. American comedian and actor, Steven Wright, tells us:

"Depression is merely anger without enthusiasm."

When I understood the connection between my feelings of apathy and depression, and my years of suppressed anger, I developed a mantra for myself which I used in situations where I would normally have shrugged my shoulders and walked away. The mantra was: *Don't be sad, get mad!* It helped me recognise when I was feeling angry instead of denying it.

It is hard for most women to recognise, let alone admit, that they are angry. Angry women are perceived as threatening, especially to men who generally cannot handle an emotional woman. Women throughout history have been condemned if they express their anger, especially towards men. They are labelled 'unfeminine', 'bitches', 'shrews', 'cows', 'nags', 'witches', 'harpies', 'strident', 'ball crushers', 'neurotic', 'hysterical', 'hormonal', 'dragons', 'man-haters', 'over-emotional' and 'lesbians'.

No wonder we have grown up afraid of our own anger. To be considered acceptable, we must be nice, feminine, ladylike creatures, always smiling and kind. I started to notice how, in some American movies, beautiful women keep on smiling their whiter-than-white smiles even when they are furious or in tears. That shows the level of confusion we still feel. We must never let on that deep inside we are seething with rage at the contempt and injustice with which we have been treated, often from early childhood. Our anger is so deeply buried that most of us are usually not even conscious that our health symptoms, frustration and feeling stuck are caused by unacknowledged rage. Instead we learn to feel guilty, unworthy, self-doubting, ashamed and powerless. Nothing blocks the awareness of our anger as effectively as guilt and self-doubt. In her book, *The Dance of Anger*, Harriet Lerner observes:

"Our language, created and codified by men, does not have one unflattering term to describe men who vent their anger at women. Even such epithets as 'bastard' and 'son of a bitch' do not condemn the man but place the blame on a woman – his mother!"

Our early conditioning that stops us from feeling our anger is disempowering. It is much easier to control and manipulate a woman who feels guilty, ashamed, unworthy, self-doubting or depressed. Outwardly angry women may be agents for change and revolution. Great examples are the suffragettes of the early twentieth century, and the feminist movement of the 1960s and '70s.

Women and men in touch with their anger at least have the advantage of knowing how they feel. Only the minority know how to make their anger work for them. The rest stay stuck in patterns of angry outbursts, blaming, complaining and frustration, all the while achieving nothing. Everything stays the same. Greek philosopher, Aristotle, who lived in the fourth century BCE said:

> *"Anyone can become angry. This is easy. But to be angry with the right person, to the right degree, at the right time, for the right purpose, and in the right way … that is not easy."*

Over two thousand years later we are still stumbling around trying to figure out what to do with anger.

To address a situation that hurts us we must have clarity, direction and control over our anger so that it becomes a vehicle for change. Ineffective expression of anger cements the patterns of behaviour with the people against whom we feel angry. The more we scream, shout and blame, the more they become defensive, angry or, even worse, cool, calm and collected. Either way, they do not take an out of control, angry woman seriously. She is contemptuously put down with the labels 'hysterical' or 'hormonal', both of which are guaranteed to make her even more angry.

We are taught from an early age that anger is a destructive emotion. We did not learn that there is a difference between our feelings of anger and the anger-driven behaviour for which we were punished. Anger is meant to empower us, to be acted *upon*. It is not meant to be acted *out*. Learning to harness and manage anger increases your personal power. In her book, *Managing Anger*, Gael Lindenfield tells us that each of us

> *"has the right to feel angry when we feel frustrated, hurt, attacked, oppressed, exploited, manipulated or cheated"*.

She also tells us that we have the right to feel angry when our needs are ignored, when we are let down, when our health, welfare, happiness, peace or survival is threatened, when we see other people's rights being abused or threatened, when we see things that we value being damaged or abused, or when we lose someone or something that we value.

Releasing emotion

Because emotion is 'energy in motion' one of the best ways to move the energy is through movement. Taking regular exercise has many beneficial effects. It is great for physical health because it gets the blood moving, removes toxins more efficiently, feeds the brain, tones and removes tension build-up in the muscles and creates more energy. It also releases endorphins in the brain which make us feel upbeat and help to dissipate stress.

To really make a difference, you need to do something physically active every day. Taking regular exercise puts people off because they think they have to get all hot and sweaty in a gym. Having structured exercise in a gym does suit some people, but it isn't for everybody. If you are not used to exercising, start slowly and build up gradually. I walk most days of the week. It's a habit I started in my early twenties when I first started working. I hated sitting all day in an office. As soon as I got home from work, I would put on my trainers and go walking/running for up to forty minutes. Brisk walking or running in the fresh air is still one of the best forms of exercise you can do. Unless you have mobility problems, most people can walk and some can run. You can divide up your walking time through the day, although a longer period of time is the most effective way to move emotional energy.

Regular stretching helps dissipate tension stored in muscles and joints, so helping to keep them flexible and supple. Other ways to get moving and stretching include dancing, gardening, racket sports, cycling, swimming, an exercise bike or treadmill, kick boxing, Pilates, Tai Chi, Qi gong and yoga.

Daily exercise and stretching will help you feel calm and more centred, in tune with your thoughts and emotions.

Chapter 7

Buttons and beliefs

"Your beliefs become your thoughts. Your thoughts become your words. Your words become your actions. Your actions become your habits. Your habits become your values. Your values become your destiny." Mahatma Gandhi

The mind is like an iceberg. The tip above water represents our conscious mind, wherein lie the thoughts and beliefs of which we are aware. Below the waterline is our subconscious, so called because it is below the level of consciousness. Deeply buried within the subconscious are a whole other set of influences: our deeply embedded beliefs and emotional hot buttons, acquired and accumulated over many years, starting in infancy. They form our programmed conditioning, the patterns that keep us deadlocked in self-limiting or self-sabotaging behaviours, even when we are desperate to change.

Beliefs

The Oxford English Dictionary defines beliefs as: *"An acceptance that something exists or is true, especially one without proof."* For example: I believe in aliens from outer space. We can change the world through loving kindness. It also says that belief is: *"A firmly held opinion or point of view."* Examples might be: All dogs should be kept on a lead. People should not drink and drive.

A belief is, therefore, any thought, concept or idea to which we become attached. Our beliefs are the sum total of the way we think and what we believe. They are our opinions, points of view and our truth about the way things are, even if others disagree with us. Our beliefs can be conscious or they can be buried in the subconscious. At the conscious level, if someone asks us what we think of a certain politician, or of eating chocolate cake for breakfast, we will have a ready opinion based on our political beliefs, or the type of food we believe is suitable to start the day.

Subconscious beliefs, by their very definition, are hard to uncover because they are deeply buried beneath our conscious awareness. When we try to figure out why we are always short of money, despite a good income, it could take a while to uncover subconscious beliefs such as: *I can't be spiritual and have money. Spending money is my only source of pleasure. I don't deserve financial wealth. I mustn't be better than my parents. Money corrupts and is the root of evil. I must always share what I have with others.* Such beliefs cause us to get rid of money the moment we have it, even when we are trying to save for our future.

Both our conscious and subconscious beliefs about ourselves and our place in the world form the basis of our internal self-map or life script (explained in Chapter 5). These are our core beliefs. They are usually set by around age seven and drop outside of our conscious awareness. While our conscious beliefs may be modified or revised through adolescence and young adulthood, our subconscious core beliefs, hidden out of conscious awareness, tend to stay pretty much the same throughout life. As we start living a conscious life, we may become aware of their influence and decide to change them.

Mind filter

Our beliefs act as a mind filter, which is the gatekeeper for the ego. The role of the mind filter is to sift all of our experiences, life events and impressions through our beliefs or life script. To ensure our safety and survival, it is constantly checking that the outside world fits with our beliefs about how things should be. Our mind filter selects, adopts, ignores, accepts, removes, discards, judges, and criticises people and events, depending on where they fit into our belief system. Someone may critically judge and therefore shun the homeless because, in their belief system, they believe that homeless people cause their own problems. While in someone else's belief system, they see the homeless as victims of an uncaring society, and need all the help and support we can give them.

Self-sabotage

We have an assortment of beliefs, some positive and some negative: they can support us in our personal and spiritual growth, or they can cause us to stagnate, self-sabotage and limit ourselves. Self-sabotage is the behaviour we use to numb down uncomfortable emotions. These behaviours provide temporary relief but don't work in the long run because we haven't dealt with the real feelings from which we are trying to escape. They keep us stuck in a cycle of frustration, pain and suffering, yet we feel unable to change. There are many variations on the theme of self-sabotaging behaviours. We each have our own well tried and tested methods. Here are a just few examples: *Comfort eating and drinking. Junk food addiction. Excessive sugar, caffeine and alcohol consumption. Being accident-prone. Procrastination. Passivity (giving in to others). Starting arguments just to let off steam. Being judgemental and critical. Deliberately provoking or hurting others to relieve tension. Over-responsibility. Never daring to speak up. Not finishing what you've set out to achieve. Overspending. Running up debt. Gossiping. Computer games. Phobias and obsessions. Pornography. Smoking. Never asking for help. Yo-yo dieting. Going to bed too late and never getting enough sleep. Too much busyness as distraction. Aggressive behaviour. Driving dangerously. Gambling. Promiscuous sex. Recreational drugs. Perfectionism where you keep moving the goal posts. Adrenaline addiction. Toxic relationships. Too little or too much exercise. Focusing on the negative. Criminal activity. Dwelling on past wrongs. Always feeling guilty. Social withdrawal. Constant partying at the expense of other aspects of your life. Never relaxing. If it's all going well, trash it!*

Always right

While growing up, we all unconsciously and unquestioningly absorbed many of our beliefs like a sponge from the adults around us. We continue to live according to those beliefs into adulthood, often unaware of the effect they have on our reality. Because many of our deeply-held beliefs were laid down as absolute truths during our formative years, even if they do not support us now, our mind always wants to prove our beliefs to be right, even at the cost of pain, compulsion, self-defeating behaviour and other dysfunctions.

A child with a highly critical parent may have subconscious beliefs: *I am a bad girl. I am unlovable. I can never do anything right.* When she reaches adulthood, this may translate into a search for love through promiscuous behaviour, pushing people away because she feels unworthy of love, a feeling of never getting the kind of love she needs, always having to prove herself by going one better than everyone else, or never feeling satisfied with her achievements. She ends up in relationships that feed her beliefs. She can't get the love she wants because, deep down, she is a 'bad girl' and doesn't deserve unconditional love.

Sari was on yet another diet and was already sabotaging her ability to lose weight with the belief that she had no willpower. She could bring up numerous examples of the times she had tried to shed kilos and failed, which reinforced her belief that she had no willpower. Her mind deselected all the times she had used willpower to stick at a job or a relationship, and made a success of it. She ignored the number of times she had used willpower to haul herself out of bed when the alarm went off, to control her irritation when the kids were cranky, or to stick with a project through to the end, even though she was exhausted. Fuelling the conscious belief, 'I have no willpower', was a whole raft of subconscious beliefs about her inability to perform or measure up to externally imposed standards: the 'not good enough' or 'unworthy' beliefs.

When our self-limiting beliefs are buried in the subconscious they can wreck our attempts to move forward. We may want to be in an intimate relationship, but each time we get close to someone a subconscious belief gets in the way and sabotages our relationships: *I will be suffocated if I get too intimate with anyone. People I get close to either leave me or die. There's always a high price to pay in loss of freedom when I love someone. I can't risk being hurt or abandoned again.* Consciously we have no idea what is going on. We believe that we must be flawed in some way because we are 'useless at relationships'.

Excavation

Once we declare a willingness to start digging down to find the subconscious beliefs that are holding us back, the mind starts throwing them up at random moments for us to examine and decide if we want to keep them. Part of my excavation process was to have some Amanae BodyWork sessions with Eric, a Californian living in Belgium. Amanae is hands-on work to release emotional blockages in the body caused by old wounds and stuck emotional energy. During one of our sessions, I suddenly realised that I had been carrying around a belief: *I will not be lovable if I am successful.* I had no idea that belief was buried in the basement of my mind. No wonder I had held myself back for many years in my relationships and my working life.

On another occasion, I was sitting in a workshop for business coachees run by our business coach, John, an empathic and twinkly-eyed Irishman.

I was enjoying the exercise exploring the power of thought, when I suddenly became aware of a childhood belief: *Calm down. Don't get too excited, it might all go wrong.* It emerged into the light of my conscious mind like a mole digging its way out of the dark earth. I realised how much I suppressed childish joyful glee and anticipation about all sorts of events because my inner child had learned to be cautious about expressing strong emotion. Then I remembered listening to a talk while staying on the beautiful Channel island of Jersey. It was given by Richard, a British inspirational speaker. He told us a story of how he booked a holiday somewhere exotic and spent the next three months in happy anticipation of the wonderful time he would have. When he finally got there it rained every day, the hotel was next to a building site with noise and dust, the staff were rude and the food was awful. In short he had a terrible time. When he returned home and regaled his friends with the tale of the holiday from hell, they were all very sympathetic about what a waste of time and money it was. His response was (and I paraphrase): *"Not really. I had the most wonderful three months of anticipation, enjoying the holiday before I got there."*

As I made the connection with Richard's story and my subconscious belief, I decided that from now on I would allow myself to enjoy every moment of excited anticipation. I no longer needed to protect myself from disappointment or let-down.

Hot buttons

What makes it difficult to change our beliefs, even our conscious beliefs, is that they are attached to our emotional hot buttons. Our hot buttons are made up of deeply ingrained, negative, repetitive beliefs held in place by emotional superglue. They operate below the level of conscious awareness and are the expression of our deepest fears, especially the fears of being rejected or abandoned, of being unloved and unlovable, unworthy, powerless, and not good enough.

We all have emotional hot buttons. Most adults probably have between twenty and twenty-five of all different sizes. Our buttons are the emotional scars or wounds collected during our many experiences of growing up. To the outside world our experiences may not seem to be very traumatic, and they don't need to be for a button to form. Our experiences carry an emotional weight that stays in our psyche right through adult life. For example, being laughed at by our classmates for the way we looked, or for stuttering when giving a speech, could be enough to form a 'stupid' or 'misfit' button. Our child's mind filter made the decision that we were inherently flawed and unacceptable because of our looks, or we should never again attempt public speaking because it is just too humiliating.

Being told that we would 'never amount to anything so don't bother trying' might form a worthless or undeserving button. Many high achievers have a 'failure' or 'unvalued' button. The belief that causes them to drive themselves hard to achieve is: *I have to be better than all the rest to be good enough.* 'Failure' and 'unvalued' buttons can go the other way and fuel the belief: *There's no point me trying, I will never get it right.* The subsequent behaviour may take the form of apathy, sabotaging our efforts, and a low level of achievement.

List of hot buttons
Below are some of the most common hot buttons. You may recognise some of them. You may also have a few more of your own not mentioned here.

Abandoned	Helpless	Not good enough	Unattractive
Abnormal	Ignored	Not special	Undeserving
Alone	Impatience	Not unique	Unfeminine
Attacked	Inadequate	Nuisance	Unimportant
Awkward	Incapable	Out of control	Unlikable
Bad	Incompetent	Outcast	Unlovable
Betrayed	Inefficient	Perfectionist	Unmanly
Controlled	Injustice/unfair	Powerless	Unrecognised
Crazy	Insecure	Punctual	Unsafe
Deprived	Invisible	Rejected	Unsupported
Disregarded	Lazy	Responsible	Unvalued
Disrespected	Lonely	Rebel	Unworthy
Dominated	Loss	Slow	Useless
Excluded	Manipulated	Socially inept	Victim
Expert	Mediocre	Stupid	Vulnerable
Exposed	Misfit	Ugly	Weak
Failure	Misunderstood	Unacceptable	Weird
Foolish	Money	Unappreciated	Wrong

Emotional charge

There is nothing inherently wrong with, for example, being alone, awkward, expert, misfit, perfectionist, punctual, lonely, responsible, slow, vulnerable, weak, weird or wrong. They can be our strengths as well as our weaknesses. It depends on the emotional charge attached to any of these words that creates a hot button, which then ends up controlling us. If we believe we are a misfit and it impacts the way we see ourselves, then clearly the connotation is negative. We will be constantly looking for reassurance that we fit in with society's views on what is considered 'normal'. Misfit becomes a hot button that will be triggered by someone's comments about our out-of-fashion clothes, our unusual eating habits, or our sexual orientation.

If, however, we are comfortable with who we are, no hot buttons are attached to those words. We won't go into a negative reaction if someone calls us misfit or a bit weird, although we might point out that their implied criticism is disrespectful.

Our hot button triggers are individual to us, meaning that not everyone reacts to the same stimuli. For example, in a small team of six people working on a project, one team member, Sally Ann, assumes the role of 'expert' (even though she doesn't really know much more than the others). She proceeds to boss everyone else around, imposing her ideas on the rest of the team of how things should be done. Of the other five team members, Tom, Dick and Jan get agitated and reactive. Tom is reacting to his controlled, manipulated, vulnerable, weak and unmanly buttons, which is how he used to feel when his father criticised him for not standing up to bullies at school. His behaviour is sarcastic, disrespectful and uncooperative.

Dick is reacting to his dominated, powerless, unfair, insecure and not good enough buttons, which is how he used to feel when his mother ignored his abilities in art and told him he should be focusing on science. His behaviour is to withdraw, go quiet and offer nothing to the team effort unless asked specifically.

Jan's hot buttons are incompetent, unworthy, useless, slow and exposed. She is reacting to a bossy school teacher who made fun of her in front of her classmates about her quirky mannerisms and inability to grasp (apparently) easy concepts. Her behaviour is to smile sweetly at Sally Ann, then fume and gossip about her to anyone who will listen. She won't confront Sally Ann in person.

The fifth member of the team, Karen, takes it all in her stride. Sally Ann doesn't trigger her hot buttons because she grew up with two sisters. All three of them were fun, loud, bossy and expert at everything, but nobody was allowed to override anyone else. They each respected the others' special qualities. Karen sees the insecure, worried little girl behind Sally Ann's bossy and expert acts. She gently ribs Sally Ann when she starts being overbearing, while supporting her good ideas and genuine enthusiasm for the project. Sally Ann feels safe with Karen and relaxes in her presence.

Tom, Dick and Jan, unaware of their hot buttons, can't understand how Karen is able to get on with Sally Ann while they can't. They don't see that they are reacting from their child and adolescent selves, which is when the hot buttons were first formed.

Pulling the threads

Even if we had a relatively happy childhood, each one of us is carrying around repressed pain, fear, shame, hurt, guilt, disappointment, resentment and anger that are stored as energy in the subconscious. These emotions keep us unconsciously reacting to our hot buttons. When one of our hot buttons gets triggered, we are activating those buried emotions, much like poking at an old wound. An override switch goes on and we end up overreacting emotionally. Whether we suppress or express the emotion we feel, it will send us down the well-worn track of doing the same thing, in the same way, to produce the same result.

Because the reaction happens so fast, most people don't see the steps they took to reach their reaction and subsequent behaviour. When we are in the throes of reactivity, it feels as though we have no control. The feelings rise up and overwhelm us before we even realise it.

To understand your hot buttons, take a moment to think of a situation when you were feeling highly emotionally charged over something. Maybe you got very angry and lashed out, or you felt very hurt and withdrew. Others may tell you that your reaction is out of proportion to what has taken place, but you feel perfectly justified in feeling resentful, angry, bitter, hurt, guilty or ashamed. You find yourself unable to let the incident go. It churns over and over in your mind for hours, days, weeks, months and even years afterwards. Each time you bring up the memory your hot buttons get triggered all over again.

Once you recognise that you are in a hot button reaction, take a deep breath, and observe the sequence of internal events. It's like untangling a knotted ball of wool by gently pulling out all the threads.

One of the first signs of your hot buttons being triggered is a reaction in the body, which manifests your mental and emotional state. Signs may be butterflies or clenching in the stomach; a sudden feeling of tension in the abdomen, like an iron fist gripping the intestines; a sudden rush of blood to the head; heart pounding; tightness across the chest; sudden headache; constriction around the stomach or throat; tightening of the neck and shoulder muscles; feeling hot or cold all of a sudden; or sweaty hands. You may feel the reaction in more than one place at the same time.

This is the stress response being activated, along with your hot buttons. Your inner child or adolescence is in fight or flight mode, convinced its life and security are threatened. You are overwhelmed with emotion, and your adrenal glands are pumping adrenaline and cortisol around your body.

The sequence of a hot button reaction starts with an external stimulus. For example, a younger colleague makes what he believes to be constructive comments about some of the points in your report. His comments trigger your 'not good enough', 'incompetent' and 'disrespected' hot buttons.

Your hot buttons are attached to strong emotions: anger, resentment, shame, hurt and fear. The surge of emotion fuels your conscious thoughts and beliefs: *How dare he criticise my work. I have been doing this job for twenty years and know what I am doing. Does he think I am no good at writing reports?!*

Overwhelmed by self-righteous indignation, your behaviour is to write your colleague a strong email pointing out all his faults. You tell him in no uncertain terms that you have been doing the job since he was still a toddler, and you don't need someone who is still wet behind the ears telling you how to write a report.

Later you calm down and feel guilty. As the hot button reactivity dies down, you realise he is an enthusiastic young guy who was only trying to be helpful. You overreacted. Your behaviour reinforces your subconscious beliefs that you are not good enough, that you don't deserve respect and, deep down, you fear that you may be incompetent, because that is how you learned to doubt yourself while growing up.

I think or I feel

This would be a good place to take a look at the difference between thoughts and feelings. Many of us get confused about this. We may say things like: *I feel it would be a good idea to put up a fence to keep the kids out. I feel that we should encourage future athletes by investing in sports facilities.*

In both these examples, we should be saying: *I think that* ... because we are stating a thought, belief or point of view. If we were expressing a true feeling, we would say: *I feel angry about kids coming in and vandalising this garden: I think we should put up a fence to keep them out. I feel sad and discouraged when I hear of child athletes having nowhere to practice: I think we should invest more in sports facilities.*

This is not being nit-picky. It is about knowing how our mind and emotions work so that we can unravel the complex intertwining of thoughts, feelings, conscious and subconscious beliefs, and emotional hot buttons.

How old am I?

In charge of all this reactivity is our ego trying to protect us from old hurt from when we were much younger. This means that most of us are being driven by our child or adolescent selves. Our ego uses the same patterns of reaction now, even though they are no longer applicable in our adult life. A question that helps to gain perspective on a hot button reaction is: *How old am I right now?* As we remember the first time we felt like this, it is easy to see how our inner child or adolescent is running the emotional show in that moment.

When Maggie realised that she had not been invited to Carol's dinner party, even though a mutual friend, Josie, was going, she felt a surge of anger, helplessness and betrayal. Her heart pounded, her neck got stiff and her stomach tied itself in knots. Her conscious thoughts were: *I could never be friends with Carol again ... After the hours I spent with her crying on my shoulder over her divorce, now look at the way she is treating me!*

Maggie felt like calling Carol and telling her what a bad friend she was, but fortunately restrained herself. Instead she spent a few quiet moments trying to figure out which of her hot buttons were going off. She identified 'unappreciated', 'unlovable', 'unimportant', 'unfair', 'betrayed', 'injustice', 'rejected' and 'victim'. But the button that was shouting the loudest was 'excluded'. Suddenly Maggie remembered two occasions, one when she was nine and the other when she was twelve years old, when she was excluded by friends from their birthday parties. The pain of exclusion and the feelings of rejection, betrayal, and injustice that went with it, came flooding back. Maggie realised in that moment that she was being driven by her hurt and angry nine- and twelve-year-old selves. Realising that how she felt had nothing to do with Carol, she chose to take no action and instead stay with the pain of her feelings until the hot buttons subsided.

A couple of days later, Carol called Maggie to ask her to dinner the following weekend because there was someone ('a lovely man called Pete'), she wanted her to meet. She also said: *"I would have liked you to come this Saturday, but I am playing cupid to a couple of other friends, Josie being one of them, and Pete isn't available until the following week. Can you come?"* Maggie was so relieved she hadn't reacted to her hot buttons. She was able to respond with gracious thanks, and a promise to bring dessert and a decent bottle of wine.

Reacting or responding
In this case, Maggie didn't react and was able to respond differently. What is the difference between reacting and responding?

Reacting is a knee-jerk, emotional reaction triggered by our subconscious patterns or programmes. Somebody says something, our hot buttons ignite, and we are off, thinking and doing the same as we have always done: the same old railway track to nowhere, the same old hamster wheel. Nothing changes. Reacting comes from our ego and a place of fear, and it usually makes things worse. When we react, we create a lose–lose situation where trust is destroyed, and we reinforce our subconscious beliefs about being a victim, or of not being good, worthy or lovable enough.

Responding is being able to take a step back, let the reaction die down, and gain perspective. We find that quiet space in our mind where we can decide from a place of calm if we need or want to make a considered response. Responding comes from a place of love and is mindful of the outcome we want to achieve. We create a win–win situation that reinforces self-esteem in both parties, and creates trust in our relationships.

Emotional need, expectation and self-esteem
There are more layers to the complex knot of subconscious beliefs, feelings, hot buttons, conscious thoughts and behaviours. These are our unmet emotional needs that drive our expectations. Our beliefs and hot buttons

were formed from unmet emotional needs when we were younger. Mostly our unmet emotional needs are buried deep down in the lower part of the iceberg, our subconscious. They drive our expectations of how life should be, how we should be, and how others should behave towards us.

Basic emotional needs are universal and are hardwired into our brain from birth. Fundamental to human growth are to feel physically and emotionally safe, secure, and loved. As we grow up, we need to receive affection, and to feel accepted, appreciated, understood, respected, supported, treated fairly, and valued. We need to matter to our caregivers and the society within which we live. We also need to develop independence while being able to emotionally connect to others.

Having at least some of our emotional needs met while growing up formed the basis of our self-esteem, which is our sense of self-worth.

While many people use the terms self-esteem and self-confidence interchangeably, I think there is a difference. Self-esteem is based on our innate sense of worthiness, value, self-trust and self-love. High self-esteem means that we feel comfortable in the choices we make about how we live. We feel good in our own skin, no matter what others might think about us. Self-esteem gives us confidence to try new things, and to achieve new skills and abilities.

Even if we suffer from low self-esteem, we can still learn to have confidence in specific areas of life through the experience of success. While self-esteem can rise with self-confidence in our capability and competence, the two don't necessarily go together. I have met many highly successful people who appear to be brimming with confidence, yet scratch beneath the surface, and inside is an individual with low self-esteem, trying to feel good or valued enough through their external achievements.

With high self-esteem we are able to experience intimacy or closeness with others. We don't need others to satisfy our unmet needs so are able to be authentic in all our relationships. We recognise our own self-worth and don't need to manipulate or control through playing mind games: we say what we mean and we mean what we say.

Those with high self-esteem feel good about themselves and are able to imbue their life with a sense of purpose or meaning. It doesn't have to be purpose or meaning on a grand scale. They are aware that everything they do has an impact on others and on the planet, so all thoughts and actions are carried out with conscious purpose and meaning.

Because even the best of parenting can never be perfect, we all grow up with some unmet emotional needs buried deep in our subconscious. Those with uncaring, neglectful or abusive parenting will have many more unmet needs bubbling away beneath the surface. We unconsciously turn to others to meet our emotional needs, especially in our close relationships. When others can't meet our needs, it triggers our 'not good or lovable enough' hot buttons. We are engulfed by our fear-driven emotions, feeling anxious, vulnerable, helpless, hopeless, resentful and powerless.

Believing that someone else must fill our emotional black holes makes us feel desperate and needy for love and approval. We may become people pleasers, always ready to placate and subjugate ourselves to another's control, in the hope of receiving a few crumbs of affection or recognition. Conversely, those who keep people at arm's length by being tough and fiercely independent, may also harbour a child within who didn't have their emotional needs met. They have learned to suppress their neediness behind a suit of armour.

Expecting someone else to meet our wounded child's needs is usually unrealistic. When we feel needy, we are functioning at a vibrational energy level that attracts other equally needy people. This means that we usually end up in codependent and dysfunctional relationships, where each is either chasing the other for love and appreciation, or pushing the other away. Neither is able to give what they can't even give to themselves. It causes pain and suffering. To attract someone who is kind, generous and has healthy self-esteem, we must first learn to meet our own unmet emotional needs.

The blame game

When others do not behave according to our (usually undeclared) expectations, our hot buttons are triggered and we end up blaming the other person for how we feel: *My daughter makes me so angry when she doesn't tidy her room. My parents still criticise and control me, no wonder I don't feel confident. When my boss points out my mistakes, he makes me feel really hopeless. My partner drives me mad when she talks too much first thing in the morning.*

We are programmed to always blame the person or situation that triggered our emotional reaction, believing that they are the cause. This is how we explain our unpleasant feelings. It is easy to blame our past, other people or the world for feeling bad, even though we are the sole generator of our feelings and our response. Yes, that's right, we are the sole generator of all our feelings. At this point our mind steps in and says: *Ah, but that can't be true because look what he or she did, no wonder I am upset or angry.*

Blaming others for how we feel is an ancient, highly developed mechanism for trying to protect our feelings of vulnerability. We close our heart to love so we won't ever feel hurt, rejected or abandoned again. This never works. Mahatma Gandhi said:

"Nobody can hurt you without your permission."

When we believe that what another person says, thinks or does to us (aside from physical violence) can hurt us, we give away our power to that person. Our heart stays stuck. We live in fear of being exposed as emotionally weak, frail, defenceless and vulnerable, not realising that every human being on the planet feels the same way.

Another person's behaviour or a situation are not the cause of our reaction. They merely act as an external stimulus to activate our subconscious unmet needs and expectations, which usually ends up in our hot buttons being pushed. We talk about people who know how to push our buttons, not realising that we do have a say in the matter. We can choose whether or not to react to their provocation.

Projection and blame
Another aspect to the blame game is projection. Perhaps you have been in a heated exchange with someone where they tell you what is wrong with you and what you should do to put it right. You come away feeling controlled and manipulated, and with a sense that that they weren't really talking about you. Or perhaps you have done the same to someone else, gone on about their behaviour and giving out advice about how they could fix it. You then felt temporarily relieved because 'that told them!'

Most of us get caught up in projection. The human race has been projecting its fears, emotional unmet needs, expectations and worldview (how things should be) onto each other, probably since we first set foot on the planet. Projection in this context was first described by Freud as a psychological defence mechanism whereby one 'projects' one's own undesirable thoughts, motivations, desires, and feelings onto someone else. The ego cannot handle the unpalatable truths or feelings that we are experiencing.

As this is usually below the level of consciousness, we are not aware of the process. Our ego creates a split which allows us to believe that the cause of the discomfort or anxiety is coming from someone else. We then project our feelings, thoughts and beliefs onto that person, blaming them for how we feel.

Projection is a form of blame and temporarily reduces anxiety by allowing the mind to avoid the discomfort of consciously admitting personal faults. For example, the alcoholic who blames his spouse for his addiction: *You are fat and unattractive, you drove me to drink.* The 'power bitch' manager who feels insecure about her ability to manage and yells at a (competent) team member: *Why can't you get anything right!*

Projection allows us to stay in denial, which is also a defence mechanism that means we don't have to acknowledge our own failings.

When my husband and I moved into our forty-year-old house, we decided to remodel the garden which involved taking down an uncared for cypress hedge between our house and our neighbours. As the work was proceeding, I received a phone call from the young guy next door who was very upset that we were cutting down the hedge. He was quite hostile and aggressive, threatening to tell the local authorities (even though we didn't need their permission). I thought it was a bit odd as he and his wife had always been very friendly towards us. While he was talking I was able to stop myself taking it personally and getting into an argument with him. Instead I suggested that they both come around later so we could discuss the issues in person. When they rang the doorbell that evening they looked shamefaced and were very apologetic. It turned out that not only had their beautiful little cat just died, but they were also planning to split up and would have to sell their house. They were distraught. In that moment I could see clearly how they had projected all their anxiety and unhappiness on to our cutting down a hedge as a way of distracting themselves, albeit unconsciously, from their own suffering.

Projection is a means of justifying anger, aggression, hostility and bad behaviour against others. We make others the focus of our fear and stress, blaming them to relieve our own tensions. Projection originates in our duality consciousness, the 'them and us' mentality, which is fuelled by survival fear.

It is very hard to keep projecting our fears and unmet needs onto others when we become aware that we are responsible for our feelings and reactions. That means we can't blame anyone else for how we feel. Bummer! The buck really does stop right here. Taking responsibility is not the same as taking the blame. We are not responsible for the hand we have been dealt, but it is always up to us how we play it. We cannot control our eye colour or height. Nor can we change our parents or our past. We can, however, make the decision to stop projecting our unmet needs onto others and find ways of meeting our own needs.

Reflection
Reflection is the other side of the projection coin. The world and the people in it are our mirror, reflecting back our strengths and our weaknesses.

Take two women who work for the same boss, Frank, a man who tends to be rather introvert and slow to give praise. One of the women, Veronica, is outgoing, empathic and tends to see the good in everyone. She gets on great with Frank. He opens up to her and even praises her work from time to time. Her comment about him is: "*Oh he's a big teddy bear really, just a bit screwed up from his divorce.*"

The other woman, Kathy, sees the world in a negative light. Everyone is out to get her. She is resentful about having to work and hates Frank. Needless to say he is rather afraid of her and tends to ignore her as much as possible. Her comment about him: "*He is the most dreadful, uninspiring, uncommunicative man I have ever worked for.*"

Same boss, two different reflections. One has her kindly, sympathetic world reflected back, while the other has her negativity and resentment reflected back to her.

While people may reflect your goodness and highest ideals back to you, there are other angles to reflection. What if you are like Veronica, basically kind and open to the world, and yet you find that people keep projecting their negative stuff onto you? You feel like the dumping ground for everyone's anger and stress. You feel disrespected and powerless to stop this kind of projection. This is how I used to feel. I carried around this 'nice girl' self-image and I couldn't understand why random strangers, as well as people close to me, would pick me out for a 'projection attack'. Then one day I asked myself two important questions: *What is the reflection here?* and *What is the world trying to tell me about myself?*

Suddenly I saw the gift in people's aggressive or hostile behaviour. While they were projecting their own fears and anxieties onto me, a 'safe target', they were also reflecting back to me my self-doubts about expressing my own anger. They were showing me that I was afraid to stand up for myself, that I needed to find the courage to assertively express my feelings and to set my boundaries. Even though I was brought up not to fight back, I deserved to be treated with respect.

On a darker note, those being mean to me were also reflecting back to me my own shadow side, the not so 'nice' aspects of me: thoughtless, bitter, arrogant, judgemental, unkind, mean, resentful, critical, bearing grudges, betraying, always right, untrustworthy and dishonest. I could be all of these, especially when my buttons were triggered. Recognising these aspects of myself was painful: they don't call it the dark night of the soul for nothing. In this case it was many dark nights and days, over many months. What a shock to meet myself head-on. My 'nice girl' image was severely tarnished and it was time for me to do something about it. I was not embracing all aspects of myself, the bad as well the good. I was not being authentic. Once I was willing to recognise the concealed messages, I was able to see that those who projected their hostility and aggression on to me really were my gifts.

Embracing my shadow side was important if I was to become a more integrated version of myself. It was, and still is, a very humbling experience. It was a long way down climbing off my high horse, and very scary letting go of the ego's story of always being right and others wrong. I could no longer play the victim or justify some of my actions of the past.

At the same time, I started to make the distinction between others' projected stuff on to me, and what they were showing me about myself. I drew a line between my stuff as my responsibility and their stuff as their responsibility. I learned to set my boundaries so I didn't put up with other people's rude, disrespectful or hostile behaviour towards me. Forgiving myself for my own past bad behaviour was much harder.

The lessons didn't happen overnight. It took many years to arrive at a place where I am mostly conscious and aware of my mind games, programmed conditioning, hot buttons and behaviours. I am still practising. Every day provides an opportunity to reinforce healthier, more self-supporting responses to people and life events, and to forgive myself.

When we are willing to ask ourselves the question, 'what is the reflection here?', then we have already evolved further along our path than the projector has yet to do. Projectors rarely, if ever, ask the question, 'What feelings am I trying to avoid by putting the blame on someone else?' It takes a certain level of consciousness to see when we are projecting, and what we may learn from the reflections of those around us.

Changing habitual patterns

In Chapters 3 and 6 we met the Observer, our conscious self who is able to stand apart from the workings of our ego. She notices how we get into our cycles of hot button reaction and self-sabotaging behaviours. When we are trying to change a behaviour that keeps us stuck, most of us have to tendency to beat ourselves up, but the Observer just quietly notices without comment, judgement or emotion. It takes practice to observe without getting drawn into the mind's dramas and stories. As the Observer we just notice with compassionate interest what is happening. We don't have to change anything. We can speak to ourselves in a genuinely curious and compassionate way: *Ah, I am doing that again, isn't that interesting? There's that thinking that keeps me stuck. I find it so curious that my mind wants to keep playing that story. My mind is going around and around in circles. I can't switch it off and I am getting upset about it. Isn't that fascinating?*

Our Observer can start to identify our patterns of thought, belief, emotion and behaviour: *That's my 'I am not good enough' thinking. I can see how that holds me back.*

To lighten the mood, I attach a random number to whichever programme I am running as a result of my hot buttons being triggered: *I'm playing my number 95 programme, the 'I'm responsible for how other people feel programme'. I can relate that to how powerless and angry I feel.*

Making the link with when the pattern or programme was first installed in our brain helps to understand what age persona is running the emotional show for us. For example: *Ah, the way my boss is treating me has provoked my 'I must be aggressive rather than show how insecure I feel' pattern. I am 13 years old again and being bullied at school. I feel insecure and resentful.*

Another example: *My reaction has been triggered by what my partner said. I can see the link to programme 64 when my parents didn't support me either. I am 8 years old again and feel very vulnerable, anxious and alone.*

Sometimes just observing and understanding the origins of our self-sabotaging behaviours is enough to change them. Often there comes a moment when we experience a shift of energy and reach a point when we have truly had *enough*! This is when we make a decision that we do not want to continue this self-defeating behaviour because we are no longer willing to continue causing ourselves pain and suffering. This is a momentous turning point because now we are ready to find a new way of dealing with our old patterns of emotion and behaviour. This is the beginning of the end of self-sabotage.

Releasing our deepest fears

When we learn to identify and respond differently to our buttons rather than have them grip us by the throat and control us, we empower ourselves to take responsibility for how we feel. This doesn't mean that we never again have a hot button reaction or go into our habitual behaviour patterns again. We don't suddenly wake up one morning, a perfect version of ourselves, free from all our petty grievances and quirky reactions. We are spirits having a human experience. One minute you may feel in love with life and touched by Spirit, the next you may feel lonely and down in the pit of despair. As we learn to accept ourselves with all our imperfections and foibles, and with awareness of our own internal processes, we can begin to recognise when we are getting into our hot button programming. We can take a step back from our normal behaviour and learn to be with the feelings. We ride out our fear, irritation, anger, sadness, guilt, shame, rejection, loneliness or abandonment, all the while staying kind and compassionate towards ourselves. This is tough for those of us who were never taught to be comfortable with our emotions.

When we lean into the sharp points of our feelings instead of running away from them, we start to make friends with them. We learn to accept ourselves when we feel bad as well as when we feel good. We get to know our feelings and be comfortable with them instead of being afraid of them.

In Chapter 6, I talked about releasing the tension of emotions through exercise. Moving the body helps dissipate the energy of emotion in the moment. When it comes to releasing deep-seated and blocked emotions, physical activity is often not enough. I use guided visualisation and inner journeys to connect with my own and my clients' deepest fears.

I describe the method here for you to try yourself at home. Some people find even the thought of meeting their fearful emotions face to face far too confrontational. If you have any doubts at all, please find a good therapist or coach with whom you can take this journey.

The first step is to take quiet time when you won't be disturbed. I use scented candles, but this isn't a prerequisite. I also invite my angels and guides to be with me, and I play my favourite meditation music, these are also optional.

Next focus on your breathing and consciously let your body relax. This is the basis of all meditation, guided visualisation and inner journeys. As you relax, you bypass the ego filter and allow the subconscious mind to reveal its hidden layers. This level of relaxation also allows you to receive messages from your higher or soul self, and your invisible guides or helpers. Most of us are only able to gain access to these realms during an inner journey.

As you feel yourself relaxing, tune into the feeling that is agitating your peace of mind. Identify it, whether it be anxiety, resentment, anger or sadness, and then invite it to reveal its full power. Notice in your body where you feel it. You can tell the emotion that you really want to feel it, and that it doesn't have to hold back.

During this exercise there is a temptation to get stuck in the ego's story attached to the feelings. You replay the hot button reaction, and feel overwhelmed by all the emotions that go with the story. If you can, gently detach from the story and bring your attention back to where in your body the feeling is being generated. Go right into the feeling. Let it move through your body without resistance. Notice any images in your mind's eye of what the feeling looks like.

Most people experience the feeling as a forceful energy that moves around the body. Ask it to move through and out of the body, either down through your digestive system or up through your throat and mouth. The result can be any combination of intestinal gurgling and gas, crying, laughing or yawning. You may find yourself crying as though your heart will break, or yawning as though your jaw will dislocate. This is the negative energy being released from its stuck place in your body.

When I do this releasing exercise, as the energy moves all around my body, I feel tingling in my arms, legs, up through my neck and under my scalp. I stay with it and keep yawning or crying to allow the energy to escape. Eventually I feel calm and energised at the same time.

Working with our emotions in this way is very empowering. We stop blaming others and we begin to meet our own needs for love, affection, security and understanding. In so doing we grow in confidence and self-esteem.

Chapter 8

Dare to be authentic!

"The authentic self is the soul made visible."
Sarah Ban Breathnach

Who are you? This sounds like a straightforward question and in the external world of everydayness it is. The question is based on your identity as you perceive it, and as can be officially confirmed through documentation like a birth certificate or passport. If you were filling out a job application or credit card request, your answer would start with name, age, gender, place of residence and contact details. Depending on the requirement of the forms being filled in, you might add your role, function in life, occupation, social status, family position, nationality and financial history.

These are the facts of your existence. And then there is the person you perceive yourself to be. The 'you' with whom you identify is made up of a complex matrix of memories, impressions, experiences, abilities, dreams, desires, thoughts, feelings, and mental and physical attributes. You and your life are unique to you. Nobody else has had exactly the same set of experiences as you.

Overlayering this matrix of your life is your own interpretation of your experiences, memories, beliefs and feelings. In Chapter 7, I talked about the mind filter which forms our programmed conditioning based on our innate fears about who we think we are. Through the mind filter, we suppress aspects of ourselves that we believe are unacceptable, and focus attention on those aspects that we hope are acceptable.

Self-image
Who we think we are is based on our interpretation of the facts of our existence and our experiences. This interpretation becomes our self-image, literally how we see ourselves. It is also the image that we present to others. Our self-image is something that we have built up during our for-

mative years to help us fit in and get along in the world. It can be self-supporting or self-limiting, and doesn't always reflect how others see us. Our culture reinforces our attachment to the concept of image, our own as well as that of other people. We forget that there is a real person lurking behind the façade, someone who feels just as vulnerable as we do and is doing their best to hide it, just as we are. We may admire the celebrity who has money, stardom and a glamorous lifestyle, only to hear that she suffers from depression, can't create lasting relationships or has committed suicide. We may envy the beautiful and successful business woman, then we discover that she is full of self-loathing and suffers from bulimia. Or we may be surprised by the shy quiet kid who stuttered at school but turns out to be a brilliant diplomat, earning a really good living, because he learned to believe in himself.

When our self-image is a true reflection of who we really are, it is a very powerful thing indeed. We have no need to "*hide our light under a bushel*" (to quote the New Testament). Our authentic self shines through. 'Authentic' is defined as genuine, honest, pure, real and true. The authentic self is an alignment of mind, body, emotions and soul. When we allow ourselves to live authentically, following our heart and soul, we feel connected, happy, and self-empowered. We speak our truth and have no reason to apologise for, or to be ashamed of, who we are. We are honest and honourable towards ourselves and others. We have a strong sense of self-worth and do not give our power away to other people or to circumstances. We feel safe enough to be real and authentic in our world.

Creating personas and roles
Remember someone telling you as you were about to go to your first job interview or on your first date: *Just be yourself?* Such wise advice, but then came the tricky part: *Who am I? Would the real me please stand up?* How can I be myself when I haven't the foggiest idea who I am? It is all so confusing.

The real me, or you, consists of many different personas wrapped up in one package. In Latin 'persona' originally meant a 'mask', particularly in reference to an actor playing a role. Most of us learned to hide our true selves behind any number of personas. They gave us something behind which to protect ourselves from our fear of being judged and rejected. No one must see how vulnerable, ashamed or unlovable we really feel when we adopt our perfectionist, arrogant or humorous personas. Because we learned to cover up our authentic self during our formative years, we grew into adults with no conscious awareness of our personas. We believe it when we say, *that is just who I am*, unaware that we may be living according to a self-image that is not an expression of our true self.

Here are some of the personas behind which we may be hiding. This is by no means a definitive list. You may realise that you have some of your own that are not mentioned here.

Always right	Helpless	Rescuer
Aggressive	Humorous	Responsible
Argumentative	Ironic	Sex kitten/hero
Arrogant	Intellectual	Shy and quiet
Bitch	In control	Spiritual
Bully	Know-it-all	Sporty
Busy	Laid back	Successful
Capable	Manipulator	Sunny girl/guy
Confidante (trusted friend)	Martyr	Superior
Confident	Mr. Fix-it	Super-confident
Complainer	Nice girl/guy	Super-efficient
Cool	Party animal	Stressed out
Cynical	Perfectionist	Strong / stoic
Drama queen	Poor little me	Stupid
Distant and aloof	Popular	Theatrical
Expert	Professional	Tough girl/guy
Exhibitionist	Proud	Tyrant
Funny girl/guy	Princess	Victim
Gossip	Rebel	Worrier

Here are some examples of how we learned to hide our authentic self.

- The sensitive, dreamy child who learned to avoid being picked on in a boisterous high school by becoming the 'funny girl' or the 'rebel' of the class, when she really wanted to stay quietly in the background.
- The 'arrogant' doctor whose 'expert', 'distant and aloof' attitude is covering up for the pain of giving into family pressure to follow in the family footsteps, when he really wanted to be a sculptor.

- The 'cynical' and 'withdrawn' IT professional who chose against pursuing a career in music, because at school he was afraid of being judged by his classmates as a cissy.
- The 'expert'/'know-it-all' who came from a family that didn't value the input of a child's point of view and learned to hide her feelings of 'invisibility' by speaking loudly and authoritatively just to be heard.
- The 'nice' girl whose parents were too busy to give her any attention and who is always over-explaining herself in an attempt to compensate for feeling unloved, in the hope that someone will give her love and recognition.
- The 'charming' man who is unconsciously so afraid of intimacy that, when a woman gets too close, Mr. Charming disappears and is replaced by a verbally and psychically abusive alter ego, determined to keep her at arm's length.
- The bright girl teased at school for being a swot who became acceptable to the cool girls when she discovered she had a natural talent as their 'confidante'.

Persona or authentic self?

We are all made up of different selves within our authentic self and, depending on the circumstances, we can move among any number of personas to keep things running smoothly. We all know how to shift into 'professional' and 'perfectionist' mode so we can be 'capable' at our job, and we step into our 'nice' persona so we can get along with our co-workers. We may feel 'super-confident' in certain circumstances, and then be 'withdrawn' and 'stressed out' in others. When we put on our socialising persona we can become 'party animal' or 'sunny' girl'.

The difficulty arises when we are not clear if we are being our authentic self or operating from one of our personas. It is possible to do both.

The easiest way to know if we are living through our personas rather than from our authentic self is by checking in with how we feel. If our default setting is 'authentic self', we feel light and at ease with who we are. When we live through our personas we never feel quite ourselves. It feels as though we are 'playing a part', one with which we are so familiar that we just keep on doing it because it is what we know best. The 'real me' is out of focus, a fuzzy image buried in our subconscious. It takes a lot of energy to stay straight-jacketed into personas that do not reflect our true self. It is exhausting and disempowering, and creates a huge amount of internal stress. We may feel tired, heavy and apathetic most of the time without ever realising why.

If we sit quietly and really focus on heart and soul, we feel a sense of emptiness and disconnection, as if we have lost something important but not sure what it is. Indeed, we *have* lost something: we have lost ourselves, sacrificed a long time ago on the altar of conformity at all cost.

Selena lost herself. A naturally bright and quiet child, Selena's father died when she was four years old. It left a huge void in her life and she missed him terribly. When she started school, young Selena was bullied by older kids in the playground. Her teachers did nothing to protect her and compounded the problem by telling her that she was too sensitive. With her authentic self shattered, Selena suppressed her sensitivity and looked to her uncle as a role model. He represented strength and confidence in a tough world, and she unconsciously copied his rational and intellectual approach to life.

Selena's young mind would not have been able to see the subtleties of her uncle's being, his emotional adaptation to the world he inhabited. She just saw that success depended on following one's head and not one's heart. Her survival, interpreted by her child's mind, depended on her becoming a high achiever and ignoring her softer, intuitive side. Adult Selena followed her uncle's example into the corporate world where she worked long hours and travelled extensively. She was a success but never felt as though she really belonged anywhere. By the time she was thirty-five, Selena had a complete burnout with debilitating depression.

Following some intensive work, Selena started the slow process of reclaiming all the fragmented parts of herself. A simple question, *"What does your heart say?"*, made her realise that she already knew what was best for her. Slowly she started taking back her power by reconnecting to her innate sensitivity. She realised that she genuinely enjoyed the excitement and challenge of a corporate environment. Her reconnection to her authentic self proved to be a winning combination as she inspired and motivated people at work. In her personal life, she nurtured her soul through dancing and painting.

When we deny our authentic self and live through our personas we self-sabotage. We feel stuck and yet we cannot allow ourselves to feel our vulnerability, insecurity, unworthiness or self-doubting. We slap on a smile for the world, all the while secretly eating our way through the contents of the fridge. We entertain our friends with our genial good humour then, when alone, we worry ourselves into ill health about our mounting debts. We responsibly carry on working at a job we hate just to please our family, while developing chronic fatigue and muscle pain for which no specialist can find a cause. Or we cause others to suffer by being mean and tyrannical, in an attempt to shift the restless feelings of loneliness and discontentment.

The person who denies their true self can often come across to others as fake or inauthentic. There is an uneasiness about them. Even if you have difficulty identifying your own personas, you can probably think of people with whom you sense a falseness: their smile is just too bright, their eyes do not reflect what they are saying, their body language is protective even when they are acting 'open' and friendly, they are just a bit too loud or jolly, they seem to be saying all the right things but their vibes (to use a 1960s term) don't tally. Something just does not ring true and you don't feel comfortable around those people. They are hiding something: their authentic self.

Letting others define us

As we start peeling back the layers of our self-image to excavate our authentic self, we realise just how much we have let others define us. Whether it happens at home, at school, or in the community, most of us have experienced being told who we are and how we should behave. Over time we believe what we are told and we do our best to live up, or down, to the expectations set by others. We judge ourselves harshly, the way we have been judged, and believe that we should be different to the way we are. This affects our self-worth, self-esteem and self-confidence: our deepest sense of self. How many times have you thought: *I am not good at this kind of thing. I couldn't possibly do that. I should be taller, shorter, prettier, more handsome, slimmer, finely boned, stronger, elegant, cleverer, or braver* (choose the adjectives that you would like to be but aren't)?

Elaine had an abusive upbringing. She was always the 'difficult' one in her family. She became the scapegoat for her family's collective neuroses: whatever went wrong she was always blamed, even though she had done nothing wrong. She remembered being excluded from family get-togethers because she was a 'naughty girl' and nobody wanted a naughty girl at the party. She was never good, clever, pretty or successful enough. As a child Elaine ate to compensate for the lack of love and self-esteem. She gained a lot of weight, which earned her the additional label from her family of 'fat and ugly'. She learned to be invisible and withdrawn in the hope that this would keep her safe from attack. If it hadn't been for a grandmother, whom she saw during school holidays, and who loved her unconditionally, Elaine said she might not have survived childhood. Her life was so miserable that there were times when she wanted to end it all.

It took years of psychotherapy support for adult Elaine to be confident enough to believe enough in herself to go for a highly prestigious job. She earned much respect from her colleagues and had been promoted twice already. Yet she defined herself as short, fat, unattractive, difficult, flawed, no willpower, hopeless at relationships, not very bright, introverted, and could never succeed at anything. She had adopted her family's view of herself, even though this was not who she really was. It took time and determination to reconnect with the little girl who was born beautiful, full of life and eager to learn. Gradually Elaine saw how she had allowed others to define her and how she had created a self-image that was far from her authentic self. She gradually learned to question all the definitions that had become her self-image, and she understood the craziness that had driven others to define her. As she changed, her confidence grew, she lost weight, looked healthier and her authentic radiance shone through. Some members of her family shunned her because they could no longer control her. Others responded to her new self-esteem with greater respect. In his book, *A New Earth*, Eckhart Tolle tells us:

> *"Give up defining yourself – to yourself or to others. You won't die. You will come to life. And don't be concerned with how others define you. When they define you, they are limiting themselves, so it's their problem."*

When we can overcome the distorted definitions heaped upon us when we were too young and vulnerable to reject them, we tap into the power of our authentic self. Letting go of our protective personas isn't always easy. It can be scary to find that we are not who we thought we were. Even though we were miserable, at least it was familiar territory. Taking the first cautious step out of our dis-comfort zone is akin to trailblazing a whole new dimension. This is when the real journey begins.

Shining our light

Marianne Williamson, author of *Our Deepest Fear* writes:

> *"Our deepest fear is not that we are inadequate. Our deepest fear is that we are powerful beyond measure. It is our light, not our darkness that most frightens us. We ask ourselves, 'Who am I to be brilliant, gorgeous, talented, fabulous'?"*

As we learn to discard our out-dated self-image, we discover just how powerful we really are. It's enough to send even the most adventurous among us scuttling back into the relative safety of our low self-esteem, defined and designed to stop us from upsetting the status quo.

In Chapter 4, we saw that the ultimate fear is fear of death and how all our other fears stem from this. We fear our power because it means we will stand out and may be judged for daring to be ourselves. We want to be like others so we won't be rejected. We turn ourselves inside out, cutting off essential bits of ourselves in an effort to 'fit in'. Even if a child is raised in a happy, easy-going family, once they get to school the pressure to conform is enormous. Often sensitive children are bullied at school and rarely do schools have an effective anti-bullying policy to protect the children entrusted to their care. The philosophy still tends to be that kids need 'toughening up' and should learn to 'stand up for themselves'. But some can't, and sometimes children commit suicide because it is just too painful trying to fit in and be accepted.

As adults, too many of us are still compromising our authentic self in an effort to fit in, afraid to stand out and be different. Sarah Ban Breathnach, author of *Something More* says:

> *"We're not meant to fit in. We're meant to stand out!"*

How can any of us stand out and make a difference in the world when we are trying to conform to some crazy, 'decided upon a whim' requirement set by people, who themselves are covering up their own insecurities and neuroses: the same people who have smothered their own authentic self? So we play it small, not daring to shine too much. Marianne Williamson continues:

"Your playing small does not serve the world. There is nothing enlightened about shrinking so that other people won't feel insecure around you. We are all meant to shine, as children do. And as we let our own light shine, we unconsciously give other people permission to do the same. As we are liberated from our own fear, our presence automatically liberates others."

I lost count of how many times in my life I was shushed by people close to me who couldn't handle my exuberance. Fortunately I discovered amateur musical theatre quite early on in my adult life. This gave me an outlet for my theatrical self-expression along with other folk, who also wanted to express their suppressed extrovert. Later I was also able to use my exuberance and passion in my work. *Our Deepest Fear* tells us that it is not only alright to shine and stand out, but that it is essential. By shushing myself down so other people wouldn't feel uncomfortable, I was causing myself a lot of anguish and doing a disservice to others. If I gave myself permission to be me, it would help others to let their own light shine forth.

Our authentic self is our core being, our true essence, our soul. We even talk about 'baring our soul' when we are confiding in someone because, in that moment of revealing how we feel, we are allowing a glimpse of our authentic self. We become our most powerful and effective self when we give ourselves permission to be who we really are. We impact on those around us when we speak our truth and admit to our vulnerability. Some examples: *I always feel really nervous when I first stand up in front of a large group of people. I'm having sleepless nights worrying about my ability to do this job. Sometimes I feel like the most awful parent on the planet. I seem to manage to put my foot in my mouth and upset people without meaning to. There are many things I wish I had done differently. Sometimes I find life so hard that it plunges me into depression, and I have to take a step back and nurture myself.*

We are inspired by those who can admit their foibles and yet seem completely comfortable with themselves. There is no pretence. What you see is what you get. Authenticity shines and empowers us to move through our fears and live up to our potential, whatever that might be.

The theatre of life

In *As You Like it*, Shakespeare said:

> *"All the world's a stage, and all the men and women merely players:*
> *they have their exits and their entrances; and one man in his time plays*
> *many parts, his acts being seven ages."*

We all of us unconsciously create the stage described by Shakespeare. We adopt our roles and personas, and we attract people to entrance and exit according to the roles we have assigned them. All of us, the entire cast, may be subconsciously searching to find our 'lost self' and to make ourselves feel whole (as discussed in Chapter 2). As adults, we try and heal the wounds of our childhood by attracting those who behave like our family members. We adopt our personas and reactive behaviours in the vain (and subconscious) hope that our partners, friends and colleagues will see through the act to the authentic person hiding there. We hope they will give us the love and understanding that we lack.

Everybody with whom we are close is there acting out the parts we have given them: the overbearing mother-in-law, the distant and aloof partner, the mother who smothers, the authoritarian father, the sibling who hates, we chose them all. At a conscious level, the players in our theatre have no idea why they are in our life or we in theirs.

As we get in touch with our authentic self, we operate more from our heart and start to see the vulnerability in others. The overbearing mother-in-law becomes a woman who is desperate to feel wanted, the distant and aloof partner is so afraid of intimacy that he is emotionally paralysed, the mother who smothers is afraid of losing her offspring's love and being alone, the authoritarian father is scared stiff of losing control and having his vulnerability exposed, the sibling who hates is reacting to his own programmed conditioning about 'never amounting to much'.

Our authentic self stops the ego's need to be right and instead, is able to offer compassion and understanding to those we find 'difficult'.

Patience and self-acceptance

Letting go of the protective personas is rarely a quick fix. It requires a lot of commitment to self, patience, time for solitude and practice. To let go of our personas and live as our shining, authentic self we need a willingness to surrender our illusion of control, and an acceptance based on trust that everything is exactly as it is meant to be.

Patience is in short supply these days. We live in a hyperactive world, conditioned to believe that we must do everything quickly, and we expect instant results. Patience is an anathema to the ego which is fuelled by fear and mistrust that take us further away from our spiritual connection. It takes practice to keep bringing ourselves back to patience when the ego demands our attention.

Patience allows us to let go of expectation and control. We become willing to work with our mind, body, emotions and spirit to become whole. Each time we feel the frustration of the process 'taking too long', we have another opportunity to slow down and notice how impatience upsets our sense of wellbeing and peace of mind. It is so easy to let the ego take us into resistance: we resist taking the leap of faith towards a connection with our own spiritual and authentic self. During guided visualisations it is astonishing how many people see the leap of faith as a body of water cutting them off from a beautiful place full of bright sunlight. Depending how disconnected they are from their soul self, the water may be a narrow, shallow, slow-moving stream or a wide torrent of fast-flowing river. Often they feel the pull of invisible forces holding them back, which they realise is the fear of letting go and taking the leap. Those that do reach the other side report feeling an incredible sense of peace, connection and love. Living in the light of love, as opposed to the darkness of fear, is our birthright. We do not have to search outside of ourselves to find it. It is already a part of who we are.

With patience comes self-acceptance, which is a state of being where we no longer resist what is but instead look for solutions, change what we can change, but let go of trying to control that which is outside our control. Accepting ourselves just as we are is not something we are used to doing. We are brought up feeling as though we have to spend our every waking moment proving to others and to ourselves that we are worthwhile. I used to equate doing things for people with an expectation of being loved in return. I usually tried to please the wrong people who were never going to love me anyway. Then I learned that I was lovable without doing anything. I didn't have to measure my self-worth against the accumulation of imagined brownie points. I was already worthy of love. If someone couldn't love or like me, then that was really okay. I could let them go and be happy on my own. I didn't need to keep trying harder. Self-acceptance is an important step towards being our authentic self.

With self-acceptance comes the realisation that we do not have to define ourselves by moments in time when we made a mistake, screwed up royally or acted against our own best values. It is just too easy in our judgemental minds to label ourselves as, for example, bad, a failure, stupid, useless, addicted, anorexic or hopeless. We hear that our actions define us. I think our actions reflect our state of mind and what we feel about ourselves in the moment, but they do not define who we really are, any more than our personas define us. When we reconnect to our authentic self, and live from a place of trust and acceptance, our actions reflect that sense of self-belief.

Stillness and solitude

In Chapter 3, I talked about stillness and taking time alone for self. Stillness and solitude are not a luxury, they are a necessity if we are to listen to the guidance from our wise self, our unseen helpers and Spirit. Sometimes solitude can feel like loneliness, which is a sign that our ego has cut us off from our soul self. Other times solitude feels nurturing. It is in the quiet moments alone that we can hear or feel the nudges from our guides. In *Eat, Pray, Love,* Elizabeth Gilbert said:

> "I'm tired of being a skeptic. I'm irritated by spiritual prudence and I feel bored and parched by empirical debate … I couldn't care less about evidence and proof … I just want God. I want God inside me. I want God to play in my blood stream the way sunlight amuses itself on water."

I could not call what I wanted in my life 'God', but one evening, as I sat in my home office, which is also my sacred place in my home, I made a decision: I wanted to stop prevaricating and accept Spirit into my life as a guiding force. In that moment of acceptance my room filled with a warm presence. The energy was palpable. I 'knew' then that I was part of something more than my mind and physical existence. I felt it and was literally awe-inspired. I looked at my cat relaxing on a wicker chair and asked her if she felt it too. She gazed back at me with her enigmatic cat smile as if to say, *"Now you get it!"*

143

Chapter 9

Self-empowerment

*"Dear God, please spare me from the desire for love,
approval or appreciation. Amen."* Byron Katie

The astrologer looked at my chart with me. I couldn't make head or tail of it having never studied astrology. He pointed to a vast area between some planets and told me that I had a serious problem with giving my power away. As I had gone to see him following yet another incident where I felt totally disempowered, I was rather amazed to see it there in my chart. At the time I forgot to ask if I could change that trait, but the question became irrelevant as over the next few years I learned to empower myself. I have since discovered that, through conscious awareness, we can overcome the traits and characteristics of our astrological charts. This means that nothing is set in stone as far as our destiny is concerned.

Exploring external power

Talking about power can be confusing. We have such negative connotations of power, from the bullying teacher, the abusive spouse, or greedy corporations and governments, who abuse their authority and power. We associate power with 'external' power, meaning power 'over' someone or something. This is not surprising when you look at the evolution of human society.

We say that someone is powerful because they have money or have managed to climb the social ladder to reach an elevated position in a hierarchical order. Hierarchy is itself a male-based power system that probably originated in the brain circuitry of our hunter-gatherer ancestors. Male brains are wired to form groups with a clear hierarchy headed by an alpha male. Our hunter-gatherer ancestors would have set off in pursuit of the tribe's lunch in hunting parties made up of male tribal members. They would have worked as a unit with each individual knowing his role in the group and closely following a leader. The alpha male would have had high testosterone levels, which is the go-getting hormone that drives libido, the urge to invade territory, to build and destroy, and the need to compete and win at any cost. He would have had great physical and mental strength which would have given him power and status in the tribe. Basically brute force, a strong sex drive, and the ability to feed and protect the tribe won every time. Eventually a younger, stronger, more testosterone-charged male would come along and compete for the coveted position of alpha male.

For around three million years, we lived as hunter-gatherers and only settled down and started farming during the Neolithic period of human history, around ten thousand years ago. Things haven't changed all that much since then. Biologically the pre-frontal cortex of the human brain has evolved and got bigger. This is the part of the brain that controls cognitive function, meaning that we have increased our intellectual capacity for thinking, learning, reasoning, problem solving, decision making, memory and language. Apart from adding a few rules and a thin layer of civilised veneer, the circuitry for power and hierarchy doesn't appear to have changed at all.

Most cultures around the world are still based on giving power and status to those who push, shout, persuade, cajole, or manipulate the loudest and the hardest. When money was introduced in place of bartering, around seven thousand years ago, it soon became a symbol of power. This has led to a consensus where we allow people power over us if they have high testosterone, are competitive and aggressive, and have money. They are granted the power to make and break rules, to influence people's lives right the way through society, and to indulge their selfish desires and greed, even at the expense of entire populations and our home, planet Earth. They of course may also influence society and people's lives for the good. Many important social and environmental changes have come about because people have had both vision and the social power to make their vision reality. Male energy is a wonderful thing when it is in constructive mode. It is highly destructive when it is allowed too much unregulated power. Allen and Barbara Pease tell us in their book, *Why Men Don't Listen and Women Can't Read Maps*:

> *"Testosterone is the hormone of success, achievement and competitiveness, and in the wrong hands (or testicles) makes men and male animals*

potentially dangerous ... Male aggression is mainly responsible for men's dominance of our species."

The average woman's brain, fuelled predominantly by oestrogen and pro-gesterone, is wired for cooperation, consensus, connection and nurturing. We don't have the levels of testosterone that men have, which is a disad-vantage in a male-dominated hierarchical system. The women who have a lot of male energy, or have more testosterone than the average woman, make it to the top by learning to behave like men. Women who lack male levels of testosterone and drive, but want a share of the power, have used men's biology, their testosterone-fuelled sex drive, to manipulate them to get what they want. Either way, women have learned that self-protection and self-realisation in man's hierarchical system means that they must find ways of having power over others in order to succeed.

For most of us then power is perceived and experienced as an external process, something we must acquire through achievement and success. While there is nothing wrong with feeling empowered through external achievement, this is not the same as self-empowerment, which is an inter-nal process that does not require the accumulation of external approval and validation.

You are already wise
When I searched online dictionaries, I eventually found this definition: *"Self-empowerment is deriving the strength to do something through one's own thoughts and based on the belief that one knows what is best for oneself."*

When I ask people what they believe would be best for them, their first reaction is often one of anxiety and confusion at the idea that they might already know the answers to their questions. Byron Katie, author of *Loving What Is,* says:

> *"Anything you want to ask a teacher, ask yourself, and wait for the answer in silence."*

We already know everything we need to know for self-empowerment. We are already wise. We don't need others to give us permission to be our most magnificent self. How can this be? How can we be our own teacher?

Our disempowerment starts with our ego, which tries to protect us for survival within our tribe. The result is that we separate from our authentic self and from Spirit. We become fragmented, like a cracked mirror. With our ego firmly in control, trying to protect our self-image from further deterioration, our fragmentation leaves us feeling anxious, separate, lonely, disempowered and stuck in fear.

Generations of programmed conditioning mean that most of us grow up believing that we are not good or worthy enough. Most of us learned to mistrust ourselves and our own judgement, forgetting that we already know what is best for us. As we learned to hide our true selves under layers of programmed conditioning, our self-doubt means that we look to our parents, family, friends, teachers, the government, institutions and 'experts', to tell us how to live. We grow up believing that we cannot trust our intuition, and that we must listen to the 'logic' and 'rational' of others.

Jemma, a highly successful forty-three-year-old accountant working for a multinational company, had all the qualifications, experience, and expertise that gave her prestige and status in her working environment. But she was not happy. Following a divorce and a series of disastrous love affairs, Jemma was in deep despair that she would never be able to find true love. Despite all her external achievements, Jemma felt like she was forcing herself into a mould that wasn't really her. But who was she? The only time she felt anything close to her own authentic self was when she volunteered at the local home for abandoned dogs. She felt a deep connection with animals that she rarely felt with people. She was also drawn to tai chi and worked with a wonderful teacher, a calm spiritual woman who stirred something profound in Jemma: a feeling of her heart opening and a sense of who she could be. This was the self that she had buried so she could live up to the expectations of others. Feeling the stirrings of her heart and soul sent Jemma into anxious resistance. *"How can I know that my authentic or spiritual self is any good?"* she cried. Her fear drove her to neglect her health. She ate badly, skipped meals, and her blood test results showed just how deficient she was in some major nutrients. Her health was suffering. She had no energy, had PMS for two weeks out of four each month, and felt depressed.

Jemma's biggest fear about listening to her 'teacher within' was that if she stopped chasing external achievements, there would be nothing left of her. She would no longer exist. When she sat in silence and asked herself what she needed to do to change, the message that came loud and clear was that she wanted to tap into her nurturing female energy to help abandoned animals.

Like many externally successful young women, Jemma had abandoned herself a long time ago. Her ego had closed down the little girl who was full of passion for life and nature, because she believed that being tender and compassionate would not win approval or success. Now her soul was calling to her to reclaim her lost self and become whole. Jemma realised that the urge to change had become more powerful than the urge to stay as she was. She wanted to feel powerful on the inside and to express herself in the world, whoever 'herself' turned out to be.

Giving away our power

Like Jemma, most of us suffer from a sense of powerlessness because we do not trust ourselves. We go through life feeling as though we are lacking something. We give our power away to others in the belief that they will help us feel whole. Yet if most people feel like we do, how can they give us what they too perceive themselves to be lacking?

The idea that we can give away our personal power is a relatively novel concept for most people. We don't even imagine that we have personal power to give away. We assume that power is given to us and can be taken away from us just as easily. We don't realise that our feelings of anger, anxiety, helplessness, resentment, depression, shame, exhaustion, and above all powerlessness, are symptoms of giving our power away. We give our power away when we:

- Believe that we aren't enough as we are and spend our lives trying to prove ourselves.
- Believe that happiness comes from the approval and acknowledgement of others, even people we don't particularly care about (the 'what will people think' syndrome).
- Believe that others know what is best for us and continually seek the opinion of others, especially before making a decision.
- Believe that we are not lovable until someone loves us, even though they can take away their love just as easily as they gave it.
- Don't trust or believe in ourselves, despite our achievements: and we underrate or discount our achievements as unimportant.

- Think that being with the 'right' person will solve all our problems and make us feel complete.
- Live from a place of fear or anxiety about what might happen: wars, crime, disease, society or relationship breakdown, terrorism, poverty, a loved one dying, even when our lives personally are not affected by any of those things in the moment.
- Feel like a victim to life's circumstances, blaming everyone and everything (society, our family, the economic crisis, global events, politicians, institutions) for our misfortunes.
- Live in a constant negative state of mind, always complaining about people and events over which we have no immediate control.
- Believe that there is no gain without pain, and that life is about struggle.
- Think that being 'nice' or 'good' is safer than being quietly (or loudly!) assertive in the face of careless cruelty, emotional manipulation or hostility from others, including our loved ones.
- Give in to the will of others, or avoid confrontation to 'keep the peace', while denying our own needs, wants, dreams and desires.
- Apologise when we have done nothing wrong. How often do you start a sentence with "I'm sorry …" even when you have nothing to be sorry about? For many of us it is a deeply ingrained habit.
- Constantly explain and justify ourselves, especially in the face of conflict and aggression.
- Try and be perfect but then keep moving the goalposts because we can never be perfect enough.
- Keep ourselves busy as a way of distracting ourselves from our true feelings, and the call of our heart and soul.
- Derive our sense of self from material possessions, especially the 'latest' of something, or from our status in society.
- Take things personally believing that others can hurt us through words (this does NOT include physical violence).
- Keep people at a distance so they cannot see our vulnerability or how 'bad' we really are.
- Try and change people to make them more agreeable to us, and then resent them for not being how we want them to be.
- React to the perceived 'transgressions' of others with aggression, hostility, screaming, shouting and throwing things, instead of assertively setting boundaries.

- Live in the past, hanging on to old grievances and resentments, and keep replaying them as though they happened yesterday.
- Either dream of, or actually take, revenge on those we believe have wronged us.
- Believe we have no choice and that our actions are determined by external forces: people, events, God or fate.
- Put off being happy until something happens: we finish this job, lose weight, stop smoking, retire, kids have left home, pass this exam, our partner changes, we have more money, move house, achieved all our goals, got divorced, found our soul mate.
- Become addicted to substances as a displacement or distraction from how powerless we really feel: caffeine, alcohol, sugar, chocolate, comfort foods, recreational and prescription drugs, possessions, activities or people.
- Fear death believing that it represents the end rather than a different beginning.
- Fear getting older because we believe that old age has to mean becoming decrepit and dependent on others, or because we can't accept our lines, wrinkles and sagging.
- *"Live a life of quiet desperation"*, to quote Henry David Thoreau, wishing we had the courage to just be ourselves and follow our dreams, if only we could remember who we are and what we really want.

Victim consciousness

Giving our power away puts us in victim consciousness, which is not the same as being a victim of circumstance, such as an accident, crime or natural disaster. In that case we are a victim in the moment, but then we rally, pick ourselves up, and continue with life as best we can.

Victim consciousness originates in fear, and is a reflection of our deeply-held beliefs about our lack of personal power to make choices that nurture our heart and soul. Being a victim is something that is stamped into our subconscious from very early on in life. We see how others emotionally manipulate, project and play power games, and we believe that 'this is how to get by'. We too learn to feel less vulnerable by having power over others through playing the blame game or emotional manipulation. Our behaviours fall below the level of consciousness. We don't even realise that we are being emotionally manipulative or allowing others to do the same to us. As a result, we stay stuck in fear and anxiety while not really understanding its source.

Pseudo-power

In victim consciousness, we are operating from a place of powerlessness. We try to control life, people and events through pseudo-power which is a false sense of power that has nothing to do with authentic power. Pseudo-power is external power over others in an attempt to feel powerful while making the other person feel small. It is sometimes hard to recognise because it is everywhere, from the top echelons of society down to the bully in the playground. All forms of bullying, harassment or demeaning others are a form of pseudo-power, whether they come from your mother, boss, colleague, partner, friend or the guy who is serving you behind a counter. Behind pseudo-power is usually an anxious, insecure person with unmet needs trying to make themselves feel more important.

Pseudo-power is disempowering. It creates mistrust and a lack of respect in our relationships with others and with ourselves. Others may give in to us, but this then becomes a martyr-sacrifice relationship, which stifles growth for all concerned. Worse, we don't give ourselves the opportunity to learn to trust ourselves.

Selfless, selfish and self-hood

One disempowering message many of us received while growing up is not to be selfish. We must always put others before ourselves. Learning not to be selfish is the grossest betrayal of ourselves as we learned to fear and deny what we want, in case it doesn't fit in with the needs and wants of others. Because we are not taught healthy self-hood, where we learn to honour ourselves as well as others, many of us tend to swing between being a selfless martyr and a selfish tyrant.

When we operate from a place of selflessness, we are either unaware of our own wants and desires or we tell ourselves that we can't have them because that would be selfish. We sacrifice our own dreams and needs to keep others happy. Behind our sacrifice is an unconscious martyr hoping for a 'pay off'. In martyr mode we make it clear that we have sacrificed plenty to please the other person and are now expecting something in return. We want the other person to see how much we have given up for them, and reward us with more love and attention. This rarely happens, because most of the time nobody seems to even notice, let alone appreciate the sacrifices we have made.

The unconscious driver is to provoke guilt and shame in others as a way of manipulating them to do as we want. Examples are the doting mama who sighs and complains to her offspring, *"After all I have done for you and this is how you repay me!"* (by marrying that girl or going to work abroad); or the resentful father who expects a *'return on his investment'* (by joining the family firm or adopting his values) from the children he has put through expensive education.

Being successful in getting others to do what they want may give the martyr a temporary feeling of power. When others refuse to be manipulated, the martyr ends up feeling powerless, taken for granted and resentful, having failed in their only strategy for getting the recognition they believe they deserve.

Selfish

The person in selfless martyr role, not getting their needs met and feeling powerless, may eventually grow so frustrated that they decide to get even in some way: payback time! This is when they swing into selfish tyrant mode trying to make themselves feel more powerful. They may express their frustration through shouting, screaming, making threats, bullying and taking revenge. Those who dare not express themselves in an overtly selfish way will use passive aggressive methods: manipulation, deception, withdrawal of love or services, sarcasm, and surreptitiously creating disruption and discomfort for the person perceived as having caused their uncomfortable feelings.

Some people rebelled early on in life against being a victim of selflessness. No way were they going to let anyone else control them. They erected boundaries that are more like barriers, rigidly set and upheld so that no-one can take advantage of them. They live at the selfish end of the spectrum, often arrogant, bad tempered, bossy, bullying, irritable and unapproachable. They are protecting their feelings of insecurity and vulnerability by pushing others away before they can be hurt. They find intimacy difficult because they can't let down their guard. Most people stay clear of those living at the selfish end of the spectrum because it is just too difficult to engage with them.

Self-hood

The most empowered and balanced place to live is in the zone called self-hood. I also like to refer to this state as being 'self-centred'. Culturally we use the term self-centred to mean arrogant and selfish, but in this context I prefer the sense of being centred and balanced. Self-hood, or being self-centred, occurs when we decide to step out of sacrifice and take the time to be clear on what we really want. We then ask for it assertively, in a way that respects the rights of others to refuse us. We always take responsibility for how we feel, not blaming someone else.

Self-hood occurs when we realise that in order to care for and respect others, we must first care for and respect ourselves. We must know and set our boundaries, meaning that we are very clear about where we draw the line with what we will and will not accept from other people. We learn to say a firm 'no' with loving kindness. We learn to give ourselves the time and space to top up our emotional resources so that we are able to choose to give from an open heart, without sacrificing. Or we make the conscious decision not to give, knowing that this is the best long-term outcome for everyone concerned.

It is normal to swing from selfish to selfless and back again from time to time. This usually happens when our hot buttons are going off, and we find ourselves being dragged down the same old track of emotional reaction and behaviour. We get hooked into other people's dramas and manipulation, either caving in to them, or fighting back with our usual defence strategies: arguing about who is right and who is wrong, or feeling hurt and withdrawing. We end up feeling drained and defeated. With awareness, we can start to recognise when we are allowing ourselves to be thrown off balance and decide what to do about it. Instead of our habitual knee-jerk reaction, which usually leaves us feeling uneasy and ashamed, we can empower ourselves by taking the time to calm down and think about how, or whether, we want to respond.

You have a choice
How many times on the news or in dramas have you heard someone commit an atrocity against someone else and then say, *"But I had no choice"*? How many times have you taken a decision that caused you or someone else to suffer and thought that you 'had no choice'?

Sam gave up a well-paid job to work closer to home because the hours she worked were having a negative impact on her family. She said, *"I had no choice"* and fell into martyr mode, resentful because nobody recognised the sacrifice she was making: not her husband, her parents, and certainly not her children, who were too young to understand the concept of sacrifice and martyrdom.

When we believe that we have no choice we give our power away to our beliefs and to external influences. Yet we always have a choice. Sam could have chosen to stay with her job and risk her family's happiness. Equally she could have chosen to find a part-time job, or to create a business she could run from home. Sam had plenty of choices and she chose to leave the job she loved so she could spend more time with her family. Even though she knew she had made the right decision, Sam continued to give her power away to her beliefs that she had no choice. Instead of resentment, which was affecting her happiness, Sam could have rejoiced in her ability to choose wisely from a place of love for her family and for herself.

When we think we have no choice we feel powerless, as though outside forces have conspired to manipulate us to be or do something against our will. We get stuck in the obligation and duty of 'should', 'ought', 'must' and 'have to': *I should really go on a diet but I love my food too much. I have to pick the kids up from school but would rather stay and finish this piece of work. I must run fifteen errands in my lunch hour when all I want to do is eat my lunch in peace. I ought to contact my mother but I know she will end up complaining for an hour.*

We drain our energy by believing that we have no choice in the matter. I found that when I replaced 'should', 'ought', 'must' and 'have to' with 'I choose to' or 'I want to', it helped me understand that I have chosen everything that I do, from major life-changing decisions down to the most mundane of tasks. I could feel a shift in energy from one where I felt buffeted around by my emotions, other people and circumstances, to one of empowerment. I put myself back in the driving seat over my decisions and how I felt about things.

Everything we do is a choice. Every day we make a million and one choices: what time to get up, what to wear, how to travel to work, how to react to people, what to eat, whether or not to exercise, where to live and how to manage our finances. Saying 'I choose to' or 'I want to' changes the energy from powerlessness to self-empowerment. Life just seems easier even though external circumstances have remained the same.

Circle of influence and the illusion of control
The Serenity Prayer, composed by Reinhold Niebuhr, asks:

"God grant me the serenity to accept the things I cannot change, the courage to change the things I can and the wisdom to know the difference."

Most of us waste a lot of energy trying to change things that are outside our circle of influence. We cannot control physical features like our height or age, or external circumstances such as traffic jams, the job or housing markets, other people, the weather or global politics. Learning to let go of the illusion of control is one of the greatest challenges for the hyperactive Western mind: we think we have just got life on track when a financial crisis hits and we lose our savings, or someone we love dies suddenly.

The only things over which we have direct control are our thoughts, beliefs, feelings and behaviours. Sometimes we are so out of balance, tired and frustrated, that it doesn't feel as though we have a choice at all. We react from our hot buttons, and feel guilty or a failure. In that case we can let ourselves off the hook and choose to accept that we don't feel in control, and that we are out of balance and behaving in a way that we prefer not to. We can then choose to relax into that state of flux and wait it out. Eventually it will pass and we can become self-centred again.

We are addicted to the concept of control because it gives us, at least temporarily, a sense of security: if we stay in control the baddies can't get us. Most of us are brought up to hide our vulnerability and insecurity behind a façade of strength and invincibility. Those of us brought up in the stoic tradition learned to 'put on a brave face and never let the bullies see you cry'. We fear losing control because we associate it with irrecoverable mental and emotional breakdown. All the ego constructs that keep our illusions of control and security intact would come crashing down. Our worst fear is that we would no longer exist, at least not in the form that we recognise ourselves. Our carefully fabricated self-image would collapse leaving us an amorphous blob gibbering in a dark corner, unable to function or accomplish anything. Worse, we would not be acceptable to others and would have no place in our version of society.

Having experienced burnout and depression, I see breaking down as an opportunity to wake up and become truly conscious (I talk more about this in Chapter 11). With a new sense of awareness, we can literally 'break down' the old paradigms and let go of all our illusions. We feel more in control by letting go of the idea that we can control anything outside of our circle of influence. We empower ourselves to make conscious choices from a place of clarity and healthy self-hood. We realise that being comfortable with our vulnerability is the beginning of self-empowerment. Our vulnerability becomes our strength because we are being authentic: *This is me, world, take it or leave it because I am literally worn down from hiding behind someone who isn't the real me.*

The desire for love, approval and appreciation

Ah, but there's the rub: how to be our authentic self when most of us think we need the love and approval of others just to feel good about ourselves. Somebody praises us and we feel ebullient, or at least appreciated. That is until someone else criticises us, and we are down in the depths of despair, feeling useless and helpless. Our whole sense of self is based on the capricious views of others. We literally give our power away to others who really don't want it, yet our whole self-image may be dependent on their opinion of us. All too often, we give away our power to those who will use our insecurities to emotionally manipulate us and 'make' us do things we don't want to do.

Janet was a sweet, kind woman whose soul purpose was to make others happy. Her work colleague, Sophie, used Janet's kind nature to bully and manipulate her to do what she wanted. She pointed out all of Janet's character flaws and apparent errors in her work, and then tried to palm off all the work that she didn't want on to Janet. When Janet tried to say no, Sophie spread slanderous stories about her, making her out to be a lazy, incompetent person who skived off work at any opportunity. Janet found herself being shunned by co-workers who didn't know her very well because they believed Sophie's lies.

Janet didn't know how to say no or be assertive. She was afraid to go to their boss because she knew the boss favoured Sophie and would never believe Janet's grievances. She didn't dare go to her union rep either because she feared Sophie would make her life even more of a misery. Janet felt devastated and had lost all her self-confidence, resulting in comfort eating, weight gain and constant stress-related health problems.

Behind her lack of assertiveness, Janet held on to the belief that if she could only be nice enough and give in to Sophie's demands, she would eventually gain Sophie's approval, and the bullying would stop. Sadly, Janet's health became so bad that she had to take early retirement: a gentle soul unable to stand up for herself in a harsh environment of pseudo-power bullying.

Byron Katie's prayer, *"Dear God, please spare me from the desire for love, approval or appreciation. Amen"* is a plea to let go of giving away our personal power to our need for others to like or accept us. We feel disempowered by trying to second-guess what other people must think of us. When we are focused on what we think the other person must be thinking, we act in a way that we hope will gain their love or approval. We want to be liked and are willing to suppress our own shining authenticity to try and fit in with what we think somebody else wants us to be.

This is a form of control so common that most of us don't even recognise it as trying to control others. None of us can ever know for sure what someone else thinks or feels about us, nor should it matter. It is not our job to be in someone else's head trying to figure out whether they like us or not. That's their job. Instead of worrying about what other people think, we can turn it around and start to wonder what we think of them: *Do I like this person? Is this person behaving in a respectful way towards me? Is this someone I trust? Is this person on my wavelength? Will we get along?* When we start seeing ourselves as worthy of only the best behaviour from others, we no longer need everyone to like us. We stop using other people to try and make ourselves feel more lovable or good enough.

Self-empowerment means taking responsibility for how we feel about ourselves. We stop giving our power away to others to make us feel anything less than worthy. For many years Jude gave away her power to her need to be seen, heard and appreciated by her significant other. When she didn't receive the recognition in the way that she thought she deserved, she felt resentful and unloving towards him. When she stopped trying to control how he reacted to her, and started loving, appreciating and approving of herself, she felt empowered. How can we expect someone else to give us something that we are unable to give ourselves? It is such a mind control game: *I don't know how to love myself, but you had better get it right by showing me you love me.* While no man or woman is an island, there is only one person who can truly love, approve or appreciate you, and that is you. This is a tough truth to embrace. As Jude learned to value herself, her self-esteem grew, and she started noticing how her partner showed his love, it was just different to her expectations.

We often hear of someone who met the love of their life and then the moment they moved in together, started trying to change them. Or the person complaining about certain family members who won't adhere to the family 'rules' about how they should behave. We even want strangers to behave according to our values, getting really agitated over their awful driving habits, their eating as they walk along the street, or what we consider to be their terrible taste in clothing.

Trying to control other people is a fruitless exercise and yet most of us are guilty of indulging this particular fantasy, sometimes consciously, but often without any awareness of how we are disempowering ourselves. We want others to feel a certain way in response to any given situation. We hate it when they don't feel the way we think they should and can spend hours, weeks, months and even years trying to influence (control) how someone feels: *My mother should be happier and start making friends in the lovely new care residence that's costing me a fortune. My husband should share his feelings more instead of shutting me out. My son should call me more often. My partner shouldn't be so gullible and spend money on status symbols. My sister should like me and be nicer to me. My kids ought to be grateful for the opportunity to learn to play the piano and stop whingeing about it. My boss shouldn't get angry about the new guy's mistakes.*

Until we have lived someone else's life for them, we have no idea what makes them tick, even less can we control how they feel. It is so easy to know how someone else should feel, think or behave: we are all experts in judging, criticising and giving advice. We like to pretend that we are doing it 'for their own good' but in truth, must of us are trying to control others so we can feel more comfortable. When the other person does not respond to being shown the error of their ways, we may resort to nagging and manipulation, and when that doesn't work we feel frustrated and powerless.

Organisation and too much busyness
It is clear that we can't control the weather or external forces, nor can we control other people, not without creating a great deal of resentment. But what about being in control of our daily lives? Many people lead pressurised and busy lives that require military precision and attention to organisational detail. The fear is that if we were to let go and relax for even a minute, nothing would get done and we would spend a life

bumming around, achieving nothing. The carefully constructed house of cards would come tumbling down: the kids wouldn't do their homework, get to school or to their activities; we wouldn't get to work; we wouldn't study for our exams; our dreams and aspirations would never be realised; our projects would never be finished; and life as we know it would disintegrate.

Of course there is some truth to this. Our lives have all become much more complicated. We live in perpetual busyness, afraid to stop, afraid to lose control. How does this work with the illusion of control? After all, it is no illusion that we are juggling a gazillion balls in the air and are convinced we can't let a single one of them drop.

Control in this situation depends on what is driving us. Too many of us hang on to the illusion of control from a place of fear, often fear of failure, or of being imperfect, unlovable or unacceptable as we are. We derive our sense of self-worth from appearing to be busy and in control, but the energy feels heavy and stressful. This kind of control acts like a shield, trying to protect us from our fears. We daren't let go and relax because then we would be confronted by our fears. It can't work indefinitely because eventually something has to give, often our health or our relationships.

Normally a high-energy, passionate man, Chris was suffering from stomach problems, fatigue and general apathy. He had been promoted to team manager, which he found stressful. He was also working longer hours, which meant he missed out on being involved in the upbringing of his three children. Ideally, Chris preferred to work as part of a team and was not very good at people management. His sleep was suffering and he felt like his life was spinning out of control. Like many of us, Chris found it hard to admit that he couldn't handle everything because he was brought up to believe that he should be strong and never give up. With his health deteriorating, he knew he was on the verge of a breakdown if he didn't make some changes.

Admitting that he was losing control was Chris' first step to regaining his health and motivation. He managed to negotiate a contract at work that allowed him to work three days a week from home as part of a team project. This gave him more time to spend with his children. He also decided to create time each day which he called 'self time'. He used this time for cycling, meditating and gardening. At first he noticed how letting go of some of his busyness and simplifying his life made him feel very anxious. Many of his self-doubts bubbled up to the surface and threatened his new-found peace of mind. Gradually, as Chris relaxed into his new way of life, he realised how much more effective he was both personally and professionally. He achieved more and felt more in control than he had for many years.

Our ego hangs on to the illusion that all our busyness means we are in control, even as we continue to feel anxious, powerless and out of control. When we learn to stop the looped thinking and the programmed conditioning, and just focus on what is really important to us, life becomes easier. We don't stop functioning as an energetic and productive human being. Instead we are more able to relax, switch off the hyperactive mind and achieve much more from a place of ease. Letting go of the ego's need for control in all its various forms is very liberating. It allows us to start operating from our right brain, which is connected to our intuition, creativity, guidance and universal knowing. We become inspired to choose different paths that lead to more fulfilment, happiness and contentment.

Self-discipline, commitment and willpower

Self-empowerment is being aware of where we give away our power and becoming clear how we want to reclaim it. Living a conscious life and reconnecting with our own innate power is not something that we do for a week or two. It is an ongoing process that starts with a desire to discard the baggage we have been carrying around all our lives. The desire to change becomes stronger than the desire to stay stuck in the same old patterns. Anaïs Nin, author and diarist, wrote:

"There came a time when the risk to remain tight in the bud was more painful than the risk it took to blossom."

Why suffer by staying bound in our old self-destructive or self-limiting patterns when we can blossom and grow into our most empowered self? While we may want to make the changes happen right now, the ego will hang on to its usual self-protective strategies until we are able to replace them with something else.

During a guided visualisation, Judy, who felt weighed down with anxiety, obligation and guilt, described her baggage as two enormous suitcases, too heavy to carry, plus a huge rucksack, and a very large handbag.

When she tried to open the suitcases, she felt very anxious and her mind wouldn't let her see the contents. She still had a little way to go before she was ready to let go of her burden.

Conversely, I knew I was making progress at letting go of some of my old programmed conditioning when I had a dream in which I got on a train and, some time into the journey I exclaimed, *"Oh, I left my baggage on the platform at the last station!"* I didn't use the word 'luggage' in my dream, it was definitely my 'baggage'.

Most of us have experience of trying to change deeply ingrained self-sabotaging habits, whether it's going on yet another diet, giving up alcohol, controlling a bad temper, or living within our budget. Changing any behaviour that has served as a habitual release or distraction from deeper feelings of anxiety or low self-worth can be challenging. This is because our fear-driven thinking has conditioned us to believe that change requires even tighter control and plenty of willpower to defeat our aberrant and imperfect self. We go into battle with self in the mistaken belief that we are fighting an enemy within. When we fail yet again to achieve new more self-supporting habits, we beat ourselves up and add another notch to the tally of all the ways we are imperfect.

The teachers at school who inspired us were usually kind, respectful and knew how to make their subject interesting. They were committed to their profession and to their students. The teachers who turned us off a subject were usually uninteresting, uncaring and made us feel as though we didn't matter. When we commit to ourselves with the kindness and caring shown by those inspirational teachers, using healthy self-discipline from a place of self-love and acceptance, it becomes much easier to make the changes we desire, permanently.

The word 'discipline' has negative connotations of punishment and being controlled by others. Self-discipline on the other hand represents a framework that supports our evolution. Through self-discipline we create a safe structure within which to question our assumptions about ourselves, and to practise our new habits of thinking and behaving. While the negative discipline meted out to us during childhood made us feel disempowered, healthy self-discipline provides the strength that empowers us.

Commitment to staying on our chosen course is a form of unshakeable mental and emotional focus. Our commitment is strongest and most effective when it is inspired by our soul's desire to help us move forward from the place where we are stuck. Our soul self wants us to grow, learn and evolve.

The word 'willpower' can also have negative connotations, usually as part of the armoury we use to beat ourselves up, as in: *I don't have any willpower because look how I failed again*. Willpower, literally the 'power of our will' or desire to achieve, is the foundation of commitment. Without the holy trinity of self-discipline, commitment and willpower, we keep swinging between extremes of selfishness and selflessness, guilt and shame, all the while wasting energy and focus.

Success and failure
While we may achieve that to which we wholeheartedly commit, commitment itself does not necessarily guarantee success in the conventional sense of the word, which means setting goals and then taking the steps to achieve them. We may want a certain qualification so we spend all our spare time studying, while working full-time. We take the exams and either pass or fail. We have either succeeded at attaining our goals or we have failed. Our minds very quickly translate fail into: *I am a failure*.

Most of us learned to dismiss our successes or achievements, and focus on our imperfections. We were not encouraged to celebrate our successes or even our attempts at something. We grew up with: *Don't boast. Don't blow your own trumpet. Don't get too big for your boots. Pride comes before a fall. Don't get big headed.*

Adults might dismiss a child's school-work as not yet good enough, even though they may have made progress from the previous year. Teachers can be just as insensitive. My son is a gifted artist. He draws with plenty of eye for detail, shading and perspective. My daughter does line drawings in three seconds flat and immediately a smug looking cartoon cat appears on the page. Her skill and technique are completely different to her brother's but, instead of loving her artistic ability, she believes she can't draw, and all because a teacher once told her she would never be any good at art. She was six years old at the time.

Most of us grew up learning to measure our achievements against external standards set by other people. We then proceeded to label ourselves as a success or failure according to the precepts of others. We give our power away to external influences to validate and approve, or to reject and disapprove of us. At least that is the way for many of us whose minds have been trained in the competitive world of *'either you are in or you are out'*.

The problem associated with the words, 'success' and 'failure', is the connotation of personal worth. We all have many things that we aspire to that don't work out as we planned: our relationships, the way we handle a delicate situation, being a caring and attentive parent, starting a new project or business venture, attaining external accreditation, getting the job we wanted, losing weight, eating healthily, taking quality me-time, running a marathon, cycling from London to Kathmandu. How we view the 'not working out' depends on how we define success and failure.

Those who take pride in their successes are those who are able to rise above the narrow definition of the words success and failure. They have learned that it's not just the big things that count. The everyday successes that we may discount as unimportant can all add up to an increased sense of achievement and self-worth. My clients come up with things like: learning to make a good pasta sauce, using the stairs instead of the lift at work, being kind to an annoying co-worker, watching less TV, getting to bed a bit earlier and feeling more rested, cutting down on their daily glass or two of wine, drinking more water, walking away from an argument without getting hooked in, staying calm in a traffic jam, seeing the absurdities of life instead of taking everything so seriously, making healthy choices when eating out, helping their children with homework even when they feel too tired to concentrate, finally making that hairdressing appointment, and stopping to notice the beauty all around them.

Success does not always mean external achievement, although it is important to celebrate and enjoy those too. Success in this context is to do with who you are, and not just what you do. It is a state of 'being', where you are happy and content with who you are, no matter what your external circumstances. The state in which you are content may not be the same as anyone else's, it all depends on your personal desires and values.

The person who believes they can only be worthy if they have 'more of' or be 'better than' is setting themselves up for feelings of failure when they either can't achieve, or they lose everything they thought they needed to bolster their sense of self. There is a line in *Desiderata,* a beautiful piece of wisdom written by Max Ehrmann:

"If you compare yourself with others, you may become vain or bitter, for always there will be greater and lesser persons than yourself. Enjoy your achievements as well as your plans."

Comparing ourselves with others leads to feelings of imperfection, of being 'not good enough' and failure. A successful human being is one who feels worthy and lives according to their own values, truth and moral compass, no matter what others may tell them. They know their external achievements form just part of a complex web of a life made up of many achievements, successes, mistakes and failures. All of them carrying equal weight and importance on the road to self-realisation.

An opportunity to learn

Most of us are comfortable with the idea that we can learn from our mistakes. We are able to apply that maxim in many areas of our lives. For example, we bake a loaf of bread and it's too hard to cut, the next loaf is better and the third one is really edible. Or we learn a new piece of software and start using it on a new project. It crashes and we are really annoyed but we figure out what went wrong, or we go back to the old software and continue with the project.

Then there are our trigger areas that cause us to give up and spiral down into the pit of self-doubt, failure and self-rejection: the one too many failed relationships, diets, job applications, business ventures or financial investments. These are the perpetual patterns or themes that run through our lives causing us to make the same mistakes. We feel as though there must be something wrong with us because there we go again, making the same old hash of it. How on earth do we empower ourselves when our most fundamental fears of not being good enough, being rejected and abandoned are threatening to overwhelm us? We feel like a complete failure in these trigger areas of our lives.

But what if there is no such thing as failure, only an opportunity to learn? At a soul level, what if we chose our mistakes and consequent suffering to bring to our own attention how we need to evolve? Here are a few possibilities of what any of us may be here to learn:

- Let go of the influences of the past. This includes the voices in our head that continue the saga of lies about who we are and our innate worthiness.

- If life is a struggle, always pushing us into self-doubt and despair, then perhaps we are on the wrong track and maybe it is time to switch the points.
- Make friends with our shadow side and embrace the truth of who we really are: no more pretence or hiding behind a false self-image.
- Forgive ourselves and others, and be free from victim consciousness.
- Stop sacrificing, and start empowering ourselves through assertiveness and setting boundaries.
- Develop a strong sense of self-belief no matter how others may judge us, after all it is only their opinion.
- Love ourselves unconditionally, and develop healthy self-discipline to create a structure within which to blossom and thrive.
- Be kind to ourselves and others, even in the face of hostility.
- Let go of the need for love, approval or appreciation to feel worthy.
- Learn patience, kindness and acceptance towards self, moving from the state of fear to the state of love.
- Trust that everything is exactly as it should be, and that everything happens for a reason, even though it is not yet clear what that might be.
- Live within our own circle of influence because controlling anything else is an illusion.
- Make quiet time with no distractions and go to a peaceful place in our mind free from nagging mind chatter.

When we see every so-called failure as an opportunity to learn something about ourselves, we stop seeing ourselves as a victim of circumstance. We start the process of self-empowerment. Our heart opens with compassion and, just as those kindly teachers once helped us to learn, so our inner teacher helps us to learn through kindness and understanding. Gradually we feel a sense of peace in our heart and we start to feel good in our own skin.

Chapter 10

Confident communication

"The most basic of all human needs is the need to understand and be understood. The best way to understand people is to listen to them." Ralph Nichols

We are all suffering from 'Attention Deficit'. When was the last time you felt truly heard, seen and understood? With our egos fully in control, most of us have no idea how to listen nor do we very often feel heard. We are not getting the right attention, in the right way, and at the right time to nurture our personal and spiritual growth.

When I ran *Confident Communication* workshops, I gave the participants an exercise where they worked in pairs. Each of them took it in turns to talk about an emotionally reactive situation for a full ten minutes, while their partner said nothing. The listener could nod, smile or show other signs of listening, but they were not to utter a word. After ten minutes, they changed over and the one who had listened now talked, while their partner listened. The results were very interesting. Those who talked said it was wonderful to be able to talk freely and without interruption. They said they felt as though they were being heard and understood, something that happened rarely in their lives. Those doing the listening said it felt really awkward and difficult to just listen without jumping in with encouraging comments, questions and advice, or giving their own take on what was being said.

When we need to be heard, many of us turn to a psychotherapist or coach, someone who has training and listening skills. They can listen to what is *not* being said by tuning into the emotion behind the words and by noticing body language. They then ask questions that allow the client to find their own solutions and insights. So many times a client will say: *Oh, I never thought of it like that!* Suddenly they are able to refocus the lens and see things from a different perspective.

We may turn to friends when we want to talk. We are lucky indeed if we have a friend with an innate ability to listen. All too often our friends get drawn into the drama of our story and take sides, or they give advice: *Well if I were you, I would .... You know what you should do ... Why don't you ...* in the belief that they are helping us solve our problem or making us feel better. They then become frustrated when we don't follow their well-meaning advice. Most of us have fewer than a handful of people who can listen with that special ear that makes us feel that we have been heard and understand. This kind of listening is a gift that helps us to process our experiences and find our own equilibrium. Stephen Covey, author of *The 7 Habits of Highly Effective People*, says:

> *"Most people do not listen with the intent to understand; they listen with the intent to reply."*

Have you noticed in a conversation that after you have said something, the other person's response often has nothing to do with what you were saying? They have their own agenda and they will speak no matter what. I recall a couple my husband and I met on holiday. They were extrovert, entertaining and good fun to be around. By the end of the five days we knew everything there was to know about the two of them: where they went to school, what their parents were like, their career paths, where in the world they had lived, their views on most topics under the sun, all about their pets, their food and beverage preferences, and much more. As we were travelling home I asked my husband if he thought they knew anything about us, and we both laughed. They hadn't shown any curiosity about us at all. Whenever either of us asked a question or brought up a topic of conversation, they plunged straight in with their own thoughts, beliefs and experiences. They listened only briefly with an intent to respond. They are not alone. Most people don't know how to really listen to understand, and far too many don't give it much thought.

'Attention Deficit' causes family feuds, wars, hostility, aggression and random violence. We aren't truly listening to each other. We are feuding on the inside with ourselves and project our feelings of lack on to others. Stuck in our egos, filtering and interpreting, most of us can't listen, nor can we communicate compassionately and assertively. Until we learn the art of empowered communication, we continue on the merry-go-round of blame, resentment and retaliation, or despondency and withdrawal.

Emotional oxygen

Stephen Covey again:

"When you really listen to another person from their point of view, and reflect back to them that understanding, it's like giving them emotional oxygen."

Too many of us are gasping for emotional oxygen. Without it we can feel very lonely and isolated, adrift in a world where we don't feel seen or heard. It doesn't matter if we are in a relationship, in a crowded place or on our own, 'Attention Deficit' can force us into painful withdrawal and depression. It can also drive us to be loud, argumentative, obnoxious and attention-seeking: anything to get some acknowledgement of who we are and how we feel. Deep down we believe that if only we could find someone to truly listen to us, then we could be at peace.

Just as we hope that others may give us the sense of power, self-belief or love that we perceive we are lacking, many of us also hope that finding someone who listens will assuage our deep-seated need to be heard. A good friend, therapist or coach will give a temporary sense of acknowledgement, but the real healing can only start when we stop wanting something from someone else that we aren't giving to ourselves: the gift of listening to, understanding and believing in ourselves.

When we connect deeply with our authentic self, our heart and our soul, we start communicating with ourselves in a way that nobody else can. We listen to ourselves with empathy, caring and compassion. When life is throwing us too many challenges we talk softly and kindly to ourselves, reassuring that all will be well, that we are safe and we will get through the crisis. When we can't make a decision, or our life is crumbling around us, we take ourselves by the hand and offer ourselves wisdom and guidance so that we can move forward with confidence and insight. We give ourselves emotional oxygen.

Mis-communication

We are the only species on the planet with the power of intelligible speech, so how on earth have we got it so wrong, and why can some people seem to communicate with ease when the rest of us struggle?

We have all had the experience of saying something to someone, only to find that they have misinterpreted our words and meaning. They may even have got annoyed at us for something we didn't say or mean. We go back and double-check what we said and how we said it, and then wonder how the message ended up garbled like Chinese whispers. I learned early on to be very precise after experiences where clients said that I 'told' them they 'had' to follow certain advice about what to eat or what to do. Even though my coaching is never directive, their mind filter system, based on programmed conditioning from their childhood, heard and interpreted an 'instruction' from an 'authority figure' and reacted accordingly.

All of this makes language an imperfect medium for communication, which is rather a strange statement when most of us focus on what we say as being of prime importance. Communication is much more than words. It is the energy and intention behind the words that count, and they are conveyed through our tone of voice and body language. There is a big difference for example between saying: *I see* (meaning 'I understand') in a soft, sympathetic manner compared to *I see!* (meaning 'oh here we go again') in a hostile, scathing tone of voice. In each case the intention behind the communication is clear. We feel either the sympathetic or the hostile energy of the words being spoken.

Great communicators

It takes a high level of awareness to realise that not everyone thinks or feels the way we do. It takes an even greater level of awareness and empathy to be willing to listen to someone on their terms, with compassion and understanding, even if we don't agree with them. Great communicators know how to listen with the intent to understand. They know that their own filters can distort the message someone else is trying to send them and they will check with phrases like: *What I heard you say is … is that what you meant?*

They may check that their communication is being received as intended. They may ask: *I am not sure if I am explaining myself very clearly. Did you understand what I meant?* rather than assuming all is well. This gives the other person a chance to focus and check whether they really did get the message as intended.

We instinctively trust great communicators because their communication is congruent, meaning that their body language, tone of voice and words are all aligned and sending the same message. There is no unspoken underlying energy to react to because their thoughts, feelings, words and voice are all saying the same thing.

Above all, great communicators have empathy and understanding, which means they are able to create a feeling of safety and trust. They make it safe enough for a free flow of dialogue to occur so that others can state their opinion without fear of retribution or reprisal. In conversations where there is a lot of emotional reactivity they take control of their hot buttons, putting them to one side because to give into them would distort the communication. They understand how important it is to maintain respect and they use phrases that indicate a willingness to listen and understand, such as: *I see how you might feel that way after what has happened. How can we find the solution that works for both of us?*

Fudging communication

Most of us are expert at fudging our communication. The dictionary definition of 'to fudge' is: *"To fail to deal with something in an open and direct way, especially to conceal the truth or mislead; to speak or act in a way that is meant to avoid dealing with a problem directly; to change something in order to trick people."*

As most of us are not deliberately dishonest, why would we want to fudge something as important as our communication?

The world is biased in favour of the outgoing, talkative and go-getting types. It does not nurture the quiet, thoughtful, philosophical or empathic listeners. Our education systems do not teach us to listen or show empathy. In Chapter 1, I introduced the concept of HSPs, highly sensitive people, also known as introverts and the emotional empaths of this world. HSPs tend to get knocked down and pushed aside in the stampede of extroverts competing with each other to get their own point of view across. Life is a battle and they must win or perish. Most of us learned very early on in life that it was risky to speak our truth or to reveal how we really felt about something for fear of showing weakness. We feared being judged, ridiculed and rejected. We weren't taught effective and assertive communication that allowed us to stand up for ourselves, to set boundaries and to firmly enforce them. We learned to fudge our communication, which causes dissonance and confusion.

This is especially so when it comes to dealing with anger. Managing our anger and learning how to use it for the good is a challenge for most of us. When our hot buttons are pinging away and we are feeling angry, resentful or anxious, most of us slip into one, or a combination of these well-worn mis-communication styles: *Passive, passive-aggressive, or aggressive.*

Passive behaviour: suppressing

The passive mis-communicator suppresses their truth and says nothing, silently absorbing the energy of their anger and resentment so they won't upset the status quo. Passive mis-communication is fuelled by a fear of confrontation and a desire to please others, even though they may be hurting themselves.

The passive person has lost touch with their own needs because they are too afraid to ask for what they want or deserve: respect and the right to express their point of view. They say 'yes' when they really want to say 'no', avoid arguments and conflict, and find it hard to admit to being angry because to do so would engender feelings of guilt and unworthiness. They have trouble making decisions, even over minor things, which can be infuriating for those around them. Ask the passive communicator what they would like to do today and they will usually answer, *I don't mind, whatever you want to do,* when secretly they would love to go to the latest art exhibition.

The effect the passive communicator has on other people is that they wish this person would say what they really mean because it is exhausting trying to second-guess what they want. Because the passive person suffers from the distorted belief that they are less entitled than other people, others may trample over their fuzzy boundaries, violating their rights to respect and consideration.

The passive communicator feels disempowered and turns their anger inwards resulting in apathy and depression. They may suffer from a variety of health problems with no obvious physical cause. Often they will be affected by chronic anxiety and all sorts of phobias as they displace blame for their distress on to neutral objects, people or places.

Passive-aggressive behaviour: sniping

My favourite mode of mis-communication was sniping at people, the passive-aggressive approach, because I was too afraid to confront them directly. I was in touch with my anger but afraid to express it. Passive aggression is the mis-communication style most of us use because it feels safer than outright aggression, even though deep down our anger fuels a strong desire to whack the other person over the head for their bad behaviour. As most of us tend towards non-physical violence, we end up using a method of communication that, at best gets us nowhere, and at worst leaves us and the other person hurt, confused, angry and resentful.

Passive-aggressive behaviour can be summed up as veiled hostility. The other person can feel the hostility simmering beneath the surface but has no idea why we are upset. (If they are also a passive-aggressive mis-communicator, they may well have an idea but feign innocence.) Hostility makes the passive-aggressive person unreasonable to deal with. Their resentment may be disguised by withdrawing, playing dumb, procrastinating, agreeing to something but then not complying, omitting to pass on information: all strategies designed to frustrate or annoy the other person without being held directly responsible. Their suppressed anger may be more obvious as they use sarcasm, sulking, manipulation, sly digs, giving the silent treatment, avoidance of eye contact, put-downs, being a gossipmonger, not listening, guilt-tripping, being stubborn, long-suffering sighs, back-handed compliments and complaining.

The passive-aggressive person expects others to read their mind and will make life difficult if their expectations aren't met. They may provoke others to aggressive behaviour and then pretend they had nothing to do with it: *I have no idea why you are getting so upset! What on earth is the matter with you?! You are overreacting! You are way too sensitive! Can't you take a joke?!*

When none of these tactics works, the passive-aggressive mis-communicator turns the anger and hostility inwards. They may become obsessional, perfectionist and demanding. Their underlying anxiety will lead to stress-related health problems. Dealing with the veiled hostility of passive-aggressive behaviour creates mistrust and, either aggressive retaliation or withdrawal from others.

Aggressive behaviour: exploding
Aggressive behaviour is different to passive and passive-aggressive behaviours. While passive and passive-aggressive behaviours are ways of deflecting confrontation, aggressive behaviour is an 'in your face', direct form of confrontation. The person who habitually uses this style

of mis-communication will come across as permanently angry or irritable. They have a hair-trigger temper and any excuse is a good excuse for them to explode. Aggressive behaviour is 'acting out', instead of assertively 'acting upon' anger, and dumping it onto others causing fear, anger and resentment.

If the aggressor is unable to get away with their aggressive behaviour, they may resort to passive-aggressive behaviour instead. This style of mis-communication is not the same as the kind of anger explosion most of us have experienced at some time, usually when we feel pushed to our limit of tolerance and endurance. While not a recommended way of getting our message across, it can occasionally serve the purpose of making people to listen to us when all else has failed.

Aggressive behaviour as a persistent mis-communication style is confrontational, loud, abusive and explosive. It is deliberately intimidating, threatening and coercive. Aggression is designed to hurt, humiliate, put down and make someone else feel inferior so that the aggressor can feel more powerful. Being on the receiving end of aggressive behaviour is frightening. It is the behaviour of bullies and cowards who have no awareness of the extent to which their behaviour hurts and damages others. When the aggressor is out of control the aggression can escalate to physical violence, hurting or killing someone, or damaging property.

Aggressive behaviour is destructive and offensive, and is a form of emotional and psychological violence. The aggressor hides behind their aggressive behaviour to avoid taking responsibility for their own feelings of inadequacy. Nor do they take responsibility for their violent behaviour for which they blame provocation by others: *You drove me to it! It's all your fault.*

Favourite verbal tricks of the aggressive mis-communicator are '*dialogue breakers*', expressions used in a scathing, condescending, contemptuous or sarcastic tone of voice designed to make the other person wither, and hopefully leave them alone. Here are a few examples: *You should …! You never …! You always …! You make me so …! Why can't you ever …?! It's all your fault! What's your problem this time?! Well normal people think/do …! You're completely wrong, as usual! What's got into you now?! I don't understand you at all! Who do you think you are?! You've got a nerve! Oh here we go again! I see! I suppose it's all my fault, is it?! What now?! Oh we're back to that old chestnut are we?!*

This is a hostile, hurtful way of treating anyone. Too often those we love are on the receiving end of this kind of verbal abuse. The moment someone uses a dialogue breaker, any chance of good communication is severed. The mis-communicator feels relieved because they avoided having to deal with a confrontational issue. The receiver feels angry, resentful and discouraged. They may eventually walk away and not return. Many relationships end because partners are unwilling to use kindness and compassion in their communication.

Whatever your favoured combination of mis-communication style, you know that none of them can ever create safe, honest and effective communication. We cut dead the possibility of a free flow of dialogue between us and the other person. Our fear and self-doubt push away the possibility of listening and responding from our hearts with compassion. We may be able to guilt-trip or intimidate someone to do what we want, but in the process we create mistrust, hostility and the risk of someone taking revenge. Disconnected from our powerful and authentic self, we lack the belief that we can effectively communicate with those we find difficult, intimidating, threatening or just more confident than we are. Trust and safety elude us, and we end up feeling frustrated and powerless. Our relationships and our health suffer as a result.

Fuzzy boundaries
The reason most of us fail to communicate effectively is because we have fuzzy boundaries. We allow all kinds of disrespectful or manipulative behaviour from others, or we unconsciously behave in a disrespectful and manipulative way because we don't know how to assert ourselves. Fuzzy boundaries are very disempowering: they make us feel afraid, resentful or angry towards those we perceive as trying to demean or control us.

A boundary is defined as a line that marks or limits an area. In personal terms, boundaries are the limitations that we set on how other people may treat us and how close we let them into our personal space. Our boundaries provide the differentiation between who we are and our responsibilities, and those of others. To maintain effective boundaries, we decide how we will respond when someone steps over them.

When I was studying at the Institute for Optimum Nutrition, a behavioural expert came to talk to us about being a professional nutritionist. She did an exercise on boundaries where she divided our group of about twenty students into two rows facing each other, each row about three metres apart. She then asked one side to start walking towards their partner standing in the row opposite them. The stationary partner was to say 'Stop!' the moment they felt as though the other had come close enough. When my partner started walking towards me, I became uncomfortable at about a metre and said 'Stop!' Some of the group said 'Stop!' sooner than that, while others said nothing at all. It was a real eye-opener to see one person allowing another to barrel straight into them, pushing them over, without saying anything. This was a practical demonstration of fuzzy boundaries: how we let others push us around emotionally as well as physically.

When our boundaries are firmly defined, we are able to express ourselves assertively from a core place of safety, self-worth and self-trust, while honouring the other person as a unique individual with their own set of needs and desires. We put ourselves first. We are selfish in the 'selfhood' sense of the word knowing that, when we respect ourselves, we respect others as well.

Too few of us were taught how to set our boundaries while growing up. Our parents, teachers and other kids tried to control or manipulate us into meeting their needs, even if it hurt us or went against our own sense of justice and integrity. We learned to: *Respect your elders. Be quiet and do as you are told! Don't answer back! Stop causing trouble! Don't tell tales! Stop complaining! Don't make waves! Just smile and be nice!*

Because we feared rejection and wanted to be loved, we learned to squash down our own needs and give into those of others. We learned to say 'yes' when we wanted to say 'no'. We suppressed our anger and resentment when we wanted to shout, scream or argue back. We learned to stay quiet and comply when we wanted to speak our truth. We either retreated into depression because we couldn't fight back, or we rebelled, made a lot of noise and behaved in a way that we knew would hurt others because nobody was listening to what we needed. Our developing boundaries were trampled underfoot before they had time to be fully erected.

Depending on our upbringing, we soon learned that either none or only some of our feelings counted. We accepted how others treated us in order to get along and fit in. We may have felt disregarded, humiliated and our boundaries violated, but were unable to put into words what was happening or describe how we felt. We just knew that something was wrong but we had no capability of making it right.

As adults, fuzzy boundaries lead us to make poor life choices because we don't trust our own judgement. We enter relationships that play on our lack of boundaries, giving in to the other person because we don't know how to say 'no' and mean it. At work we don't know how to deal with difficult, hostile or aggressive individuals. Going into work each day becomes filled with dread and stress. Fuzzy boundaries cause no end of suffering as we feel inadequate, anxious and unable to change how others treat us. We resort to the only strategies we learned: passive, passive-aggressive or aggressive mis-communication, with predictable results.

Assertiveness

There is another way, and that is assertiveness. Our society often mistakes aggression for assertiveness. True assertiveness is never aggressive. It never intentionally sets out to hurt or put down the other person because it is grounded in compassion, kindness and a sense of connection with self and other people, no matter what they may be saying or doing. There is a real sense of optimism in assertiveness which gives it a high vibrational energy.

Assertiveness is a way of being based on alignment of thoughts, feelings and actions. It enables us to express our feelings, needs and wishes clearly and with confidence, when it is appropriate to do so. And this is always a judgement made by each individual: whether it is appropriate to express ourselves or to stay quiet.

Assertiveness is a respectful way of communication with oneself and with others. It is always gracious, always responsible. It honours the other person while maintaining personal boundaries and self-integrity. It respects other people's rights and is never passive, aggressive or manipulative. It is direct and to the point while maintaining personal boundaries against being hooked in to the manipulative tactics employed by others.

Assertiveness maintains an openness that allows space for the other person to feel heard and understood. We keep our emotional hot buttons under control and do not bring up past behaviours with which to bash the other person. If we are angry we say so, avoiding sarcastic comments or false smiles. Our facial expression, tone of voice and body language are aligned with what we are saying.

Assertiveness seeks to understand and find win–win solutions. It means being able to graciously accept that the other person may not concede to our request or point of view. Assertiveness honours self as well as the other person: we do not get drawn into self-defending or retaliation in the face of criticism or verbal attack.

Assertiveness does not waste time arguing. Arguing is just a form of self-defence or attack so that the other person will listen and concede our point of view. When we are being non-assertive we take things very personally and get stuck in our hot button reactions. We must prove that we are right even though by definition that means the other person must be wrong. The ego loves to score points, be right and win. As each person tries to be heard, they feel pushed into a corner and the argument escalates so that nobody is listening: everyone loses. Between individuals, trust is destroyed, hearts can be broken and nothing is resolved. Between groups of people or nations, this kind of arguing can lead to violence, war and death.

With assertiveness we stop worrying what others think about us and we drop the need to be self-defensive. It becomes easier to deal with conflicts because we can rise above the need to be right. It becomes easy to let the other person believe what they believe, even if it is not our truth. What they think about us is not who we are. Zoe, a naturally peace-loving woman, went through one of my early coaching programmes and commented: *"I learned to be more assertive and not to engage in time and energy-wasting 'no-win' conflicts, either at or outside work. I feel healthier, happier and more confident than I have for years."*

Being assertive is an act of courage that carries the risk of other people's displeasure some of the time: not everyone will like you for speaking out, no matter how respectful you are. To be assertive means being willing to stand apart from the crowd and speak your truth. Mostly people will respect you because they trust you to be honest. You are straightforward to deal with, no veiled hostility, no mixed messages.

Assertiveness does not shy away from confrontation. With an eye on the outcome we wish to achieve, we learn to choose our moment and how we wish to address someone, whether firm and stern, or informal and friendly. Even if we have had cause to confront someone with their bad behaviour, we are willing to listen to their anger or grievance without taking it personally. Once we have discussed our perspective and found a solution, we do not bear grudges but forgive and move on. Assertiveness also means that we may decide that we do not want to confront the other person, that nothing positive will be achieved, and we decide to let the matter go.

Assertiveness can be learned. Generally it takes a lot of practice because fear drives us all too easily back into our old patterns of mis-communication. Like everything to do with personal growth, it can be a process of taking three steps forward and two back. Fortunately, there are plenty of opportunities every day to practise assessing a situation and responding assertively.

With assertiveness comes an increased sense of self-esteem and confidence. You believe in yourself and your ability to connect with people at a different level. They sense this and know that you are not someone who will mess them about. Their respect for you means that they don't try using their manipulative mind games on you. They feel safe enough to drop those patterns and have a real dialogue with you.

In the face of hostility
Most of us find it challenging to deal with other people's hostility, aggression, and pseudo-power behaviour. This is particularly difficult if the person in question happens to be someone you work with.

Julie's bully of a boss, Sven, called her into his office and started listing the problems with her work, all of which were either untrue or an exaggeration of incidents that were outside of her control. After he had finished Sven stared at her with cool hostility and asked: *Well, what have you got to say for yourself?!* With her heart thumping, her hands clammy and her mouth dry, Julie immediately jumped to her self-defence with answers and explanations to each of his points. Then she noticed the look of triumph on Sven's face. He had got her where he wanted her, under his thumb! He had pushed all her hot buttons and now he would be able to manipulate her. She had allowed him to disempower her. Julie realised that she would never get this bully off her back and would probably have to change her job to get away from him.

In assertive mode, Julie would have taken her right to stay quiet and think before answering. We are drilled from an early age to come up quickly with an answer to people's accusations and arguments, believing that we can stem the flow of criticism and win the other person over. The truth is that if we speak from justification and self-defence, we open ourselves up to manipulation, mind control and bullying.

If Julie had taken a moment or two of silence, she could have marshalled her thoughts and taken back control of the situation. She would not have got into defending herself or trying to prove Sven wrong. Instead, she would have expressed her intention, that she wanted to listen, understand and find a solution to the issues he was bringing up. She would also have stated very clearly that she was not willing to continue being on the receiving end of his hostility. She then would have asked him where they should go from here, and waited in silence.

The sound of silence

The sound of silence is very powerful. It puts you back in the driving seat of a confrontational situation. You take back control of the energy and refuse to enter into a dialogue with someone who is clearly out to get you.

Silence when the other person has said something emotionally charged, challenging, critical, hostile or generally inappropriate also gives them space to discover their true thoughts and feelings. It may allow them to retract and rephrase without losing face.

The next time Sven tried to have a go at Julie, she let him say his piece and then, even though she felt shaky and upset, she stayed quiet for a moment and just looked at him. Then taking her courage in both hands, she called him on his inappropriate behaviour: *"I am shocked at your attack. I expect support from my boss, not groundless criticism."* She then let the silence linger until she saw him start to fidget with discomfort. She waited, not saying a word, while he figured out his next move. Being Sven, he tried again, insisting that some of his points were correct. By now, Julie was feeling very confident and assertive and actually laughed, which caused Sven even more discomfort. She said: *"You do know that everything you said is completely unfounded, so what is your real motive for having a go at me? If we have a problem, let's talk about it like adults and sort it out."* She then waited again in silence.

This approach takes nerve. Aggressors hate being called on their tyrannical behaviour because they have no justification for being disrespectful or intimidating. Sven blustered and turned very red. He realised that he had met his match and apologised, making excuses for his behaviour. Bullies are the biggest cowards: the moment you stand up to them, they usually back down. If you need your job and it is hard to find another one, your options may be limited. However, one thing is certain, you will never give away your power by answering before thinking, or by defending yourself in the face of aggression.

Compassionate communication

Marshall Rosenberg, psychologist and creator of non-violent communication, says:

"What I want in my life is compassion, a flow between myself and others based on a mutual giving from the heart."

Compassionate communication is the next stage in assertive communication. We take the step towards compassionate communication when we have let go of our ego fears and programming, and opened our hearts. We know with absolute confidence that we cannot be hurt, manipulated or bullied by others through a verbal interaction, no matter how hostile the other person might be. We no longer need to be right or to defend ourselves. We recognise the mind games that people play and are not affected by them. Our personal boundaries are firmly in place and we begin communicating from a compassionate perspective.

We tap into our own heartfelt humanity, seeing the other person as someone who is also a spirit in human form, trying to survive and get along in a complex and confusing world. Where they are in their spiritual evolution may be different to where we are. Our communication takes on a quality that goes way beyond the superficial chitter chatter of everyday life. It comes from a place of love and compassion for self, and for the rest of humanity stuck in its predicament of neediness, desire and fear. The Dalai Lama XIV said:

"This is my simple religion. There is no need for temples; no need for complicated philosophy. Our own brain, our own heart is our temple; the philosophy is kindness."

Active listening

Compassionate communication means we are in a relaxed and open state of mind towards whoever we are dealing with. Knowing that most of us are suffering from 'Attention Deficit', we bring a willingness to connect by becoming an active listener. We are no longer waiting to jump in with our opinion or to change the subject so we can talk about something that interests us more. Active listening means having empathy with the other person. It is the ability to focus on the other person and really hear what they are saying, both the verbal and the non-verbal messages. It is the ability to put ourselves in the other person's shoes and to understand what they are trying to convey, even if we don't agree with them. We try to understand what their experience means to them.

Active listening means taking ourselves out of the equation. We listen without fear because we do not take anything they say personally, even direct criticism. We suspend our own emotional hot button reactions and let the other person know that they are free to express themselves without judgement, advice or reprisal. This is a tough challenge for most of us brought up to comply, defend or attack in our communications.

We understand the unspoken need to be heard and understood behind the words and behaviour. Some will express their need by complaining, talking too much or too loudly, always explaining or justifying themselves, always needing to be the centre of attention, or speaking over others. In their company we may feel as though our energy is being drained.

Others have built up so many layers of protection around themselves that they must never show any vulnerability. They subconsciously express their need to be heard and understood by being aggressive, hostile, unfair, never listening, unpleasant, and difficult to get along with. We may feel irritated around these people, usually because they trigger our hot buttons.

These behaviours usually stem from very deep, unmet needs and low self-esteem. When we start looking at people from that perspective, we start to feel sympathy for their confusion. Of course, we may also feel irritated or drained, after all we are only human, and old habits die hard! Nevertheless, we stop feeling inferior, superior, powerless or helpless, and instead see a person who is struggling, just as we are, to deal with their demons.

Just to be clear, this is not the same as condoning bad behaviour. As an assertive person, sure of your own boundaries, you will not accept other people's bad or violent behaviour towards you. If someone is threatening physical violence, you must protect yourself by getting away as fast as possible. Being compassionate and assertive is not compatible with allowing someone to harm you.

Confrontational situations

Compassionate communication is a heartfelt method for confrontational situations. It creates trust by empowering the other person to listen to their own heart instead of their ego. It builds trust and safety by helping the other person work through their emotional reactions. They don't have to censor their thoughts or words to save our feelings. It helps them understand what they really mean and want.

We can empathise with how the person might be feeling, although we cannot assume that we understand fully the other person's experience. Nor can we know what is right for them. We attempt to gain clarity by asking questions like: *I'm not quite sure I understand what you mean by (... repeating their exact words ...). Tell me more about .... When you say you felt ...... what did you mean exactly? What happened exactly? How did you react to that? How did you feel about it? How do you feel about that now? How do you see yourself dealing with this?*

Compassionate communication never gives advice, even when asked. Deep down, the other person knows what to do, they just don't realise it yet. As an active listener we encourage them to explore all the options and to follow their intuition using phrases like: *It sounds as if ... I get the impression that ... What would happen if you were to ... You must have felt/ be feeling ... That sounds like a ... experience.* This gives them a chance to explore what they really mean and feel, while rejecting some of your interpretation.

Hannah was fed up with her colleague, Rose, sniping at her about her time-keeping, especially as she was an impeccable time-keeper. One morning Hannah said to Rose: *"Rose, how about I buy you a coffee and we can talk about what's going on between us."* Startled Rose acquiesced and they went to the cafeteria together, where Hannah opened the dialogue with: *"Rose, I am fed up with you remarking on my time-keeping and would love to know what is really going on. Do you have an issue with me?"* Confused, Rose ummed and ahhed before finally blurting out that she had expected to get Hannah's job when it became vacant six months ago. She was upset that it was offered to Hannah, an outsider to the department. Hannah expressed her sympathy at Rose's disappointment. She then talked some more about what Rose really wanted in a job, and what she could do instead. They parted on good terms and Rose became a friendly and helpful colleague.

If Rose had reacted with hostility, calling Hannah names or trying to make her wrong just for having this conversation, Hannah could have asked directly why Rose was being hostile towards her. She would have avoided defending herself against Rose's attempts to attack her integrity. Instead she would have reiterated her intention to want to understand Rose and find a solution, but that she was not willing to continue being on the receiving end of her hostility. She would then have asked Rose where they could go from here, staying quiet to allow Rose to find her own solution that would allow them both to move forward.

If Rose had come up with a genuine complaint about Hannah's behaviour, for example, *"You never say good morning to me when you come into the office"*, Hannah would have been willing to own her part and apologise for disregarding Rose. This is not the same as accepting blame and responsibility for what has happened, or how the other person feels. This is about admitting honestly that we made a mistake and got it wrong.

Assertive and compassionate communication is empowering. It makes us feel strong, capable and worthy. Everybody wins and we are able to open our hearts a little more and let kindness be our philosophy.

Chapter 11

The need to fall apart

*"When things fall apart, when things are shaky, we
are on the verge of something"* Pema Chödrön

While on my journey of intense personal and spiritual growth during my
fifties, I was suffering from the effects of chronic fatigue and burnout. I
was tired all the time, lacked motivation and joy, and was sometimes in
a deep, life-draining depression, just because I didn't have the energy to
feel anything else. It felt as though something had plugged into my energy
supply and was leaching the life force out of me. Anyone who has suffered
from chronic fatigue knows how disabling it can be. I was doing everything I knew as a nutritionist to heal myself from this condition, which
was caused by adrenal exhaustion due to long-term emotional stress, and
heavy metal toxicity from having my amalgam fillings removed. I felt as if
I were falling apart, and I realised that, for different reasons, many of my
clients were feeling the same.

Falling apart really sucks. Breaking down is frightening. Being human
none of us wants to experience the sense of vulnerability and powerlessness
that comes with no longer feeling in control of our mind, our body, our
emotions, or our life. Falling apart is an inevitable part of being human
and has special significance for those on their path to living a conscious
life. As we begin to live our truth something has to give. We can no longer
keep up the pretences of our carefully woven self-image. Living a lie is no
longer an option. There is no room on our spiritual path for any of our
mind games, whether with others or with ourselves. We are laid bare, raw,
stuck with this personality, in this body and with this soul calling us.
There is nowhere to run and hide, and we cannot escape from ourselves.

We can try and resist, or we can view falling apart as a trauma with a
purpose: a means towards breaking down the old paradigms, a reconnection to our authentic self, and a move towards living a conscious life.

Falling apart can often happen in mid-life anywhere between the ages of forty and sixty. This is particularly so for women as hormones start to decline during menopause. Men may also experience a mid-life breakdown as their testosterone levels decrease. However, it is not exclusive to mid-life as many of my clients are in their twenties and thirties when they fall apart.

Sometimes falling apart is triggered by a life crisis, such as losing a job, going through a relationship breakdown, children leaving home, financial hardship, serious illness, the death of a loved one, or moving house or country. All too often falling apart just seems to happen with no conscious awareness of the process. It can be the end result of years of chronic, unresolved stress, the kind of stress with which we are so familiar we no longer notice it until we have a shock or a change in our circumstances. Suddenly we are no longer able to cope with everyday life. We feel depressed, lack enthusiasm and feel totally lost. Sleep is affected, we feel weak, exhausted, confused, agitated, irritable and totally demoralised. This is the road to burnout and is the twenty-first century malaise. It is what used to be referred to as a 'nervous breakdown'. Burnout is so frightening that most people cannot handle the feelings of overwhelm, being adrift, apathetic and cut off from everything that has worked for them in the past. They are so exhausted and depressed that they are grateful for the offer of a life raft when the doctor hands them a prescription: anything to numb the pain and feelings of helplessness.

The nature of depression and burnout
The thing I learned about depression is that it either is or it isn't. You can't talk or think yourself out of it, whatever the cause. In this state it is impossible to will yourself to 'snap out of it' or get back to normal. You just have to go with it. In the words of the Borg (for all Star Trek fans), "*resistance is futile*". It's like falling down a disused mine shaft into pitch black. When you hit rock bottom you hang around there and just learn to survive in the dark, feeling utter despair. Eventually, after weeks or months, you realise that you are having some good and better days, and you try to hang on to them, but they vanish again like clutching at mist.

Because you can't see an end point, no light at the end of the tunnel, you start thinking that if this is the way it's going to be for the rest of your days then what's the point in carrying on? You hate waking up in the morning because you have another day full of melancholy, apathy and dreariness. I had thoughts of ending it all because I just didn't see the point of living another twenty days, let alone twenty or thirty more years feeling like this. It wasn't a life, it was a living death. Then I pictured all the people I loved and knew that I couldn't do it to them. I hung on in there with the hope that I would be able to turn this Titanic around.

If you have never reached that low, it is hard to describe how dull and numb everything feels. It's the pits. Yet even through the haze of the meaninglessness of my life, I understood that this experience would help me empathise better with my clients who were suffering from depression and burnout.

Mainstream medicine has no medical diagnosis or magic pill for people suffering from burnout. Even though each individual may have a wide range of physical and mental symptoms, they tend to be lumped under the heading of 'depression' and treated accordingly.

In 2013, The New York Times reported that 10% of the American population, and a quarter of all women in their forties and fifties, were taking antidepressant medication. A study published in the journal *Psychotherapy and Psychosomatics* suggested that the reason for such high levels of prescribing is that depression was being over-diagnosed. The BBC reported in August 2013 a record high of fifty million prescriptions for antidepressants in 2012 in the UK. Depression is a multi-billion-dollar industry. Meanwhile, many studies show that dealing with the underlying physical and emotional causes of depression, and making lifestyle changes can be just as effective, if not more so, than popping pills indefinitely.

When someone is feeling suicidal or just can't function at all, taking medication can be a lifesaver. I know numbers of people who have benefited from short-term use of antidepressants to get them through a difficult period. That said, I believe that doctors could spend more time and effort investigating the underlying causes of burnout and depression. Most people don't get even basic blood tests done to show any biochemical abnormalities. At a purely biological level, symptoms may be due to low thyroid function and adrenal exhaustion; a lowering of oestrogen, progesterone or testosterone levels; lack of DHEA and other adrenal hormones; nutritional deficiencies; low levels of neurotransmitters, especially dopamine and serotonin; low blood sugar; toxic levels of pollutants and heavy metals; and dysbiosis (an imbalance in the microbial population of the gastrointestinal tract which in turn is connected to brain chemistry). As low adrenal function can cause all of the above symptoms, it should always be investigated.

Spiritual breakdown
Giving the physical body natural healing support is an important element of recovery. I invested a fair amount of money over the years on natural supplements and treatments to help my body regain its ability to heal itself. But I soon realised that this is only part of a holistic approach to understanding what falling apart really means. Falling apart is essentially an emotional and spiritual breakdown. It is a wake-up call from the heart and soul that we are on the wrong track. We are not taking the best care of ourselves, nor are we honouring our own needs or listening to our innate wisdom. Falling apart is an opportunity to shed our old personas along with our beliefs about who we think we should be. If we allow it, we go through an internal gloopy metamorphosis, changing our whole perception of who we are and how we want to live. We may then emerge a wiser, saner, calmer, more centred version of ourselves.

I decided against antidepressant medication, despite advice from well-meaning friends. I did eventually, after many years of struggling with insomnia, decide to take a tiny dose of a prescribed sleep medication, which saved my life and my sanity. Getting a good night's sleep helped me a lot on my road to recovery. But mostly I wanted to understand the real reasons for falling apart and let it be a means to change something fundamental within me. I knew that I had sabotaged myself into burnout because I still had plenty of old programmed conditioning to deal with around assertiveness, self-love and confident self-expression.

I was fifty-nine and feeling ninety-nine. After five years of suffering from chronic fatigue I was still being driven by my fears of a future full of scarcity, which pushed me to work even harder, despite having so little energy. I had this oppressive sense of 'it's now or never', which meant that there was no time to take it slowly. I was unable to hear the whispers from my heart, my soul and my guides. I was clearly out of balance when I finally found a doctor who took the time to really listen to my tale of low energy. Dr Moreau, a conventional but supremely empathic woman in her early sixties, was the first doctor among all those I had visited who asked me questions about my work and my lifestyle. She listened carefully and finally gave me her opinion. She insisted that I was doing way too much and that I needed to ask for, and expect, more help from those close to me. She said that if I were to fully recover my vitality, I should work less and take time out to completely relax. Such obvious advice, and yet I needed to hear it from someone else because I was stuck in a self-image of an independent and strong woman who didn't need help from others. I had great problems asking for and receiving help. Dr Moreau also did all the necessary blood tests and arranged for me to have a full cardiovascular health check at the local clinic, which happily showed no problems. In mainstream medical terms I was in good health, except that I still didn't feel great.

Letting go

I took the doctor's advice and a few months later, I started off a new year by drastically cutting my workload. I stopped marketing, networking or advertising, and became a semi-recluse. I retreated from social situations, and anything that taxed my energy. I put my trust in my angels and guides, and knew that somehow it would all work out. I trusted that those people who needed my kind of help with natural health, healing and personal growth would find their way to me. And they did. This gave me a lot of breathing space to work on my own remaining emotional and mind baggage, and to get in touch with myself at a much deeper level.

I explored energy medicine for healing. Belgium has a wealth of practitioners in alternative and energy healing. In Chapter 7, I mentioned Eric, an Amanae BodyWork practitioner. He had helped me many years before to shift some blocked emotional energy that was stopping me from writing my first book. This time he tuned into and helped me open my heart centre, which is connected to my throat (voice) centre, so that I could confidently express my truth instead of swallowing it all back down. This was important because I was still struggling to assertively express myself, and this was causing me severe digestive problems, as well as depression.

I also went for BodyTalk sessions with Chantal. BodyTalk is a system of energy healing based loosely on kiniesiology that bypasses the mind and works with the body's own innate wisdom to heal. Chantal picked up emotional patterns that were acting like 'circuit breakers' in my cells, disrupting the flow of energy. These patterns were not only my own, but were ancestral in origin, meaning that they were passed on down through generations. She received images, apparently from my body, about people and details that she could not possibly have known as I had never talked about my family. It was very powerful in helping me release old patterns of beliefs, many of which I hadn't been consciously aware.

After eighteen months of listening to my intuition and following my feelings, I was working in a way that gave me great satisfaction. My energy started to come back and I felt the urge to start writing again. It wasn't over yet, I still had a lot of inner excavation work to do, but at least some of the time I now had a bit more energy to continue.

The need to retreat

Whatever the cause of a breakdown, retreating from the world is a necessity for recovery. Retreating can mean turning down social invitations and staying home with feet up, a good book and listening to favourite music. Television became my friend for quite a while, despite my ego casting judgement at watching the 'same old rubbish'.

Retreating in nature, either alone or with other like-minded individuals, helps us get in touch with our connection to Mother Earth and our own innate cycles of nature. Using retreat time to meditate regularly alone or in a group is a discipline for stillness, self-discovery and completely letting go.

This need for social withdrawal causes a lot of inner conflict. It can feel frightening to suddenly stop all our habitual dependencies on others, but when we are falling apart, going out with people and discussing everyday events no longer holds any interest. We would rather have an in-depth discussion about life, philosophy, the universe and spiritual matters. If that is not possible, we just want to be left alone. Yet when alone, we wonder if we will ever be able to re-join the human race, or whether we will ever again feel joyful.

Retreating doesn't have to be alone, it can take the form of actually going on a retreat of some kind, for a day, a weekend or for a week. There are many retreats on offer covering a wide variety of subjects, including yoga, mindfulness, meditation, tai chi, detoxing, drumming, energy healing, chanting. The list is endless. The aim of a retreat is to allow you to completely relax, and do inner work in a safe and supporting environment. Retreats can involve group interaction or they may encourage silence and solitude.

The need to retreat can last months or years, depending where each of us is in our metamorphosis. It will take as long as it takes until we are ready to re-emerge.

Forgiveness

Part of my inner excavation work was to begin the process of letting go of years of resentment towards those who I perceived as having hurt me. I also wanted to let go of the guilt I felt at my own bad behaviour and negligence towards others.

Some people find it easy to let go. I don't. My ego has a personality that I call *"The bitter one"* (from the song, "To the Moon and Back" by Savage Garden). She enjoys the drama of being the victim even when the conscious me no longer wants it. She remembers every hurt going back to age nine, and it feels like that is her age when she starts getting into the stories of who did what to her. She was full of resentment and unexpressed anger, which she swallowed rather than assert herself. This was the underlying chronic stress that was disabling my ability to deal with the more acute stresses in my life. I had to learn to forgive.

Whole books have been written about the power of forgiveness and yet it remains a sticking point for many of us on our road to living consciously. Forgiveness is a word heavy with all sorts of connotations. Most of us are programmed with the concept of forgiveness as something we do for the person who hurt us in order to be seen as 'good', or even saintly. Conversely we may fear that we are 'bad' when we hang on to grudges and are unable to forgive. Then we get tangled up in guilt because we can't forgive and we create a whole sorry mess of leaden energy that blocks our spiritual growth and joy.

We subconsciously fear that forgiving others is the same as 'letting them off the hook', that we condone their actions. This is not the point of forgiveness at all. Forgiveness is not about saying the other person's behaviour was alright. Often they may be unaware of the hurt they have caused, especially if we never confronted them or were unable to take action to stop them. They may equally be aware of what they did but felt entitled to hurt, or told themselves that it was no big deal. Most hurt is caused by those who are hurt and damaged themselves. They are living from a place below the level of consciousness. Ignorance and lack of self-awareness are no excuse for bad behaviour or abuse, but when we operate from ego fear and separateness, it is too easy to hurt others and not take responsibility for our actions.

While pondering the thorny dilemma of forgiveness, I came across the Buddhist story of the two monks. It goes something like this. Once upon a time there were two monks travelling back from the village to the monastery. They came to the river and were about to wade through the water to cross over when they saw a woman standing on the bank. She was worried about getting across the river as there was no bridge. The older of the two monks offered to help her and he carried her safely on his back to the other side where he put her down. They then went their separate ways. His younger companion was very quiet all the way back to the monastery. Over dinner that evening the older monk asked him what was troubling him. The younger one blurted out that the older monk had broken all the rules. They were not supposed to have any contact with women and yet he had physically carried one across the river. The older monk smiled sympathetically and said: *"My dear friend, you are right about the rules, but I put that woman down hours ago and you are still carrying her."*

Forgiveness is about letting go, about putting down the burden of suffering. We do not forgive for the other person, although as we release the energy of resentment something in them may shift too. We do it for ourselves, to give ourselves relief from carrying around this heavy load of pain, the pain of anger, resentment, grief, loss, fear, shame and betrayal.

Self-forgiveness

Forgiving ourselves for all the times we have thoughtlessly betrayed or hurt other people is not so easy. We live with the guilt, carrying it around like a cloak of black energy. Self-forgiveness is about owning the actions that are causing our shame and remorse, being honest about our motives at the time, learning from the mistakes, and giving ourselves permission to move on. We can choose to continue carrying the burden, or we can finally give ourselves some peace by letting it go. Time moves on, people move on too. The past really has gone, it is only our guilt that keeps it firmly in the present.

Forgiveness is not something that we achieve overnight. Like everything to do with releasing habitual patterns, it may take many months or even years of practice. When we practise forgiveness, we change our relationship with our past. I had epiphinal moments when it seemed that the camera lens shifted one hundred and eighty degrees and I saw my memories from a completely different perspective. I felt my heart open. It didn't make right what I or the other person had done, but it allowed me to feel compassion for their and my confusion.

I also had moments of profound knowing that there really is nothing to forgive. Everything happens exactly as it is meant to. All our experiences have made us who we are now. I can choose to keep adding to the burden of pain and confusion in the world, or I can practise letting it go and living from a place of love.

Surrender to higher guidance

Falling apart causes us to spin out of control. The more out of control we feel, the more we try and hang on to some semblance of control. Since my burnout, at no point had I totally thrown my hands in the air and relinquished control of my life to my higher self and a divine guidance. It took a long time before I realised that this might even be a possibility.

Then one day I was taking a walk across the fields near where I live. I love being in this place. It is high up and quite flat with fields, trees and very few houses stretching to the horizon. It always reminds me of my early childhood living on an RAF base in Suffolk which, being in East Anglia, is very flat. I have wonderful memories of collecting wild mushrooms in the fields there at dawn with my father and brother. On this particular day, there was heavy cloud cover, typical Belgian gloom, a very uninspiring day, but I needed the fresh air and exercise. I felt as low as I could possibly feel and I began appealing to my guides who were supposed to be helping me here on Earth. My prayer was, *"If you exist, please let me know now. I am not doing very well down here. I feel very alone and I could really do with some help and guidance."* Not expecting anything to happen, I suddenly 'felt' a very strong presence and turned around to see who was there. I didn't actually see or hear anything but I knew for sure that 'they' were there. The energy around me was palpable and I felt enveloped in a warm blanket of love and acceptance. My heart opened and tears poured down my face. With it came a sense of calm in my agitated brain. This was my very first 'road to Damascus' experience, the knowing once and for all that I was not alone, nor could I ever be alone. From now on I knew with absolute certainty that I was accompanied by what I started to call my Dream Team.

Dream Team

At that point, I let go of all the worry about work, survival and the need to keep pushing myself. I ignored the siren call of my spirit inviting me to develop ever more projects. I took a complete break from anxiety and I trusted that all would be well. It was such a relief. I felt free for the first time probably in my entire life.

I decided to push my luck and ask my Dream Team if, now I had made contact with them, they would be able to send me a certain number of coaching clients, and while they were at it, would they help me start up some small group programmes, and send the right people to me. Not being brought up in a tradition of prayer or requesting help, this all felt very impertinent and demanding. Who was I to ask for this kind of help? In fact, I ended up with exactly the number of clients and small group programmes that I had asked for. Gradually I learned to accept with immense gratitude that I had 'someone' to turn to. All I had to do was ask for help and then listen carefully for the answer, which came in the form of being gently nudged in a certain direction.

I also tapped into my EGS (emotional guidance system, see Chapter 6) and learned to trust the feelings attached to ideas. When I thought about a particular project, I had the distinct 'clunking' feeling as though my energy was falling through my feet. When I thought about a different project, I felt a buzz of excitement.

Trust

One of the most important lessons that falling apart taught me was to completely surrender to trust that everything would work out exactly as it was meant to. Trust is a small five-letter word carrying an enormous amount of weight and meaning. I had finally understood what trust really meant. It meant surrendering and releasing all my illusions about who I was, about being in control, and about being alone on planet Earth. I could never be alone, even during the times when my ego took over and plunged me into anxiety and loneliness. Trust allowed me to fall through the bottom of the depression pit and out the other side into sunshine and hope.

Once I had made contact with my guides I felt their presence on many occasions. In the early days of chronic fatigue, I asked them to bring their healing power to a BodyTalk session. While lying on the BodyTalk table, I 'saw' a group of five benign beings gather around. They were faceless and yet I knew they were smiling. Their bodies were less dense than a human body, slightly transparent and greyish in colour. Their energy was loving and supportive. Of course my rational mind butted in to remind me that this was all my imagination. I responded that I didn't really care where the images came from, I was just enjoying their comforting presence. Then suddenly another being joined the group, smiling and 'breathlessly' apologising for being late. Now I didn't imagine that!

The middle way
Our minds have a tendency to think in polarity terms of black and white, all or nothing, now or never, right or wrong, good or bad, either/or, selfish or selfless, success or failure, friend or enemy, busy or lazy. When we are falling apart, dropping down into that dark pit of despair, the ego hangs on ever more tightly to its well-honed survival strategy of polarity thinking. The mistaken belief is that we might save ourselves if we keep on doing the very things that drove us to this point. We end up feeling even more hopeless and out of control, battered around by extreme thinking.

There is no room in polarity thinking for what the Buddhist philosophy calls 'the middle way or path'. This is the place wherein lie the grey areas and subtleties of our existence. It does not deny the existence of extremes, but rather allows us to be comfortable with uncertainty and ambiguity. When we polarise our thinking we have to hang on to something, anything that provides even a fleeting sense of security or certainty. In the middle way we let go of the feeling of anxiety and insecurity. There is nothing to hang on to. We allow decisions and solutions to emerge without putting ourselves through stressful mental and emotional anguish.

This is not an easy path to follow, especially when we are stuck in the despair of breakdown and depression. Our mind dashes about like a headless chicken trying to analyse the situation and grasp on to a solution, any solution, but please just make the misery and the suffering go away. It is a very strange concept that maybe there is no solution, or at least that it isn't our job to find one. I worked hard to heal myself, but now looking back I believe if I had literally done nothing, stopped 'doing' and just let myself 'be' in complete trust and acceptance, I might have found my equilibrium much more quickly.

When we give up trying to force a solution on any given issue, that is when the situation can heal in ways we may never have imagined. Pema Chödrön tells us:

"*The middle way is tough going because it goes against the grain of an ancient neurotic pattern that we all share. When we feel lonely, when we feel hopeless, what we want to do is move to the right or the left. We don't want to sit and feel what we feel. We don't want to go through the detox, yet the middle way encourages us to do just that. It encourages us to awaken the bravery that exists in everyone without exception, including you and me.*"

Putting ourselves in the middle way is not a quick-fix solution to falling apart or depression, but is a first step towards noticing how our old thought patterns may have led us to the point of breakdown. We notice our polarity thinking, how it drives us to mistrust ourselves and others, so we never feel truly safe. We realise how our programmed conditioning creates fuzzy boundaries and affects the choices we make. We can no longer give our power away by blaming people or events for what we do or how we feel. We become aware of how we hang on to our dreams and desires, even when it is clear they are no longer relevant and we need to change tack. We wake up to how we are unconsciously driven by fear to chase after security and certainty when part of the human experience is to live on shifting sand. Benjamin Franklin said:

"*In this world nothing can be said to be certain, except death and taxes.*"

I would add that we can be 'certain of uncertainty'. We are here today, tomorrow may be similar, or our lives may change beyond recognition. We can't know what each day will bring. In the middle way we can go with the flow and find comfort in the fact that we don't have to try and control those things over which we have no control.

In the middle way is a gap, a place where we can rest. We don't have to do anything except let go. This is so frightening it can feel like jumping out of an airplane without a parachute. And when we finally dare to surrender and throw ourselves into the gap, something amazing happens. We jump and realise that not only do we have wings, but we are able to use them to ride the thermals, to soar and swoop, and to glide in that space where miracles happen. It is deeply relaxing and peaceful. My belief is that most of our health problems, our sorrows and our struggles exist because we lost our ability to relax completely. We forgot how to fly.

Timelessness

I sat on the beach in Cyprus floating on a cloud of contentment, the only thought in my head being the surprised observation that I could really take to being a beach bum. As someone who had always liked to be on the move, this was quite a revelation. The sun was warm, the sky and sea merged in shades of deep azure and turquoise. I was totally chilled out. Without warning, I was transported out of my normal consciousness and entered a state of 'timelessness'. In this state time no longer mattered. I was timeless. I was ageless. I have always been and always will be with no beginning and no end. All my human preoccupations, my wants, desires, preferences and requirements were totally irrelevant. It flashed through my mind that my life and death don't matter, that when I am gone, nobody will be aware of my existence. Even to my own family, within a generation, I will just be a name on a family tree, a woman who gave birth to this person who gave birth to this one. My ego's self-importance, the need for recognition, the need to be remembered when I am gone, just fell away. All my worries of the past and for the future disappeared. There is no past and no future. I had all the time in the universe. There are no limits to time. I was limitless. I felt deeply relaxed, connected and liberated.

Timelessness is the complete antithesis to polarity thinking. I started noticing how often my clients would say they were *running out of time*, that if they didn't achieve what they thought they needed soon it would be *too late*. I realised how we have all been brainwashed into thinking this way. It leads to deep unhappiness and dissatisfaction, and effectively stops us being in the moment. It also acts as an obstacle to listening to the whispers from our higher self and our guides. When I felt timeless I 'knew' what to do here on planet Earth. I knew what direction to take my work and my life, without having to weigh up the pros and cons in my rational mind. I could be in the middle way. I didn't have to move in any direction until I felt the nudges or the buzz of creative energy. All would be well. I heard *"You will always be safe and you are always loved."* My higher self and my Dream Team were on the job. They trusted me to take appropriate action when the time was right. I felt serene.

Falling apart again and again

As we recover from a breakdown or depression, we start feeling more energetic and alive. We have put ourselves back together again and our human mind wants that to be it now. Let's get back to normal and slip back into the life we were living, the comfortable familiarity where those around us know what to expect. This is a recipe for disaster. It's like trying to put a jelly back in the mould. Falling apart changes us and we can never go back to how we were. Something fundamental within has cracked wide open and something else has seeped in through the cracks to replace what was there. The butterfly cannot go back to being a caterpillar. Not unless you have chosen the path of chemical medication. Long term anti-depressant or tranquilizer use numbs the pain but can be addictive. Medication can also hamper the process of evolution towards living consciously because, by its very nature, it is designed to maintain a sense of equilibrium that attaches you to how you have always been.

When you accept the process of evolution that follows on from breakdown, then you know that your life may change in many ways, both minor and major. You also accept that falling apart isn't always a one-off event. It can happen many times in the form of mini-breakdowns or crashes. They are a reminder that we haven't yet finished evolving, that we still have a way to go. A shock can temporarily send us into a spin cycle where we swirl around in a murky whirlpool of ego anxiety, full of doubt about who we are and what we are doing here. I temporarily lose that sense of deep trust and timelessness as my old anxiety reactions suddenly whoosh up like a geyser erupting from the bowels of the earth. In that moment I have lost my connection with my higher self and my Dream Team. I feel totally abandoned, and overwhelmed by anxiety. The only way out of it is by living through it, accepting that I am only human and my journey isn't yet finished. I wait for it to subside knowing that this too will pass. When I return to centre it feels like being hurtled through outer space, crashing through the earth's atmosphere, before landing with a thud on solid ground, shaken but still in one piece and all the wiser for the experience.

Life is a series of falling apart and putting ourselves back together again. It is a form of dis-integration and re-integration. Pema Chödrön tells us:

"... the truth is that things don't really get solved. They come together and they fall apart. The healing comes from letting there be room for all of this to happen: room for grief, for relief, for misery, for joy."

In the end you are the ship and the lighthouse. You weather the bad times and, after each challenge, you guide yourself home to yourself, because that is where you are and will always be until you leave this life.

Chapter 12

A time for every purpose

"To every thing there is a season and a time to every purpose under heaven." Ecclesiastes 3

Human beings seem to be programmed with a desire to have a purpose to life. We need something to get up for in the morning, something that gives our life meaning, and something through which we can express who we are. Edgar Cayce, twentieth-century psychic and medical clairvoyant, said:

> *"Each person living in the Earth is here for a specific soul purpose; a purpose that no one else can fulfil."*

I suspect that many of us get stuck on the words 'life purpose'. It all sounds so grand, and we feel so small and insignificant. It is easy to dismiss the whole concept of life purpose as yet more pressure on top of everything else with which we are already coping.

What is my life purpose?
While some know from a very early age what it is they are here to do, most of us flounder around feeling inadequate that we aren't fulfilling our life's purpose, whatever that means. Being spirit in human form, I think our first purpose, our reason for being here, is to experience life on Earth. I think we all have much to learn in the evolution of our soul, and many of us have incarnated this time around with a mission to heal some aspect of the Planet, which can be fulfilled in many different ways. Some may serve humanity by going to far-flung corners of the globe, giving practical help to those in need. Others may work closer to home, giving some of their time and energy volunteering in the community, helping those who are less fortunate.

We can fulfil our life's purpose through our job: working in a policy-making institution, getting involved in fund raising, writing or teaching health and healing, always behaving ethically no matter what our chosen career might be, or joining an action group that represents the downtrodden in our own society.

Equally our life purpose may be to give pleasure to others through art, music, writing, dance, sports. We could choose to live always from a place of graciousness and non-judgement towards others, bringing happiness through our warmth and humour. Our life purpose might be to show others how to live from their heart by offering compassion and the gift of deep, empathic listening. We could help the dying to leave peacefully, or give practical help to elderly neighbours. Or our life purpose could be giving birth, and raising our children to be happy and well-adjusted individuals, who may then go out and follow their life purpose.

We are not all here to selflessly serve on a grand scale. People everywhere are making a difference in their own small corner of the globe: in their communities, families, social circles and in the work place.

Stan is a self-published author who, in his spare time, just loves to write novels that delight his readers. His daytime job for the last three decades has been leading a team of people in a large organisation working on environmental issues. Within his organisation, not only is he an expert on the subject, but he is known by all as the peace-maker, the diplomat, the negotiator, and the soother of fevered brows. His work on the environment is invaluable. His 'people' work, empathising, communicating and bringing all factions together around the negotiation table, is an essential part of Stan's purpose. He is bringing peace, light and pleasure to so many people on many different levels just by being true to his authentic self.

What if then our purpose is just to be who we are, experiencing life on planet Earth, while at the same time bringing love and kindness to those with whom we have contact? Whatever we do, however we choose to live, we affect those whose lives we touch. We make a difference just by being ourselves.

Maybe it doesn't have to be more complicated than that. We can feel relief and just enjoy life the way it is, with all its challenges and pleasures. While we may not be doing anything that will earn an award for service to humanity, we are nevertheless living our purpose, or purposes, in life.

Being a lightworker

For those who are still restlessly seeking their purpose or mission in life, it can be very frustrating. Many may be older souls who are tired of the fripperies and dramas of human activity. It all seems so shallow and worthless, especially when they see so much suffering around them. They live with a constant feeling of needing to do something more, of being here to help people.

These old souls may be termed 'lightworkers', those who have reincarnated through many lifetimes. Before this incarnation they agreed to bring love, light and healing to planet Earth. Then when they got here, they forgot their mission, becoming overwhelmed by humanity's focus on power, greed, materialism, violence and brutality. But they are now waking up and becoming conscious that they are here to fulfil their mission.

I have found that the term 'lightworker' aptly describes 99% of my coaching clients. Lightworkers tend to be highly sensitive people, the HSPs or empaths of this world. They feel different, have spiritual or metaphysical experiences that others contemptuously dismiss as nonsense, and often feel misunderstood by their families, friends and society in general.

When talking to a lightworker, you find that they have always cared deeply about the state of the world and every living thing in it, often since childhood. They feel great compassion and have a need to put things right. Lightworkers have a powerful sense of fairness, and cannot abide injustice and the exploitation of any living thing. They want to encourage and support others to release their fear, and let their light shine brightly. This is where many lightworkers get stuck. They hear the call but are unable to act upon it, often because they still have many of their own fears about being unworthy, of standing out from the crowd, and of going against their programmed conditioning.

Because they have a kind heart, lightworkers tend to have fuzzy boundaries, attracting those who would take advantage of their soft nature. Many can find themselves in toxic relationships that do not nurture their soul purpose. Jodie, like Stan, brought peace and harmony to her workplace. She could listen to her colleagues' dramas without getting sucked in, and was able to diplomatically help them find mutually-benifical solutions. In her spare time, she volunteered two evenings a week on a crisis helpline. She was a shining light which seemed to work against her in her relationships with men. Jodie described how her light and goodness always seemed to attract selfish and narcissistic men, *"like moths to a flame"*. As soon as she entered into what she thought would be a loving and mutually-nurturing relationship, they did their best to extinguish her light. They would become verbally or emotionally abusive, trying to demean and put her down. By withdrawing their love in this hostile way, Jodie was left feeling as though there must be something seriously wrong with her. Her despair led to lack of self-confidence and, as she slipped into depression, she lost touch with her lightworker abilities and started drinking more. First a glass of wine at the end of the day, then it crept up to two glasses, until finally she was drinking a bottle of wine each evening to numb the pain. Addictions and self-sabotage are common among lightworkers/HSPs.

Gradually, like many lightworkers beginning to wake up to their calling, Jodie decided her first step was to heal her own life and allow her light to shine again. She learnt to set boundaries to protect herself against thoughtless cruelty from others, all the while recognising the innocence and confusion of those who cause harm. As she grew in compassion for herself, she felt compassion for those who had hurt her. She stopped drinking and started taking good care of herself. She continued to shine her light at work, and decided that, in her spare time, she would retrain as a life coach to support other lightworkers. Her new self-confidence started attracting different kinds of men, those who were more emotionally and spiritually mature. But Jodie realised that she was in no hurry to settle down with anyone. It would happen when the time was right.

Many lightworkers shine their light finding fulfilment as mediators, teachers, counsellors, coaches, leaders, writers, social workers, peace-makers, health practitioners and healers of all kinds. They may also be the guy who serves you coffee, or the taxi driver who beams his goodwill and love of life at you. Because they have an affinity for the spiritual and anything that is not of the five senses, lightworkers pick up energy from people and their surroundings. This makes them true empaths and good listeners: they are able to feel what the other person is experiencing. People feel better when they have been in the presence of a lightworker, whether or not the lightworker herself knows her true identity.

Divine Timing

In the 1960s, Pete Seeger set to music the wise words from *Ecclesiastes 3* in a song called *Turn, turn, turn*, also recorded by The Byrds in 1969:

"To every thing there is a season, and a time to every purpose under the heaven:
A time to be born, and a time to die; a time to plant, and a time to pluck up that which is planted;
A time to kill, and a time to heal; a time to break down, and a time to build up;
A time to weep, and a time to laugh; a time to mourn, and a time to dance;
A time to cast away stones, and a time to gather stones together;
A time to embrace, and a time to refrain from embracing;
A time to get, and a time to lose; a time to keep, and a time to cast away;
A time to rend, and a time to sew; a time to keep silence, and a time to speak;
A time to love, and a time to hate; a time of war, and a time of peace "

Divine Timing is the concept that, when the time is right for our soul's purpose, doors will open and we will feel the urge to move forward on our path. Stephanie was tired of paper-pushing but had sabotaged all offers of promotion, feeling deep in her gut that her path lay in a direction different to climbing the hierarchical ladder. As she talked about her lack of direction, she started describing a new scheme being discussed within her organisation to start peace talks in a part of the world being torn apart by hostility and aggression. As Stephanie described the new venture, she realised that this would be a perfect opportunity for her to use all the skills and experience she had acquired over the previous twenty-five years. It would be a sidestep in terms of promotion, so no extra money or status, but that really didn't bother her. As she thought about the work she would be doing, she had an epiphinal moment of absolute clarity. She realised that this was the means to follow her true purpose in life: to help mediate and open a dialogue with people who had been at loggerheads for decades. She was amazed that this hadn't occurred to her before, but then understood that up till now the timing had not been right.

Different phases of life

If we practise listening to our intuition and our guidance, we will know when the time is right. Before that moment we may need to go through many different phases and have many different life experiences. During our twenties, thirties and forties, our human self may need to go through a building-up phase, when we are building our career, establishing our financial security, and when we have most responsibility towards others. We may be raising children and taking care of family members. This is the phase for creating a solid foundation to make us ready for the next phase, which is to open the door to our ultimate soul purpose. During that phase, as happened to Stephanie, the perfect opportunity arises that allows us to surge forward with confidence.

The life of each human being is made up of many steps that form our purposes for being here. Many of our experiences cause us pain and suffering, but none of it is wasted. Eventually, when we are tuned into that part of us that 'knows', we can be guided by our intuition to understand when the time is right for us to take up the greater challenge, the grand design of life purpose for which we chose to come here. Some people wait until their children have grown up and left home, or their career has come to a crossroads. Others wait until they receive a 'sign' which can come in many forms: a chance conversation, an article on the internet, hearing about a job offer or training course, picking up a book that inspires, or a request for help from an unlikely quarter.

When I look back on my life at all the different phases and stages, I can see how each experience led to the next, which in turn led me to where I am now. My soul in human form had already decided that I needed to go through this evolution. At each stage I was fulfilling one of my many life purposes. I did many kinds of jobs, and was a stay-at-home mum for a while, before it became clear what I really wanted to do. In my early twenties I was supposed to discover my empathy with people when I worked as a housing estates manager in a busy London borough. I was responsible for managing five hundred council properties. When my tenants came to me for help, they often commented that I was the only estate manager who ever truly listened to them. Through marrying twice, I learned valuable lessons about assertiveness in the face of old-fashioned male programming. Learning self-forgiveness for my many screw-ups taught me humility and put me on the road to living more consciously. I gave birth to two wonderful people who have their own purpose for being here. En route, I followed the serendipitous signs that led me along the path of nutrition and health, coaching, teaching and writing.

Absolute clarity

When we are able to define our purpose it brings us a sense of peace and excitement. We have a channel for our creative self-expression and our passion. All the confusion gathered over years of being told who and what we are, falls away. We suddenly understand, and with understanding we have a clarity which is so bright that we wonder how we ever could have missed it. All that bumbling around trying to be this or that, feeling the tug from our heart and soul but unable to hear it, or too afraid to listen, is no longer an issue. We feel the buzz, and we are energised to move heaven and earth to manifest what we are here to do.

When we live a conscious life, time and the universe expand. We break free from the chains that bind us and shine our light with confidence. As we live a conscious life, we learn to trust that all is as it is meant to be, even if we can't always see the bigger picture. We re-integrate our mind, body, heart and soul. We become whole and authentic, walking with a foot in both worlds, a spiritual being having a human experience, fulfilling our purpose, whatever that might mean.

www.ingramcontent.com/pod-product-compliance
Lightning Source LLC
LaVergne TN
LVHW041215080426
835508LV00011B/964